PRAISE FOR
The Lifetimes When
Jesus and Buddha Knew Each Other

"This book is shocking, and that's what I like about it. How did Jesus become the Christ and how did the Buddha attain Buddhahood? Are their stories somehow connected? These are just a few of the questions that Gary Renard and his teachers, Arten and Pursah, pursue in this book. At the very least, they challenge our willingness to consider the impact these masters can have on our lives today, not just in ancient times. I really think you're going to enjoy this journey."

— **James F. Twyman**, best-selling author of
The Moses Code and *Emissary of Light*

"Arten and Pursah are back and better than ever, with their uncompromising message and pull-no-punches attitude, all the while reinforcing the importance of seeing in the light of pure nondualism. Additionally, they share with us a very intriguing and pleasantly surprising historical connection between Jesus and Buddha that the world doesn't even know about! Gary is his usual humorous self, and as always, candidly shares his forgiveness opportunities that we can all learn from. Giddy up!"

— **Mike Lemieux**, author of *Dude, Where's My Jesus Fish?*

"The Lifetimes When Jesus and Buddha Knew Each Other is a Masterpiece. Aside from A Course in Miracles, *I don't know of any other book that comes as close to speaking in the clearest of terms about the truth of who we are and what is our purpose here."*

— **Gabriela Ilie, Ph.D.**, professor in community health and epidemiology at Dalhousie University, Faculty of Medicine, Halifax, Nova Scotia

The Lifetimes When

Jesus

and

Buddha

Knew Each Other

ALSO BY GARY R. RENARD

THE DISAPPEARANCE OF THE UNIVERSE:
Straight Talk about Illusions, Past Lives, Religion,
Sex, Politics, and the Miracles of Forgiveness

YOUR IMMORTAL REALITY:
How to Break the Cycle of Birth and Death

LOVE HAS FORGOTTEN NO ONE:
The Answer to Life

ENLIGHTENMENT CARDS:
Thoughts from The Disappearance of the Universe (a 72-card deck)

All of the above are available at your local bookstore,
or may be ordered by visiting:

Hay House USA: www.hayhouse.com®
Hay House Australia: www.hayhouse.com.au
Hay House UK: www.hayhouse.co.uk
Hay House India: www.hayhouse.co.in

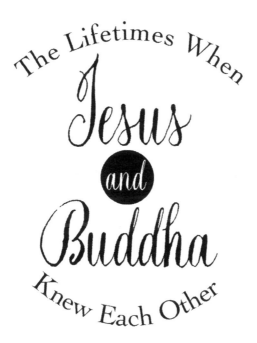

The Lifetimes When Jesus and Buddha Knew Each Other

A History of Mighty Companions

GARY R. RENARD

HAY HOUSE, INC.
Carlsbad, California • New York City
London • Sydney • New Delhi

Published in the United States by: Hay House, Inc.: www.hayhouse.com® • *Published in Australia by:* Hay House Australia Pty. Ltd.: www.hayhouse.com.au • *Published in the United Kingdom by:* Hay House UK, Ltd.: www.hayhouse.co.uk • *Published in India by:* Hay House Publishers India: www.hayhouse.co.in

Cover design: Jenny Richards • *Interior design:* Bryn Starr Best

The Library of Congress has cataloged the earlier edition as follows:

Names: Renard, Gary R., author.
Title: The lifetimes when Jesus and Buddha knew each other : a history of
   mighty companions / Gary R. Renard.
Description: Carlsbad : Hay House, Inc., 2017. | Includes bibliographical
   references and index.
Identifiers: LCCN 2017027585 | ISBN 9781401923150 (hardcover : alk. paper)
Subjects: LCSH: Spiritualism. | Jesus Christ--Miscellanea. | Gautama
   Buddha--Miscellanea. | Course in Miracles.
Classification: LCC BF1272 .R46 2017 | DDC 299/.93--dc23 LC record available at
https://lccn.loc.gov/2017027585

Hardcover ISBN: 978-1-4019-2315-0
Tradepaper ISBN: 978-1-4019-5043-9
Ebook ISBN: 978-1-4019-5041-5

1st edition, November 2017
2nd edition, November 2018

Printed in the United States of America

To Dr. Kenneth Wapnick.
I cannot be you, but like you,
I can stick to the truth.

Contents

Introduction

The following text relates true events that occurred from October of 2013 to September of 2016. Except for my narration and notes, they are presented within the framework of a dialogue that has three participants: Gary (that's me) and Arten and Pursah, two ascended masters who appeared to me in the flesh. My narration is not labeled unless it interrupts the dialogue, in which case it is simply labeled "NOTE." The many italicized words you will see indicate an emphasis on the part of the speaker.

It is not absolutely essential to believe that the appearances of the ascended masters took place in order to derive benefits from the information in these chapters, and I personally don't care what you think. However, I can vouch for the extreme unlikeliness of this writing being done by an uneducated layman such as myself without inspiration from these teachers. In any case, I leave it up to you, the reader, to think whatever you choose about the book's origins.

Although this is my fourth book with Arten and Pursah, it is not necessary for you to have read the first three, which make up the *Disappearance of the Universe* trilogy, in order to understand and enjoy this one. If you are new to *A Course in Miracles*, which is one of the teachings discussed herein, you'll find the basic foundational knowledge you'll need to understand it in the Note that follows this introduction. Those ideas will be expanded on during the dialogues. You'll see how they relate to other classic teachings, and be introduced, if you haven't been already, to the concept of nonduality.

This book should not be considered part of the *Disappearance of the Universe* trilogy, in which Arten and Pursah completed their individual stories and explained how three of their lifetimes from the past, present, and future were interconnected. Ultimately, all of our lifetimes are interconnected, but the focus of my teachers was on those three time periods for teaching purposes. They also explained how they went about achieving enlightenment, which could also be described as awakening from the dream we call life. That awakening, and how to achieve it, is also a major topic of this book.

One of the things that is unique about these discussions, and why this book stands on its own, is that Arten and Pursah have chosen to focus on two other friends of theirs, how those two beings attained salvation, and how they knew and even helped each other at certain times in history. This was a shocking revelation to me when they first told me. I'm referring to Jesus and Buddha, although those were not their real names. Incidentally, even though the name Gautama is sometimes associated with Buddha, it was not mentioned by my Teachers.

Please note that this book is not meant to be an in-depth explanation of the spiritual disciplines and traditions that are discussed herein, but rather a history of how two great masters got to be who they were.

It's the opinion of my teachers that the fastest—not the only, but the fastest—way of attaining enlightenment can be found in the already-mentioned metaphysical masterpiece called *A Course in Miracles,* referred to mostly in this book as simply "the Course," or "ACIM." But there are many parallels between the Course and the teachings that Jesus (who will be referred to as "J" in this book, as in my other books) and Buddha were exposed to and came to live. The corollaries are striking at times, so some quotations will be used in this book not only from the Course but also from other texts as well. However, it's important to note that it's not until the teachings are understood in the context of pure nondualism, which will be explained, that one can look back and realize that each step along the way was necessary in order to lead to the next.

All spiritual paths lead to God in the end, and it's never the intention of this author to put down or invalidate anyone else's spiritual path or approach. At the same time, it's the uncompromising nature of *A Course in Miracles* that is one of its most important features. Without that, it would be like everything else and would not have been needed in the first place. Therefore, I refuse to compromise on its message, and I sincerely believe that J and Buddha would have it no other way.

Please note that when words such as *Oneness, Reality, Guide, Truth, Creator,* or *Spirit* are capitalized, the word is referring to the level of God Mind that is beyond the idea of separation. When these words are *not* capitalized, even the word *oneness,* it is referring to a level that has not yet acknowledged God as the only Reality. As you will see, this is the difference between nondualism and pure nondualism.

If there are any errors in this book, you can be certain that they are *my* mistakes and were not made by my teachers. I am not perfect, so this book isn't perfect either. But I believe it's the big message that matters, not the details. Indeed, many students nitpick sentences in the teachings so much that they can't *see* the message; they cannot see the forest through the trees.

Ultimately, this book is about nothing less than climbing the ladder to enlightenment; the various stages that J and Buddha went through on their way up the illusory ladder; and how we can learn from their experiences, thus saving thousands of years on our own spiritual journey.

I'd like to thank Hay House for their fine stewardship of my books; Cindy Lora-Renard, my wife, co-teacher, and joyous example of living the teachings; and my wonderful webmaster, Roberta Grace, for all her important support. Without them, doing this book would have been much harder. I'd like to give a shout out to William Shakespeare. I'd also like to thank my editor at Hay House, Nicolette Salamanca Young, and my copy-editor, Jeffrey Rubin, for their invaluable input, which I found to be truly helpful.

Finally, I'd like to thank my friends at the Foundation for Inner Peace in Mill Valley, California, and the Foundation for *A Course in Miracles* in Temecula, California, for their decades of important work that has resulted in making *A Course in Miracles* available to the world. Aside from my own, I'm certain they have the gratitude of millions.

— Gary R. Renard

somewhere in the illusion of California,
and not in the illusion of California

A Note from
the Author about
A Course in Miracles

What It Teaches, and Its Relevance
to Jesus and Buddha

The purpose of this Note is to explain some of the core concepts of *A Course in Miracles,* how they relate to the subject of nondualism, and how they are thus relevant to the enlightenment of spiritual masters like Jesus and Buddha. This will make it easier for the reader, experienced and unexperienced alike, to understand and enjoy the conversations in this book.

This book is not meant to be a substitute for the Course. (As I mentioned in the Introduction, *A Course in Miracles* is commonly referred to simply as "the Course" or "ACIM.") Even a true, nondualistic understanding of the Course, which is rare, will not result in enlightenment. It's only by practicing and applying the teachings in your everyday life—such as in your relationships, your experiences, and even the events you see on television—that enlightenment will happen. With that in mind, let's proceed.

ACIM was channeled by a research psychologist who heard the Voice of Jesus. Her name was Dr. Helen Schucman, and she was helped enormously by her colleague, Dr. William Thetford. He would type out the words of the Course as Helen read them to him from her shorthand notebook. The two of them had a strained relationship, and they worked in an environment that Helen described as "depressing." Then one day, Bill told Helen he thought there must be "another way." She agreed, and together they decided to find it. It's apparent that the Course came as a result of that decision.

The full story of ACIM is fascinating but long, and has been told in several books. For the purpose of this brief Note, I'll mention that it took seven years for Helen to channel the Course, but that she continued to hear what she called "The Voice" for at least five years after that. Helen also channeled two sections that were added to the Course later. It's clear that J never stopped working with her. It's also clear that because of this continuity, J was the editor of the Course from beginning to end. He corrected Helen's mistakes, mostly in the first 5 of the 31 chapters of the Text, and he was totally responsible for its consistency throughout a half-million words. (Aside from the main text, there is also a Workbook, which comprises 365 lessons, and a Manual for Teachers.) For your convenience and later study, direct quotations from the Course are noted and listed in an Index in the back of the book.

The three other major players in the history of the Course were Dr. Kenneth Wapnick, Judith Skutch Whitson, and Bob Skutch. With Helen and Bill, the five of them eventually formed the Foundation for Inner Peace, which became the publisher of the Course in 1976. Dr. Wapnick went on to become what my teachers described in my first book, *The Disappearance of the Universe*, as "the Course's greatest teacher."

ACIM is a self-study course—it's not a religion. Although people meet in study groups and start churches that they say are based on ACIM, at the end of the day the Course, like spirituality, is meant to bring about an experience that will be found not in the world, but in a certain way of looking at the world. This comes from within.

My role, as a student of the Course for the last 24 years, is to clarify and explain the Course in such a way that students are able to apply it. I can do this only because of my teachers. Without serious help, I would not have been able to understand ACIM.

Part of the style of the Course is ingenious repetition. It would be impossible to learn the Course without being exposed to its ideas over and over again. This is how the thought system is learned, which makes the Course's brand of true forgiveness possible. You'll find repetition in this book, as well as a few things that have already been said in my other books, that will help you if you use them for their intended purpose. Repetition is not only acceptable in teaching and learning the Course, it's mandatory. The approach of the Course is to undo the false you that is referred to as the *ego*, thus leading to the experience of your Divinity. That will be discussed shortly, but first let's point out that there's a difference between real spirituality and what has become accepted as spirituality in the last few decades, namely the self-help movement.

It's not my intention to put down the self-help movement. I'm not a hypocrite. I've used the self-help movement successfully in my life. It's just that I know the difference between that and the real deal, and what my teachers give me is the real deal.

The self-help movement is about getting what you want, making things happen in the world, attracting things to you that are outside of you, and achieving your goals. That approach is based on a false premise. The premise is that if you get what you want, it will make you happy. The truth is that if you get what you want, it will make you feel good only for a short time and then you'll want something else. It's like a carrot and a stick, designed by the ego. The ego thought system is based on the idea of separation: the idea that somehow we have separated ourselves from our Source, which is God, as well as from each other. And if your happiness and peace of mind is dependent on what happens in this world, you're in trouble, because the only thing you can depend on in this ego-illusion of a world is that it will shift and change. That's what it does. It's fleeting and transitory, offering only temporary satisfaction at best.

But what if it didn't matter what happened in the world? That's heresy to the ego, but what if it really didn't matter? What if you could be happy, strong, and peaceful *regardless* of what happens in the world? That would be real power. It would be real strength and freedom, and it would be real spirituality.

Having taught all over our country and the world for 14 years, in 31 countries and in 44 states in the U.S., I couldn't help but notice from many of the questions I'm asked that there is a tremendous feeling of scarcity everywhere. People then attempt to fix that scarcity on the level of form—what you could call the screen we think is our lives—by getting something that they think will somehow erase that sense of lack, such as a material thing or a relationship. However, they're looking in the wrong place. The lack is within, not without, and it's not caused by what most people think. As *A Course in Miracles* puts it, "A sense of separation from God is the only lack you really need correct."[1]

I've said that the ego is the false you, but there's another you: the real you. The real you is something that has nothing to do with this world or the body. Your body is simply a symbol of separation. The real you is something that is immortal, invulnerable, constant and unchanging, inseparable and whole; something that can't be touched by anything in this world—something that can't be threatened in any way.

When the Course starts off by saying, "Nothing real can be threatened,"[2] that's what it's talking about. It means the real you. When it goes on to say, "Nothing unreal exists,"[3] it's talking about *anything* else, anything that is not this immortal, changeless, invulnerable self. That's why the Course is a purely nondualistic spiritual thought system. It's saying that of the two worlds, the unseen world of God and the falsely seen world of man, only the world of God is true, and nothing else is true.

The world of God cannot be seen with the body's eyes, except once in a while in temporary symbols, because the body represents a limit on awareness. However, your perfect oneness with your Source can be *experienced*. Even while you appear to be here in a body, it's possible to experience the real you. And spiritual experience is very important. In fact, it's the only thing that will ever make you happy. Words won't do it; my words won't do it. As the Course says, "Words are but symbols of symbols. They are thus twice removed from reality."[4] And when you think of it, how is a symbol of a symbol ever going to make you happy? How's it ever going to make you feel full, whole, complete, and satisfied? Even a description of the reality of the world of God won't do that. It's still just words. But an *experience* of reality, an experience of what you really are and where you really are, will make you happy because it *is* full, and whole, and complete, and satisfying.

The Gnostics referred to this direct experience of God as *gnosis*, which means knowledge. But it doesn't mean intellectual knowledge or information. When the Course uses the word *knowledge*, it often uses a capital *K*, because like the word *gnosis*, it is referring to direct experience, or Knowledge of God.

How does one get to this experience, which blows away anything this world has to offer? This is accomplished by undoing your ego. As ACIM succinctly puts it, "Salvation is undoing."[5] And that's a brilliant approach, because if you could really do that, if you could completely undo the false you, then eventually the real you would be all that's left. And you don't have to do anything about the real you! The real you is already perfect; it's already exactly the same as its Source. In order to experience that perfection, what you have to do is remove the ego within your unconscious mind—the walls of separation that block your experience of this perfection. The Course takes you through a process that undoes the false you that incorrectly believes it has taken on an individual and personal identity, a separate existence from God. As we'll see in this book, that's not something you can do on your own.

This raises another question: How do you play your part in undoing the ego? This is achieved through a certain kind of forgiveness, but not the kind of forgiveness that most of the people in the world think of, if they think of forgiveness at all. The traditional form of forgiveness makes the illusory world real to your mind, thus keeping it and the ego intact *in* your mind. But true forgiveness does not make the illusory world real, and does not keep it and the ego intact.

There are people who will teach you that you should "make friends with your ego." But I've got news for them. The ego is not interested in being your friend. Your ego wants to kill you. Because if you can be hurt or killed, then you're a body. And if you're a body, then the entire ego thought system of separation is true. The only thing you can really do with your ego is undo it. *A Course in Miracles* is about undoing the ego, or the false you that has come to identify itself with the body and separation. But the real you has nothing to do with the body or separation. As the Course says many times, "I am not a body, I am free. For I am still as God created me."[6] And God created you to be exactly like God, the same as its Source forever, completely and eternally in a state of oneness.

This seemingly separate existence is actually a dream. The teaching that the world and the universe are an illusion is thousands of years old, but the Course refines that teaching into the idea that this world is a dream that you will awaken from, and it's that awakening that *is* enlightenment. This is what Buddha meant when he said, "I am awake." Today, most spiritual students think that when Buddha said, "I am awake," he meant he felt amazingly alert and ready to manifest like hell. Indeed, that's what passes for enlightenment in most of today's spirituality. But Buddha didn't mean he was more awake *in* the dream, he meant he had awakened *from* the dream. And that's not just a minor distinction. It's everything. Buddha realized that he was not the dream, but the *dreamer.* He was not actually in the dream at all. The dream was coming from him, and he was not an effect of it, but the cause of it.

This is why ACIM is completely relevant to J and Buddha. You cannot attain enlightenment without a total shift from being at the effect of the dream to being the dreamer—to being the cause. Then it becomes possible to awaken. And in order to do *that,* the ego, which is keeping you blocked in a dream state of separation, will have to go.

We can't awaken from this dream without help that comes to us from outside of the dream, from outside of the system. An analogy I like to use is this: Let's say you have a three-year-old daughter and she's in bed at night, sleeping. You peek in on her, and you can see she's having a bad dream; she's tossing and turning and has an unhappy look on her face. What do you do? You don't go over there and shake the hell out of her, because that could make her even more afraid. So perhaps you intuitively sit on the side of the bed and whisper to her. You might softly say something like, "Hey, it's only a dream. You don't have to worry. What you're seeing is not true. In fact, you made it up, and then you forgot you made it up. But you're seeing this with your mind." And when you think about it, what is she seeing that dream *with?* Her eyes are closed! And you continue whispering to her, saying things like, "Everything's all right. I'm here with you, and I'm going to take care of you." Then an interesting thing happens. Your daughter can start to actually hear your voice in her dream. The truth can be heard in the dream. The truth is not *in* the dream, ever, but the truth can be *heard* in the dream. And if your daughter listens to the right voice instead of the voice that speaks for the reality of the dream, she starts to relax. Maybe she begins to think that this dream she thought was so important isn't that big a deal after all. Then when she's ready to wake up without being afraid, she wakes up. And when she wakes up, she realizes she never left the bed. She was there the whole time. It's not that the bed wasn't there, it was just out of her *awareness.*

And when *we* woke up this morning from the dreams we were having in bed last night, all we awakened to was a different form of dreaming. *A Course in Miracles says,* "You are at home in God, dreaming of exile but perfectly capable of awakening to reality."[7] And into *this* dream, which is not reality, the Holy Spirit is whispering the same kinds of things to us that we might whisper to a three-year-old who's having a bad dream in bed at night. The Holy Spirit is saying to us right now, "Hey, it's only a dream. You don't have to worry. What you're seeing is not true. In fact, you made it up, and then you forgot you made it up. But you're seeing this with your mind." The Course tells us we are "reviewing mentally what has gone by."[8] In addition, it makes the uncompromising statement, "All your time is spent in dreaming."[9]

The reason this dream seems so much more real than the dreams we have in bed at night is because of levels. There are no levels in Heaven, where there is only perfect Oneness and no differences. But the ego's world is full of levels and differences. This is a trick to make us believe that because this dream seems so much more real than the ones at night, then it must be reality. Yet even many physicists of today will tell you the universe has to be an illusion; it can't possibly be here. Some are even becoming convinced that this is all a simulation. But whatever you want to call it, the fact is that you dream that you're born, you dream that you have this strange life, you dream that you die, you dream that you have this in-between period, you dream that you're born again, and it goes on and on. Our lifetimes are like serial dreams that occur one after the other, so we are always in an unreal state. The *form* of the dreams appears to change, but the *content* is always the same: separation. The Course teaches that this is an unreal state, and in a state of unreality and confusion there is always an underlying anxiety, whether conscious or not. Yet if we have the willingness to listen to the right Voice that speaks for the reality of Spirit, instead of the ego voice that speaks for the reality of the dream, we start to relax. Maybe we'll begin to realize that all these things we thought were so important in the dream weren't such a big deal after all. Perhaps there is a greater reality that is just beyond the dream, and yet everywhere. It's not that it's not there; it's simply out of our awareness. This is why the Course talks about "removing the blocks to the awareness of love's presence, which is your natural inheritance."[10] Your natural inheritance is nothing less than the Kingdom of Heaven, and you don't have to earn it; it was given to you as a present by God. You don't have to earn a present, but you do have to awaken to it if you think you are here. I love the question the Course asks us: "How else can you find joy in a joyless place except by realizing that you are not there?"[11]

The Course is a very BIG teaching, not the little one portrayed by most of its teachers. The Holy Spirit is Guiding us to awaken, not to be a better individual, but to be ALL of it, nothing less than One with God. And that doesn't happen overnight. We go through a process. Spirit is a higher life-form than being a body. You have to be prepared for this higher life-form, or else awakening would be too frightening. Just as a butterfly goes through a cocoon process, we do so too in order to awaken to what we really are. What facilitates that metamorphosis is the Holy Spirit's teaching of a certain kind of forgiveness. The Course tells us, "Forgiveness is the central theme that runs throughout salvation, holding all of its parts in meaningful relationships, the course it runs directed and its outcome sure."[12]

There are three basic steps that make up the Holy Spirit's kind of forgiveness. Determined practice of them will eventually result in what the Course calls Vision, and it will inevitably lead to your awakening from the dream of duality and opposites.

We can begin to do what *A Course in Miracles* says is necessary for the salvation of "the Sonship," which you could take to mean everyone and everything that appears to exist. J says, "Thus is all the thinking of the world reversed entirely."[13] You do your part in salvation, which is your only responsibility in this entire mess we seem to find ourselves in, by practicing the unique form of forgiveness the Course teaches. You don't have to save the world. That's the Holy Spirit's job. Your job is to *follow* the Holy Spirit instead of having to be the boss. Now, if you own your own business, you don't have to *tell* anybody you're not the boss, but in your mind you know who the real leader is. Many people think of Jesus as being the ultimate leader, but the truth is that he was the ultimate follower. In the Course, he says he just listened to one Voice. This is the Voice the Course wisely describes as "The Voice for God,"[14] the Holy Spirit, rather than as the Voice of God. God does not interact with the world, because God is perfect Oneness and we should be happy God is not responsible for this world. If He was, He'd be just as crazy as we are. But because God is still Perfect Love, as both the Bible and the Course say, that gives us a perfect home to go home *to*.

In this dream, the Holy Spirit can and does see our illusions, but without believing in them. We learn to think like the Holy Spirit and thus awaken to Spirit, by following the Holy Spirit's counsel to forgive. The first step in doing this requires discipline, the kind of discipline it takes to make a choice you are not used to making when the stuff hits the fan.

As a personal example, let's imagine I'm driving down the freeway in Los Angeles, where I live, and some guy cuts me off in traffic. We all know that cars bring out the best in men, and right at that moment I have a conscious *choice* to make between one of two interpretations of what I'm seeing. I can do what most people do and think with the ego, which is to judge and perhaps even react (a big mistake). Maybe, if I'm having a bad day and I'm particularly upset, I'll give the person who cut me off the finger. This can lead to all kinds of problems. What if that person has a gun? I could be dead—not that there's anything wrong with being dead. After all, when your body appears to stop and die, your mind keeps right on going, so you're never *really* "dead." But if you have things you still want to do here, there *is* another choice.

Instead of reacting with the ego, I can stop myself. That's not easy, because it goes against everything I've been taught for as long as I can remember. Stopping yourself is particularly difficult for men. Men have a problem called testosterone. If you push me, I'm going to push you back. It's built into the system. Men start wars. It seems that half of us don't know how to do anything constructive. Yet it *is* possible to make another choice. I can catch myself starting to think with the ego, and I can stop myself. That's the first step in true forgiveness, and that first step is the hardest. To take that first step on a consistent basis takes a firm decision to change and a determined effort to get into the habit of thinking with the Holy Spirit instead of the ego.

Once you've learned to stop yourself from reacting with the ego, which takes the kind of discipline and mind training that is taught throughout the lessons of the Course's Workbook, you can go on to the next step in forgiveness. Eventually all three steps will blend into one, and you'll do them as a habit without having to think much about the steps. You'll just *know* the truth and think accordingly. This is much like the Zen concept of *knowing* as unarticulated truth. But at first it's essential to learn and practice the steps so you know what you're doing, and so you know what it is you're choosing between. That's how the steps become a part of you, and you'll know they're a part of you when you miss forgiveness if you *don't* do it. One of the reasons for that is you'll know that *you* are the one who is actually getting the benefits of doing it.

If you can stop reacting with the ego, you can take the second step and start thinking with the Holy Spirit. This step involves what the Course calls the "Holy Instant." That's the instant you switch from thinking with the ego to thinking with the Holy Spirit. Now you've made the right choice. And you're always choosing, whether you like it or not. You can't think with the ego and the Holy Spirit at the same time. They represent two complete and mutually exclusive thought systems. If you choose wisely, it leads to a totally different experience of life. It can even lead to a better outcome, but that's just an effect. Our focus is on the cause. If you take care of the cause, the effect will take care of itself. The ego has been telling you that what you're see-ing is real, that the body is real, that you have a real problem you need to take care of with real people in a real world. The Holy Spirit has a totally different story: what you're seeing is not true.

Aside from describing it as a dream, the Course also describes the ego's illusory world as a projection that's coming from your own unconscious mind. Because you can't see your unconscious, you can't see that you're the one that the projection is coming from. You've made a projection of bodies and a trillion forms of separa-tion. But people are not bodies; they are still perfect spirit at home in God. This has merely been forgotten. The Course asks you, "What if you recognized this world is a hallucination? What if you really understood you made it up? What if you realized that those who seem to walk about in it, to sin and die, attack and murder and destroy themselves, are wholly unreal?"[15] Eventually it would be impossible for you to ever react to the world the same way you used to, and in choosing the Holy Spirit you would be taking the second of three steps that awaken spirit in yourself. As the Course teaches, "The term *mind* is used to represent the activating agent of spirit, supplying its creative energy."[16] By choosing spirit, you activate it in your own mind. The Course also teaches that miracles "heal because they deny body-identification and affirm spirit-identification."[17]

In *A Course in Miracles,* the "miracle" is the kind of forgiveness I'm describing: a kind of forgiveness that comes from a place of cause and not effect, the kind of forgiveness where you stop being a victim and start being responsible for your own projection. Native Americans have often said, "Behold the great mystery." *A Course in Miracles* says, "Behold the great projection,"[18] because that's all that the universe of time and space is. As some disciplines have taught for thousands of years, it's all an illusion. You may not be able to see where the projection is coming from, but you can undo any effects the projection has on you by withdrawing your belief in it, which gives it power over you.

The dream is not being dreamed by somebody else. There is nobody else, only the projection. If anyone or anything in this world has the power to hurt you, it's because you've given it that power. Now it's time to take that power back and put the power of belief where it belongs: in God. Over time, this changes everything. The Course says, "Miracles are habits."[19] Your mind is being retrained to forgive instead of judge.

As for your experience, you can get to the point where the world cannot hurt you. As the Course says about the Holy Spirit's form of forgiveness, "It denies the ability of anything not of God to affect you. This is the proper use of denial."[20] By being at cause instead of effect, you are reversing the thinking of the world. Now forgiveness is justified. If all of this is real, then forgiveness is not justified. But if it's your projection, forgiveness is totally justified. The more you get used to looking at the world as not coming at you, but coming from you, the more impossible it becomes to react to it the way you used to, and the more you realize that you're dreaming.

In 2003, shortly after the release of my first book, *The Disappearance of the Universe,* I started an online study group at Yahoo about my book and *A Course in Miracles.* It has gone on to become the largest Course study group in the world. At the group we coined a phrase for "forgiveness opportunities." We started to call each one a JAFO, an acronym for "just another forgiveness opportunity." The phrase is born of the fact that there will always be forgiveness opportunities as long as you appear to be here. However, it's possible to get to the point where these forgiveness opportunities cannot affect you. When that time finally arrives on your spiritual path, these JAFOs will be less challenging and your forgiveness will be more and more automatic, leading to a major change of experience.

I'm often asked various questions at my Workshops about what the Course means, and I usually start off by saying that the best way to know what the Course means is to go by what it says. That may seem obvious, but the Course says a lot of things people don't want to hear, and there's tremendous psychological resistance to getting it. For example, it says, "There is no world! This is the central thought the Course attempts to teach."[21] Most people don't want to hear that. They want the world, and they desire the things in it they are attracted to, hoping at the same time that the bad things won't come to them, or at least not be *too* bad. Yet the Course also says (with the Voice of the Course, Jesus, speaking in the first person), "I once asked you to sell all you have and give to the poor and follow me. This is what I meant: If you have no investment in anything in this world, you can teach the poor where their treasure is. The poor are merely those who have invested wrongly, and they are poor indeed!"[22] The Course is talking here about your psychological investment. Its teachings are always done at the level of the mind, not at the level of the physical. You prepare yourself to go home by undoing the ego and gradually letting the Holy Spirit become the dominant force in your mind, and in the end, the only force in your mind.

The world we once believed in is a dream, and nothing more. William Shakespeare, who according to my teachers was enlightened, was right on the money when he wrote these words in *The Tempest*:

> You do look, my son, in a moved sort,
> As if you were dismayed: be cheerful, sir.
> Our revels now are ended. These our actors,
> As I foretold you, were all spirits and
> Are melted into air, into thin air:
> And, like the baseless fabric of this vision,
> The cloud capped towers, the gorgeous palaces,
> The solemn temples, the great globe itself,
> Ye all which it inherit, shall dissolve
> And, like this insubstantial pageant faded,
> Leave not a rack behind. We are such stuff
> As dreams are made on, and our little life
> Is rounded with a sleep.

Those words would fit very comfortably into the Text of ACIM. The Course leads to lucid dreaming on a whole new level. Eventually you become aware that you're dreaming. Every JAFO is equally forgivable. You begin to relax. Real peace of mind is yours. Ironically, you function better in the dream because you can think more clearly, and you have the Guidance and inspiration of the Holy Spirit to lead you.

To review the first step in forgiveness: you have to catch yourself thinking with the ego and stop it! That takes discipline, because the ego is very clever and will come up with a thousand different ways to convince you that you and others are bodies, which makes the whole thing true. Yet to repeat, the Holy Spirit has a totally different identity for you to remember: "I am not a body, I am free, for I am still as

God created me."[23] This also applies to others, and the second step in forgiveness involves an understanding that what you're seeing is not true, and you need to change your mind and think with the Holy Spirit instead of the ego.

If you make it that far, the Holy Spirit will give you the right-minded ideas from the Course that are the best for you to apply to the situation or event you find yourself involved in. Or you may not have to think at all. You may simply find yourself at peace.

Eventually, as the ego is undone and the Holy Spirit begins to dominate your mind, you'll be able to hear the messages and inspiration that come from the Holy Spirit more clearly. You can even receive answers to the practical questions you have about how to proceed with your illusory life. A life lived with the Holy Spirit is a totally different experience than one lived with the ego. Now you're never alone, even if you're the only person in the room.

Your unconscious mind knows everything. It would have to, because that's where the projection of a universe of time and space is coming from in the first place. And if it knows everything, it knows that there's really just one of us. And if it knows there's really just one of us, it will interpret whatever you think about the world or another person to really be about *you*. That's a pretty sobering thought. People wonder why they're depressed, but just look at the garbage they've been thinking about other people their whole lives, without realizing it was really just going to them, and would determine how they feel about themselves and, ultimately, even establish their own identity as they would see it and believe it is! So another important aspect of the second step of forgiveness is that you understand you are forgiving the other person not because they've really done something, but because they haven't really done anything, because you're the one who made them up in the first place. So you're forgiving that person because they haven't really done anything. That's why they're innocent. This kind of forgiveness leads to a re-imaging of yourself. If they're guilty, you're guilty. But if they're innocent, you're innocent. There's no way around it. That's because of a very important law of the mind that is articulated in ACIM: "As you see him you will see yourself."[24]

Yet it's vital at the same time that you *do not stop there,* as many students do. There's another very important part to all of this that most never consider. If it's true that as you see him you will see yourself, and if you go through life thinking the world and people are just illusions, your mind will interpret it to mean that *you* are an illusion. That will leave you feeling empty and meaningless, which is a pretty good description of depression. That's why *A Course in Miracles* is a lot more proactive than most people realize. It doesn't just describe the thought system of the ego, which is the thought system of most of the world; it completely *replaces* the thought system of the ego with the thought system of the Holy Spirit. So it's imperative that you combine the third step of forgiveness with the first two.

The biggest mistake *A Course in Miracles* students as well as other spiritual students make when it comes to forgiveness is that they don't go all the way with it. Their forgiveness is too limited. That brings up the third step in forgiveness, which is based on the Oneness of Spirit rather than the chaos of an unstable and seemingly separate world. This is spiritual sight. You learn to see the way the Holy Spirit sees, and thus get in touch with what you really are. The Holy Spirit sees the love and innocence of Spirit everywhere. In fact the Course says, "Wherever He looks He sees Himself."[25]

Thus the third step is what my teachers call *spiritual sight,* and what the Course also describes not only as Vision but as true perception. You change your own experience, and ultimately what you believe is your own identity, by changing the way you think about and identify other people. As the Course tells us in the final section of the Text, "Choose once again what you would have him be, remembering that every choice you make establishes your own identity as you will see it and believe it is."[26] This is why it's vital to remember that the Holy Spirit doesn't think in terms of separation. The Holy Spirit thinks in terms of the wholeness and the Oneness of Spirit. Spiritual sight involves the way you think. With spiritual sight you *overlook* the body, as well as the idea of individuality, and think outside of the box. You think of that person not just as being *part* of the whole, but as being *all* of it.

It's possible to carry on a normal conversation with someone and still acknowledge in your mind what they really are, which is perfectly

One with God, and where they really are, which is the perfect oneness of Heaven. And if you think about people that way often enough and long enough, eventually you can't help but experience that's what you really are and where you really are. That's the way the mind works. That's how Jesus got in touch with his own Divinity. That's how Buddha awakened from the dream. That's how some of the other masters discussed in this book thought in different forms but with the same idea, that there exists the Oneness of Reality that's just beyond the veil of separation, and only this reality is true. That's nonduality. And being at cause they were not a victim of the dream, they were the author of the dream. Then, when the process of undoing the ego is complete because all of your forgiveness lessons are complete, and with no guilt left in the mind, the time comes when you lay the body aside for the final time and you are awake and at home in God for the timeless reality of eternity.

Forgiveness, when done correctly, leads to love automatically, because that is what you are. And love leads to peace. The practical application of these ideas by enough people can and will eventually lead not only to their enlightenment but to world peace, and you can play your part in the healing of the collective mind of all beings.

The world has been trying to achieve world peace in the wrong place: out there on the screen. But by focusing in the right place, the time will come when world peace is finally achieved. That won't happen in our lifetime, but that doesn't matter. You can do your part *now*. Then you can awaken and go home.

In *The Disappearance of the Universe*, my teachers and I were talking about the prospects for world peace when they said something very interesting: *"The people of the world will never live in peace until the people of the world have inner peace."* That's because the Course teaches us that what we're seeing out there on the screen we call life is really "the outside picture of an inward condition."[27] In fact, the illusory world is just a symbolic representation of what exists in the one, large, hidden mind, or what Carl Jung called "the collective unconscious." If what we're seeing is a reflection of that which is within, then as long as there's conflict in the mind, there will always be conflict in the world, whether it be war, murder, crime, terrorism, mayhem, or merely disagreements. But the day will come when enough people attain inner peace through the type of forgiveness that undoes the ego. When *that* happens, it will change everything.

I think it's very appropriate that the people who published *A Course in Miracles* called themselves the Foundation for Inner Peace. The human race has been trying to achieve world peace for thousands of years, just in this cycle of history. So we try diplomacy, and when that doesn't work we try negotiation, and when that doesn't work we try war. But people get tired of war after a few years, so we try a League of Nations. But that doesn't work, so after the next war we try a United Nations, and occasionally we seem to have peace. But it's not *real* peace. As the Course puts it, "Mistake not truce for peace."[28] Nobody ever forgets where the hatchet is buried. That's because we haven't dealt with the cause. But when a critical mass occurs where enough people in the world achieve inner peace, then outer peace will literally have to happen. As Shakespeare would say, "It must follow, as the night the day."

You have an opportunity to make a real contribution to the healing of the unconscious mind, and thus the world, with your forgiveness and your achievement of inner peace. Historians may not put you in the history books, but so what? Most of the people in the history books were war makers. We're peace makers. As the immortal Gandhi said, "You must be the change you wish to see in the world." Perhaps Gandhi was not the first one to say that; it can be traced at least back to Buddha, and probably further. But Gandhi knew it was true, and he lived it. You can do the same if you are determined enough to attain your enlightenment and the peace of God. We do not have to be intimidated by the masters who have come before us. As Jesus explains in the Course, "There is nothing about me that you cannot attain."[29]

Both Mary Baker Eddy and the Course said, "All are called but few choose to listen."[30] Are you willing to listen? One of my favorite sentences in the Course appears in the final section of the Text called "Choose Once Again." It admonishes us, "Choose once again if you would take your place among the saviors of the world, or would remain in hell, and hold your brothers there."[31] There are many people who are afraid of the idea of going to hell and don't realize that they're already there. According to the Course's uncompromising metaphysics, any state apart from Heaven is hell. But it's possible to eventually change your experience to a higher life-form: one that has no form. You can graduate from the experience of being a body to the Oneness of Spirit.

The world is full of many forgiveness opportunities, if we're willing to take advantage of them. If we have trust and perseverance, we can attain the attitude of J: "Let us be glad that we can walk the world, and find so many chances to perceive another situation where God's gift can once again be recognized as ours! And thus will all the vestiges of hell, the secret sins and hidden hates be gone. And all the loveliness which they concealed appear like lawns of Heaven to our sight, to lift us high above the thorny roads we traveled on before the Christ appeared."[32]

We can play our part in bringing genuine peace not only to ourselves but to the dream we call the universe, which will ultimately disappear the same way any other dream disappears when you wake up from it. We can achieve this by practicing forgiveness and seeing with spiritual sight. That's our only responsibility, but it's an important one. It's the natural profession of all those on the ladder to enlightenment. You're welcome to join in. The Holy Spirit will take care of the rest.

Part I

B.C.

1

The Ladder to Enlightenment

There are three great mysteries in life.
To a bird, it is the air.
To a fish, it is the water.
And to a human being, it is himself.

— TRADITIONAL BUDDHIST SAYING

There were many questions I wanted to ask my teachers, Arten and Pursah, that I hadn't. Many times when they appeared to me, I'd forget what I wanted to ask them because I was so amazed at their presence. Each experience was still surreal to me, even after there had been dozens of them. For example, I wanted to ask, How did Jesus get to be Jesus? What was his previous lifetime like *before* he was Jesus? And how did Buddha get to be Buddha? What were the experiences they had and what disciplines had they practiced that enabled them to awaken and attain their enlightenment before other people did?

My teachers had taught me that these past lifetimes were like serial dreams. We never actually incarnate into a body. We have never really been in a body, and we never will be. Our experience is a trick of the ego: a sleight of hand, an optical illusion, or as Einstein put it, an "optical delusion of consciousness." We believe we are in a body and are seeing the universe with the body's eyes, when the truth is we are actually seeing with the mind. In turn, everything we see, including our own bodies, is merely part of the same projection as is everything else in the dream universe. And they are only that: projections with no substance, much the same as in a movie theater.

In the fall of 2013, I hadn't seen my teachers for about nine months. I had a feeling they could show up at any time, and my intuition of them appearing had become very accurate. This was because I had become more in touch with Spirit and come to learn that Arten and Pursah *were* the Holy Spirit taking on a form in order to communicate. The Holy Spirit has to take on a form, or else we'd never be able to hear it and we'd be stuck in illusions forever. The most common way for the Holy Spirit to show up is in the form of ideas that come into our mind. An idea has form to it. And in some cases the Holy Spirit takes on different forms. It all depends on what is best for the person being communicated to. This is why we shouldn't compare our experiences to those of other people. The Holy Spirit knows what's best for us.

While I waited for my teachers to show up, I had no shortage of happenings to occupy my time. I had just published a book based on our last conversations, *Love Has Forgotten No One*. One of the more surprising developments was the growing interest in Asia in the Course. Suddenly my wife, Cindy, who had become a fine teacher in her own right, and I were being invited to teach in Japan, Taiwan, South Korea, and most surprisingly, Mainland China. In fact, a teaching organization in China had invited us to come for two-week tours twice a year for five years. It was a very exciting prospect to be able to go to a faraway land and see the Course, which was new there, finding its way into the minds of the people of the Far East. Chiao lin Cabanne, the woman who had translated *A Course in Miracles* into the traditional Chinese they speak in Taiwan, had also translated it into the simplified Chinese they speak on the Mainland, but it took years of tireless effort on her part to get the Course published on the Mainland. The Communist party had to be sure that the Course was not subversive to their authority. Chiao lin had also translated *The Disappearance of the Universe* into both forms of Chinese, and once the Course was approved for the Mainland it didn't take long for D.U., as it is popularly known, to be available there as well. The timing for me was perfect. Aside from Chiao lin herself, who is Chinese-American, I got to be the first well-known American teacher of the Course there.

The Mainland had been changing rapidly for years. The Communist Party had allowed capitalism to become the norm, hoping to fend off social discontent. I had heard and read that going to Shanghai now was like going to Tokyo. But there was one thing you *couldn't* do there. You could not criticize or question the authority of the Party. That could be fatal. In fact the slaughter of students by the army in Tiananmen Square in 1989 was never mentioned on the Mainland, although there were brave Chinese students studying abroad who openly spoke of it in an attempt to keep facts about it alive.

People in China were forbidden to get on most of the Internet. Sites like Google, Facebook, Twitter, and YouTube were not permitted, but that didn't stop many of the people from getting what they wanted. They could get software that would trick the Chinese censors and make it look like their computers were accessing the sites from another country. Indeed, much of the exposure to the Course and my work had happened because of this, and the people, especially Buddhists and psychotherapists, were excited about this new teaching and its deep take on ancient wisdom.

Another thing you couldn't do on the Mainland was talk in a supportive way about the Dalai Lama. Even though he had no army, the Party still feared his influence and his potentially taking back Tibet. That hardly seemed in the cards, despite the wishes of many in the West, but it made no difference. In any case, the exotic intrigue that had developed in China made me happy to be able to go there and see the Course and the Holy Spirit work their miracles of forgiveness.

Another surprising development in my life since I'd last seen my teachers was that I fell in love with a little kitty. I had always been a dog person. I had the same dog for 15 years. I loved the enthusiasm of dogs, and I found cats to be a bit aloof. But Cindy had seen an adorable, three-month-old little kitty online who had no home, and I found myself, along with her, off to the rescue. Luna, as we named her, turned out to be a total joy. She was like an unbelievably cute flying monkey. She was lightning fast and entertaining, but she could also have the attitude of royalty. Having now had both a dog and a cat, I understood the difference in how they think.

This is how a dog thinks: *Wow! These people are great. They love me, they feed me, they take care of me. They give me everything. They must be Gods!*

This is how a cat thinks: *Wow! These people are great. They love me, they feed me, they take care of me. They give me everything. I must be a God!*

During the summer Cindy and I led a retreat in Hawaii, as we did almost every year. Walking back to our room one night, we had one of our most unusual experiences ever.

We looked up and noticed two half-circular objects in between the clouds. It was like they were two halves of the same whole, yet separate from each other. They were not very high up at all, maybe a thousand feet. There were lights going through each one, and it was as if they were signaling us with the lights. I got the distinct impression that they were communicating with us, speaking a language I did not understand. We weren't the slightest bit fearful. I knew intuitively that this was a spacecraft from light-years away. I wondered if they were Pleiadians, like the ones I had met when Arten and Pursah took me for a trip around the universe. It was as though they were acknowledging us, saying hello. The episode lasted only about a minute, but it was so clear and so close that it filled us with a sense of wonder. The spacecraft disappeared instantly, as if it had never been there. But I knew that even though we couldn't understand what they were saying, we had been spoken to by alien beings in a positive way. I was willing to leave it for the right time to have the exact meaning revealed to me.

Cindy and I would often get together with her sister, Jackie, and Jackie's husband, Mark. We'd engage in far-out metaphysical conversations about spirituality, aliens, sound-healing, conspiracy theories, and the hidden forces that run the world. The conversations were normal to us, yet I remember thinking that if anyone overheard us they'd say, "What the hell are they *talking* about?" Of course that was also true when the four of us simply talked about the Course. To the uninitiated, our words would seem ultraradical, but to the advanced student, completely acceptable.

One day I was sipping my morning coffee and thinking of the past. There was a time when I used to drink six cups of coffee a day and smoke 30 cigarettes. *Wow*, I thought. *Aside from everything else, it takes time to do that!* Now I had one cup of coffee a day and no cigarettes, but I still didn't have enough time to do the things I wanted to do. *Strange illusion*, I thought. Then suddenly and without ceremony, my teachers were there, sitting on our black leather couch.

ARTEN: Hey, bro, you've had a busy year. Congrats on the new book being out.

GARY: Thanks, but I should congratulate you. After all, the best parts of it come from you guys.

ARTEN: Oh, I don't know. As one of your readers wrote to you, you're not our water boy any more.

GARY: And how are you, my unattainable beauty?

PURSAH: Still unattainable. So let's get down to business, shall we?

GARY: You sound serious. Is something urgent?

PURSAH: Not really, but we want to emphasize to you that the reason we keep visiting you is to help people keep the process going of undoing their egos, and accelerating that process. The undoing of the ego takes time, and it's easy for people to get distracted, in many different ways. We'll point out some of those ways as we go along.

ARTEN: And don't forget, that takes a combination of repetition and the introduction of new ideas. You'll be hearing both. So tell me, how are you doing forgiving your critics?

GARY: Pretty good. Besides, you know what they say about critics.

ARTEN: No, Gary, what do they say about critics?

GARY: Critics are like eunuchs in a harem. They see it performed every night, but they can't do it themselves.

PURSAH: That's not *exactly* what Arten meant by forgiving, but I appreciate the humor.

GARY: You know, Cindy and I had lunch once on Wilshire with this guy named John who she graduated with from the University of Santa Monica. The conversation turned to the fact that there are a lot of angry, negative people out there on the Internet, and he said something that really struck me. He said, "Gary, you've got two kinds of people. You've got your people and not-your people. Why waste your time and energy responding to or thinking about the ones who are not your people? Don't bother. They're not going to change their minds anyway, not until they're ready to. What you want to do is spend your time and energy on the ones who *are* your people. Then your efforts will always be well spent." That made a lot of practical sense to me. And yes, forgiveness is even deeper.

PURSAH: Well, we're going to be going pretty deep with you during this series of visits, my brother. And we're going to be doing it in a way we know you've been waiting for.

GARY: I knew it! You've been picking up on the fact that I want to know how Jesus got to be Jesus. Of course, I'll call him J. And while we're at it, how did Buddha get to be Buddha? What were their dream lifetimes like the time before that? What did they learn and apply? We all know an ounce of application is worth a pound of knowledge.

PURSAH: It sure is, and you're asking an appropriate question. When a master like J comes back for his final lifetime, it's not like he has a big learning curve. He already knows everything he has to know in order to be enlightened. That story of J teaching the rabbis in the temple when he was 12 years old is true. They even called him Rabbi, which means teacher. He already knew everything. There were just a couple of big lessons that were appropriate for him to teach and learn during that lifetime, including, of course, the crucifixion.

ARTEN: Another reason a master comes back for his or her final lifetime is to be there for others. Many people simply need to be pointed in the right direction. The master can't do the students' mental work for them; they have to do that. And the student cannot be enlightened simply by being in the presence of a master, even though some of them would like for that to be true. But the master can point the way.

That's what J, the wisdom teacher, who really appeared to exist in this world two thousand years ago was doing: pointing people in the right direction. Not starting a religion, but pointing the way. You may recall that we once described him as a light leading the children home to the Kingdom of Heaven.

PURSAH: You could also say that's exactly what he's doing today with *A Course in Miracles.* It's like he's saying, "Look, this is what worked for me. Maybe you should check it out. Maybe you'll save yourself a few thousand years." And as you know, he's often quite forceful in the *Course* with his teaching style. He's relentlessly uncompromising.

GARY: I noticed. And people are always trying to compromise on the Course.

ARTEN: Don't let that have any effect on you. It's just a dream, remember? And it's *your* dream, not somebody else's. There isn't anybody else.

PURSAH: It's interesting that you've been asking about both J and Buddha. More interesting than you think.

GARY: Okay, I'll play along. Why's that?

PURSAH: What if I told you that they knew each other in several lifetimes, and even helped each other along the path?

GARY: You're shitting me. I always thought of them as two completely separate beings, because their cultures were so different.

ARTEN: You'll find that in the end their cultures were the *only* thing that was different about them. Ultimately, we are all one. And we have a few surprises for you along the way.

GARY: By now I'd be shocked if you didn't. But tell me, how did they help each other along the path?

ARTEN: Explaining that will be gradual, because enlightenment in the illusion comes gradually. Even J and Buddha started out at the bottom, except they had one great advantage over others that guaranteed the two of them would get home quicker than anyone else.

GARY: Say it.

ARTEN: They didn't buy into the dream as much as other beings did. Yes, they believed it at first, but they didn't believe it *as much*. They had doubts from the beginning that the dream had substance, and sensed that only an insane God would make an insane world. They also sensed that God was *not* insane, and that something was amiss.

PURSAH: That simple advantage was huge, and you don't have to be them to learn it. But they learned it before others, because they had already sensed it.

ARTEN: Yes, but they still had to climb back up the ladder to enlightenment.

GARY: I don't remember much in the Course about a ladder.

ARTEN: Actually, it's in there a few times. For example: "What waits in perfect certainty beyond salvation is not our concern. For you have barely started to allow your first, uncertain steps to be directed up the ladder separation led you down."[1]

Everyone who thinks that they're here climbed down the illusory ladder of separation. In fact, it's the experience of separation from your source, which is God, that's the problem. At other times we've gone into how the separation seemed to occur, so we won't repeat it here. But the place where all people who begin a sincere spiritual search find themselves is right at the lowest rung of the ladder, steeped in a condition of duality. Duality means you believe there is a world outside of you. So you believe in a subject and an object. There's you *and* the world. Before you climbed down the ladder there was only perfect oneness; there was only God. But now you're stuck in a condition of twoness. There's you *and* God. That's true for people who believe in God. If they don't, then it's themselves and the world. Either way or both ways, they believe in separation. And the word *believe* is paramount here. As we emphasized in the last series of visits, it's your belief in the world that gives it power over you. Your belief puts you at the effect of it, and if you're at the effect of the world, it will have an effect on you. J and Buddha, on the other hand, didn't believe in it as much as the others did.

PURSAH: Everybody's got to start somewhere, and dualism is the condition of 99 percent of the people in the world, including those who are on a spiritual path. But as you know, *A Course in Miracles* is not a dualistic system. And it's not just nondualistic, it's purely non-dualistic, which we'll get to. That's why the Course says, "Be vigilant only for God and His Kingdom."[2] But that's a pretty tall order, which is why most students of the Course end up in some kind of a dualistic quagmire and never go all the way with it, including those who are convinced that they're right about the Course making something exist other than God, when it certainly doesn't.

Even J and Buddha, despite their advantage, had to appear to start in this world like everybody else; and we'll tell you how they did it. But because of their head start, they didn't make some of the same mistakes that most people do.

GARY: Such as?

PURSAH: One of the problems with the history of spiritual students is that they *think* they understand what a master is teaching when they don't. So someone will be with Lao-tzu, and after Lao-tzu is no longer seemingly hanging around in a body the student will say, "This is what he said and this is what he meant by it." And invariably the student will be coming from a place of dualism when the master was coming from a higher state. There's more than one higher state, and more than one step on the ladder, which we'll get to. But most students want to be teachers instead of students. It feels special to be a leader instead of a follower.

That's how religions get started. People think they understand Buddha, and so someday you end up with Buddhism. But Buddha didn't want to start a religion. People would ask him, "What are you?" and he would say, "I am awake." That's what he wanted for them, not hundreds of rituals to follow. He was a wisdom teacher.

And of course everybody and their brother thought they knew what J was saying, or they had an agenda that led them to say something to the contrary, and someday you have a religion purported to be about him. Yet, like Buddha, a religion was not something J would be interested in. He was also a wisdom teacher.

ARTEN: That's why most people in the West think of J as being the ultimate leader. But just the opposite was true! He wasn't the ultimate leader, he was the ultimate follower. Why? Because he listened to the Holy Spirit. The Holy Spirit was the leader, not him. And eventually he listened to *only* the Holy Spirit. He was vigilant only for God and His Kingdom, which is why he's advising you to do the same in the Course.

GARY: So dualism generally leads to religions (or at least organizations) that are falsely based on what the members imagine that a founder, who may have not even wanted to be a founder, was really all about.

PURSAH: Well put. Almost.

ARTEN: Remember one thing: everybody makes it real. As soon as people pray to a God that they imagine to be outside of themselves, they're making duality real. They're perpetuating the idea of separation without even realizing it. That's why enlightenment is a process.

We'll talk more about the different levels or steps on the ladder as we go along, but for now, remember that at the bottom of the ladder it's all subject and object, and it's all real.

PURSAH: We'll be back soon to tell you more about J and Buddha and how they knew each other. It wasn't in *that* many lifetimes, but it was very important to their progress. Don't forget we've told you about how minds travel in each other's orbit. You may appear to go apart, but because you're in each other's orbit, you're destined to come back together again.

GARY: So it's like Ralph Waldo Emerson said: "If we are related, we shall meet."

PURSAH: Very nice. And there's something else. The forgiveness lessons you are presented with in this lifetime are the same lessons you were presented with in other lifetimes. That's one of the reasons the Course mentions "the body's serial adventures."[3] The lessons don't *look* the same. Things didn't look the same five hundred years ago as they do today. But the *meaning* is the same. In turn that means—and here's some good news for you—if you could complete all your forgiveness lessons in this lifetime, you would simultaneously complete all of your forgiveness lessons in every lifetime.

GARY: Wow! That kind of comes back to the time-saving feature of the miracle, which I've never seen anywhere else.

ARTEN: Yes. When you do your forgiveness work in this lifetime, the Holy Spirit takes that forgiveness and shines it through every lifetime that you are not aware of at the moment. The Course is correct when it says, "Trials are but lessons that you failed to learn presented once again, so where you made a faulty choice before you now can make a better one, and thus escape all pain that what you chose before has brought to you."[4] That's not just true within the scope of one lifetime; it's true within the scope of all of them.

By the way, I take it you were blown away by your UFO encounter in Hawaii?

GARY: You ain't kidding! I had the distinct feeling we were being communicated with.

ARTEN: You were.

GARY: Were they Pleiadians?

ARTEN: You got it. They were acknowledging you. Saying hello. You see, they were in the neighborhood on one of their smaller crafts. And because you were on one of their big ships before, and you showed yourself to be of a peaceful mind, they consider you to be a friend.

GARY: I'm in the club? Does that mean the Pleiadians and me are in each other's orbit? No pun intended.

ARTEN: That's right. There's clearly a language barrier right now, though, so I wouldn't expect too much. They don't like to speak English, even though they understand it. So for now just think of them as being distant relatives. No pun intended.

PURSAH: We'll be back.

And with that they were gone. I found myself immediately looking forward to their return. J and Buddha together? It was too much.

During our talk I had mentioned the time-saving feature of the miracle, and it reminded me of a quote from ACIM. Many people use the famous "tiny, mad idea" quote from the Course, but few use the surrounding sentences. As my mind started to rest, I thought of these words:

> Let us return the dream he gave away unto the dreamer, who perceives the dream as separate from himself and done to him. Into eternity, where all is one, there crept a tiny, mad idea, at which the Son of God remembered not to laugh. In his forgetting did the thought become a serious idea, and possible of both accomplishment and real effects. Together, we can laugh them both away, and understand that time cannot intrude upon eternity. It is a joke to think that time can come to circumvent eternity, which *means* there is no time.[5]

2

From Shintoism to Lao-tzu: Early Peak Experiences

Desire and discontent lead to misfortune.
Seeking worldly things is folly.
Those who are rich are those who are
contented with what they have.

— THE TAO TE CHING

I wasn't a student of the ancient traditions or comparative religion. I really didn't care much about those things, and I had no intention of changing that. Still, I figured if Arten and Pursah were going to talk about different lifetimes when J and Buddha knew each other, then maybe I should do some homework—but I didn't. It usually surprises people to learn that I don't read much. There may be 20 books I've read in my life that have made a real difference to me. The truth is I'd still rather go see a movie than read a book any day.

However, the first time I ever became interested in spirituality was when I was 21 years old. That was a good seven years before I began what I would call being on a spiritual path. A friend of mine lent me a book and said, "You've got to read this." It was Herman Hesse's *Siddhartha*. It blew me away. That was the book that piqued my interest in things of a spiritual nature. Before that I hated life, hated people, and hated God. After that I still did. I was depressed and had lost interest in life, if I ever had much interest in life to begin with. It wouldn't be until I was older that my transformation would begin, leading all the way to a place where today I can honestly say I love God.

When I read *Siddhartha*, I didn't understand all the religious jargon of Hinduism, but I understood the story. I could relate to the young man who wanted to be free, and to the fact that he was rich but found it meaningless and took off to find salvation instead. To show you how green I was on the subject of spirituality, I read the entire book and still didn't know it was about Buddha. I would find that out later.

At the time I didn't think about the Holy Spirit. Yet looking back at my crazy 20s, I can see that the Holy Spirit was always working with me, saving my life. The Holy Spirit works with everybody, all the time, whether they are aware of it or not. I can see now that when I was 27, the Holy Spirit was nudging me in the right direction, persuading me to listen to my friend Dan's advice and do the Erhard Seminar Training (*est*). Without going into the story, *est* was exactly what I needed at the time. It doesn't exist anymore, but of the million people who did it, it wouldn't surprise me if at least one hundred thousand of them went on to do *A Course in Miracles*. It was a great precursor.

We all have a right mind where the Holy Spirit dwells, and a wrong mind which is dominated by the ego and its thoughts of separation. Which part of the mind controls us is decided by the third part of the mind: the part that observes and chooses. That's where our real power, the power of decision, is. You make that decision mostly in how you choose to think of others.

You can always tell which students are understanding and applying the Course and which ones are not. The ones who are understanding have no need to judge and condemn others; if they do, they catch themselves, stop themselves, and change their minds. On the other hand, the students who are resisting the message and practice of the Course are very, very good at pointing out the ego in *somebody else.* They're experts at it. "Oh, he's in his ego" is a favorite observation. But that's not forgiveness. *A Course in Miracles* is not about spotting the ego in somebody else. It's about recognizing that there *is* nobody else, not really, and the things you don't like about others are actually what the Course calls "the secret sins and hidden hates"[1] that you really have about yourself that you have chosen to see in other people through the dynamic of projection. Thus, when you forgive the other person who appears to be there, you are really forgiving yourself. I wondered if J and Buddha were open to such ideas in the early years of their spiritual experience.

I wouldn't have to wait long to find out. I was walking home from doing errands on a typically mild and sunny January day in California. I got home, closed the door, turned around and was astonished to see my teachers already sitting on my couch. Startled, I said, "Don't do that!" They just looked at me with their gentle smiles.

PURSAH: Don't you ever get tired of this perfect weather?

GARY: No, except if we don't get some rain here soon then we're all screwed and tattooed. You know, I've been hearing there's been a drought here for the last two years. [NOTE: This conversation took place in January 2014.] But I've been here for six years, and as far as I can see there's been a drought the whole time, except for maybe two wet weeks. I assume that's global warming?

PURSAH: That's part of it. But don't forget there have always been droughts, all through history, all over the world. Sometimes they're so bad that they cause civilizations to end, because the people have to go where the food and water is. That's what happened to the Mayans and that's what happened to Cahokia.

GARY: So we take nature for granted until it turns around and bites us on the gonads. But there *is* global warming, right?

PURSAH: Yes, and your drought situation is here for a long time. That big a problem can't be solved in a year or two. But that's not what we came to talk about.

ARTEN: This visit we're going to tell you about a couple of the lifetimes where our two masters met, knew, and helped each other. We'll tell you about a few more of those common lifetimes later. Sometimes they helped each other with knowledge and observation. Sometimes they helped by giving the other a forgiveness opportunity.

GARY: Yeah, I love forgiveness opportunities. I like the little drops of blood they form on my forehead.

ARTEN: People who are in each other's orbit will meet repeatedly. In the overall scheme of the illusion, you may appear to be in a body every hundred years or so, sometimes more often if you have a dream where you don't live long. Then, obviously, you have more time to dream another lifetime in that interval.

You can think of what we would call the modern era of history to be the last five thousand years. That's just this cycle of history, and you know very little about what happened before that—not that you know *that* much about what happened in the last five thousand years either. In any case, the first time period and place we'd like to mention is about 700 B.C. in Japan, for reasons we'll get into.

Now, the truth is there is no physical evidence, absolutely no proof that J, Buddha, or Lao-tzu ever existed. Some people actually believe they are made-up characters or perhaps composite characters. That's not true. They did exist in the dream and were just as real as anybody else appears to be. Historians will dispute exactly *when* they lived, which is kind of funny since they can't prove *that* they lived, but we'll tell you when they did.

Although it wasn't the first time they came across each other, for the purposes of our discussion the first important relationship between the beings we call J and Buddha took place at the time period we mentioned, around 700 B.C. Shintoism is one of the oldest religions in the world, although it's more of a tradition than a religion. Shintoism is particularly dominant in Japan. Even today about 80 percent of the people there think of themselves as being Shinto. Like any country and any religion, though, some people are more serious about it than others.

GARY: So J and Buddha were Shintos?

PURSAH: Yes. At that time J's name was Saka, and Buddha's name was Hiroji, although we're simplifying the names. And keep in mind, what's regarded as the sort of Bible of the Shinto religion, the Kajiki, wasn't formalized until much later than the time period we're talking about. It was more like the 8th century A.D. And even before 700 B.C. you had a long time where Shintoism was an oral tradition, being handed down through the generations. Two thousand seven hundred years ago, Saka and Hiroji were friends who were faithful to their religion as well as to the emperor. In fact, it wouldn't have been a good idea to not be loyal to the emperor, since he owned you. He owned everybody. For all intents and purposes, the emperor was

God. That belief on the part of the people lasted right up until after World War II.

GARY: That would explain the size of the emperor's palace. As I'm sure you know, I was there in Japan to speak about six years ago, and it took a 20-minute car ride just to go around the palace!

PURSAH: You saw a lot of Shinto shrines too.

GARY: Yeah, as well as Buddhist ones. No offense to Buddha, but I like the Shinto's orange-type color better than the reddish-brownish Buddhist temples, not that they aren't impressive too. And one of the Shinto ones was painted gold. That was beautiful. But I digress. What about these Saka and Hiroji guys?

ARTEN: One of the reasons we bring up those lifetimes is to make you aware that even Saka and Hiroji came from a place of dualism at times. Even if you don't totally believe in the dream like them, you still go back and forth a lot. Sometimes it's real and sometimes it isn't. Then it is again.

GARY: Sounds familiar.

ARTEN: Shintoism was and is big on ritual and that what you do in the world is very important. You're not going to tell anyone at that time and place that what they did wasn't important. That would be insanity to them. But it's only insanity if it's real.

PURSAH: The Kajiki is full of songs and poems that, put together with rituals and stories of ancestors, connect the people to an ancient past. When it comes to Shintoism, respecting your ancestors is about as holy a place as you can get.

GARY: I've seen moonlight ceremonies on TV of Japanese people in Hawaii lighting these beautiful little paper-boat-like objects and having them float out to sea to honor their ancestors. It was really nice.

ARTEN: And very important to them.

GARY: What you said about the oral tradition, the stories of origin and the rituals and all, it reminds me of the Polynesian oral tradition. I've seen a lot of it in Hawaii. Their history is in their hearts, not in books.

PURSAH: Very good, as is the connection to nature. Shintoism wouldn't necessarily think of it as oneness, but the sense of connection is there. There are parallels to the Hawaiian Gods of nature and to the legends of the origins of the islands; you could extend the similarities to Shamanism as well.

Although most Japanese people at the time didn't think in terms of oneness, our friends Saka and Hiroji were actually experiencing it at times. Although their mystical experiences were temporary, as with most mystics, they definitely had peak experiences that didn't have much to do with the framework of their religion. In fact, Saka had an experience of oneness with nature that was very similar to the one you had with the rain forest.

NOTE: Cindy and I were leading a retreat on the Big Island of Hawaii in June of the year before. It was at Kalani Resort in the rain forest on the Hilo side, near the ocean. The place we slept in was screened in but very open, like sleeping in the forest. Around midnight I had a sense that the rain forest and the island were speaking to me. The sound of the tree frogs (boop beep, boop beep), the waves of the nearby ocean, the rustling of the trees, and the sound of the trade winds, as well as a sound that seemed to connect it all but that I couldn't identify, all came together to make me feel that I was becoming one with all of those things, and thus disappearing into them. There was a language there. The rain forest was communicating with me. I could almost understand what it was saying. I was so close. I wanted to understand it, just like I wanted to understand the Pleiadians. Even though I couldn't quite pick it up, it was there. When I heard it together as one instead of the individual parts, it was there. Then I stopped trying to understand, and I merely understood. I never felt closer to the living organism of the Earth. Yet it was beyond the Earth.

ARTEN: In a while we'll talk about a couple of the early peak experiences J and Buddha had at the time of Lao-tzu. But one important distinction to make before that is that unlike the ideas of Shintoism, with Taoism *the Tao is formless*. So when the Taoists Saka and Hiroji, whose names we'll give you later, had mystical experiences, they thought of the dream that they returned to differently than they did when they were Shintos. It's a different level of awareness.

By the way, when it comes to awareness, there's something you should remember about all people, whether you are fond of them or not: *Everyone is doing the best they can with the level of awareness that they have.*

GARY: Quick question before we continue. You never seem to mention Muhammad, and I think you've mentioned Zoroaster only once, back toward the beginning of the visits. Did J and Buddha ever come into contact with them?

ARTEN: No. There's a good reason they didn't come into contact with Muhammad. He was six hundred years after their final lifetime. Of course that puts him six hundred years after Thomas and Thaddaeus too. It's not that we have anything against Muhammad, it's just that we weren't personally connected on the level of form; although as we said, ultimately all of us are connected. As for Zoroaster, he was one thousand years before the Japan time period we're talking about, and J and Buddha didn't know each other then. By the way, we did say you were once a Sufi Muslim.

GARY: Yeah, but that was after Muhammad. As for Zoroaster, wasn't he in Iran?

ARTEN: Yes, but it wasn't called Iran at the time. It used to be called Persia.

PURSAH: Getting back to the subject at hand, it turns out that Saka and Hiroji were both interested in the same woman. Her name was Megumi.

GARY: All right. Now we're getting somewhere. I want details.

PURSAH: The first thing you need to understand is that whether it shows or not, people feel on a very deep level. Even if they look calm, there are usually some pretty deep feelings going on, unless of course the feelings have been denied so completely that they're totally unconscious and the individual doesn't feel anything. But that's rare, and that's not the way it is for most people, even the quiet ones.

GARY: Still waters run deep.

PURSAH: Yes, and in order to get what our two friends were like at that time, you need to know the kinds of things they paid attention to. You've heard many times in the various teachings that you should monitor your thoughts. You should watch your thoughts closely for conflict, negativity, judgment, and condemnation. That's true, but what most teachers don't realize is that it's just as important to monitor your feelings. Why? The truth is you're more likely to act out of your feelings than anything!

Of course most people don't realize that those feelings came about as the result of thoughts, often repetitious, that they'd been having over a long period of time. The thoughts come first, and they make the feelings. Saka and Hiroji, being who they were, realized this. Also, being friends, they had long discussions and realizations about many things.

Their powers of observation were excellent, which is also true of most people who are firmly on a spiritual path. They're more likely to notice things most people don't pay any attention to. They're more likely to question things. They're more likely to ask, "What kind of a God could have made this kind of a world?"

Saka and Hiroji picked up on many of the teachings of the time. For example, they realized the importance of breath. They learned to breathe deeply at all times, until it was second nature.

GARY: I notice I always feel better when I breathe deeply. It took me quite a while to do that, because back when I first wanted to I played my guitar in nightclubs and dances and stuff, and they still allowed smoking in public buildings. All the smoke rose right up to where we were on the stage, and I didn't feel much like breathing deeply. But once I moved to Maine, I started to always do it, whether I was meditating or not.

PURSAH: Yes, and speaking of meditation, Saka and Hiroji became very proficient at it. It was something that would help them in later lifetimes.

GARY: So they got into a lot of things, even though, as you say, it was still dualistic.

ARTEN: Yes. The main difference with Saka and Hiroji was that even when they were on a dualistic path, they were already questioning the validity of what people call life. They were already sensing it was all an illusion, although they wouldn't explore that more deeply until their next lifetime together.

They'd notice other things too; for example, how to communicate with animals.

GARY: They'd talk with animals?

ARTEN: No. First of all, animals don't think in terms of words. Yes, they'll understand a few words that you repeat to them over and over, but that's not how they think. Animals think in terms of pictures. So if you want to communicate with an animal, then you have to practice sending pictures to the animal with your mind. If you do that and get good at it, you might be surprised. You know from the Course that minds are joined. That's true with animals, and it's true with humans and animals, because there's only one mind. So you can send a message to the animal in their language, which is through pictures.

You know how Luna always gets upset when Cindy leaves to do errands?

GARY: Yeah. It's okay if *I* leave. But when Cindy leaves, Luna has a conniption.

PURSAH: The next time Cindy leaves the two of you alone and Luna gets upset, send pictures to Luna with your mind. Send her a little movie showing Cindy coming home through the door, picking her up, and hugging and kissing her. It will remind the cat that Cindy always comes home and loves her, and this time will be no different. Practice doing it clearly. She'll get it.

NOTE: I tried this technique the next time Cindy left and Luna started to whine. Luna calmed down immediately.

ARTEN: And don't feel bad about Luna seeming to favor Cindy. Obviously, from the day you rescued her, to Luna Cindy is mommy. And to a child, whether it's a baby human or a baby kitty, mommy is everything. Mommy is God. So to Luna Cindy represents all the love in the world.

GARY: And what am I, roadkill?

PURSAH: Not at all. Another thing that animals think is that they are part of a pack. That's true whether they're in the wild or domesticated like you. You're the male energy in the house, and Luna senses it. So she looks to you for protection. If something goes wrong, she comes to you.

GARY: You know, I've seen that. Like when we had that 5.6 earthquake. It was one of those rolling quakes and the whole house started going up and down. It lasted only about 20 seconds but it was pretty wild. As soon as it was over, Luna came running to me.

PURSAH: There you go. You're not useless in her eyes after all. So now all you have to do is ask yourself, should you really be concerned about what a cat thinks?

GARY: Yeah. I'm making it real. Life's a bitch. But you're saying Saka and Hiroji used this method to become excellent at communicating with animals?

PURSAH: Yes, and I don't recommend anybody try this, but it can also be done with wild animals. The person who does it, though, should be very accomplished in this area, and Saka and Hiroji were. As for your time period, you'll be hearing more and more in the future about people communicating with animals, both at home and in the wild. The time will come when it's commonplace, but it will happen gradually.

GARY: Can you give me an example of them communicating with wild animals?

PURSAH: Sorry, but we can't. We don't want to encourage anyone to try what they did, and you know there would be somebody who would try to do exactly what they did. The purpose of telling you about that time in Japan is to make you realize that all spiritual students go through the same steps at one time or another, and all of these steps must be completed successfully. However, they will all lead to the biggest step, which everyone will get to when they're supposed to.

As for our two friends, all of their efforts were about using their minds in more and more powerful ways. You have to master each step of the ladder, including the beginnings of spirituality that go along with dualism, and this is done one step at a time. A lot of people don't want to do the work that it takes to complete each step. They want to skip to the end. They think they can just say, "I'm enlightened," and it's done. It would be nice if it was that easy, but it's not. You've got to undo the ego.

ARTEN: Also, a common mistake people make is they think if they know something intellectually, then they know it. But they don't! It's not enough to know something as a piece of information. You have to *do* it.

GARY: That reminds me of something Jackie said. [NOTE: Jackie is my sister-in-law, Cindy's sister.] She pointed out that a lot of Course students will say, "Yeah, I had another forgiveness opportunity." And then she'll ask them, "Yes, but did you *do* it?"

ARTEN: Exactly. It's not enough to know about forgiveness or even understand it, and that's rare enough. But once you do understand it, you have to get into the habit of doing it consistently. And that's true of all the steps on the ladder. As you learn them, you have to do them, or else you haven't really learned them!

As you can see from what we've said about our two friends, even with dualism there are accomplishments that can be pretty advanced. Saka and Hiroji's spiritual progress was accelerating quickly, and by the end of this lifetime they were ready for much more.

GARY: Hey, what about the babe? Did you say her name was Megumi?

PURSAH: Yes, she, Saka, and Hiroji all grew up in the same area and were friends as children. As they became teenagers, though, both Saka and Hiroji began to have feelings for Megumi, but because of their culture they had a difficult time getting close to her.

GARY: Ah, universal experiences. The same thing happened to me with the girl next door, Barbara. Unrequited love is a bitch. It's also a big forgiveness opportunity.

PURSAH: Yes, but did you *do* it?

GARY: Sure, 30 years later.

PURSAH: As for Saka and Hiroji, they both had dreams of one day marrying Megumi. To their chagrin, however, there were numerous obstacles in the way of that ever happening. We said that in those days the emperor owned everyone. Because of that it wasn't uncommon for his family to arrange marriages. Some of them knew Megumi's family and arranged for her to marry a man she had never met. Megumi loved Saka, which he didn't know, but she had no choice but to go along with the will of the emperor's family. So the wedding took place and the three friends could never see each other, leaving all of them deeply depressed.

GARY: Did they ever get over it?

PURSAH: Megumi was never really happy, but she did her duty, lived out her life, had children, and was respectable in the eyes of her and her husband's families. That was a very big deal at the time, keeping your word and your honor.

Another thing that was a big deal at the time, and still is to a Shinto, is that reincarnation is very *real.* That's because of the belief that the body is real. You know as a student of the Course that reincarnation is a dream. You're never really in a body; it's an optical illusion. But most Shintos don't know that, and neither did Megumi. So she hoped for better karma. The belief in karma actually predated Taoism and Buddhism. It's an idea that's associated with Hinduism, which is much older.

In any case, Saka and Hiroji were very disappointed about the situation, and even though neither one of them could be with Megumi, they developed a strange jealousy toward each other because they both had the same feelings for her! As you know, the ego can be very tricky. It almost ruined their friendship. In fact, they didn't see each other as much for a couple of years.

ARTEN: Fortunately they were both very intuitive and began to see the whole episode, as well as their lives in general, as a spiritual lesson. They sensed that they needed to forgive each other, even though they hadn't learned the art of doing that yet. So they did the best they could, and they did it pretty well. From then on, whether in that lifetime or others, they *always* forgave each other if they had to, and they did so quickly. Forgiving quickly is a sign of spiritual maturity, and even though they were still in a state of dualism they realized forgiveness was an essential part of spiritual progress. They also began to question the whole system and logic of the cycle of birth and death, although they'd learn more about that later.

PURSAH: This and all of their experiences from their Shinto lifetime together were very useful to them in their next lifetime together, during which they came to know the master and partial author of the Tao Te Ching, Lao-tzu.

ARTEN: The lifetime during which J and the future Buddha were students of Lao-tzu took place around 600 B.C., which was about 200 years before Buddha and about 50 years before Confucius. Once again, don't expect historians to agree on the times, but that's when it was. By the way, Confucius was a philosopher. He didn't have a set discipline or religion. Taoism, on the other hand, was a discipline.

GARY: Was Lao-tzu a believer in nondualism?

ARTEN: Yes, absolutely. He understood that *everything* that appears to have a form is an illusion, but the Tao is formless. This brings up a point we'll be making at times in these conversations. *All* of the teachers we're going to be talking about believed in nondualism. They knew that the truth of oneness is true, and nothing else is true—period. Then what happens, *always,* is that some of their students take their teachings and devolve them into dualism. Then, once the truth is changed, it gets passed on to the dream world as something that isn't the truth. That's been happening for thousands of years, just in this cycle of history, because the truth is too threatening to the survival of the ego.

The ego's specialty is changing the truth, whether it's the Vedanta, Lao-tzu, Buddha, or *A Course in Miracles.* The only solution to that is what we've been saying to you since the '90s: you've got to undo the ego, or the ego will continue to undo the truth. It can't help it. That's what the ego does. It's like a survival machine. And of course the students and teachers don't know that they're changing the truth. It's like projection. They don't know they're doing that either. They just think they're right.

GARY: And the cause is unconscious resistance to the truth?

ARTEN: Yes. Now, most people will take the word *Tao* to mean "your path," but for Lao-tzu the word was to be understood on two levels. On the level of the world, yes, it would be your path. But on the macro level, it would be the truth, the oneness beyond the illusion.

GARY: Would he call that *God*?

ARTEN: No. The Chinese, as you know from your visits there, aren't too big on God. So to a Taoist, the truth is simply the formless truth. It wasn't until *A Course in Miracles* and pure nondualism that you had the perfect oneness of God being acknowledged as the only reality, the ultimate truth. Of course, there was always a master here and there who knew the ultimate truth, but they weren't famous, nor did most of them care to be.

GARY: I always wondered about that. I mean, if you're really experiencing that the world is a dream and you're the dreamer, then why would it matter to you if anyone knew you were enlightened?

PURSAH: That's a good point, but sometimes for teaching purposes it's appropriate to say what your experience is.

GARY: You mean like Buddha saying, "I am awake."

PURSAH: Yes, and speaking of Buddha, he and Lao-tzu were very similar in their teachings. Sometimes things that are attributed to Buddha were actually said first by Lao-tzu, and things that were actually said later by Buddha are quoted as coming from Lao-tzu. In any case, Buddha eventually outgrew some of Lao-tzu's approach.

GARY: How so?

PURSAH: We'll be telling you more about Buddha later, but we'll point out one difference here between him and Lao-tzu, because it will help explain J and Buddha's experience of life with Lao-tzu. Lao-tzu was unusual in the sense that even though he understood nondualism he was also an ascetic, and he demanded that his students be ascetics. This led his students more to an experience of semi-dualism rather than nondualism, because if you believe you have to deny yourself worldly pleasures, then you're making the illusion real through your resistance to it.

GARY: It's like if you think you have to give something up, that's making it just as real to your mind as when you desire it.

PURSAH: Precisely. Yet it was Lao-tzu who first taught that it is desire that leads to suffering. And he thought it would help his students to give up desire by having them give up the world. He would say many things that argued against worldly participation, such as "The sage, because he does nothing, never ruins anything."

GARY: At last! A good excuse to be lazy.

PURSAH: Well, Buddha, who was influenced by both Lao-tzu and the Vedanta, believed the exact same thing two hundred years later; but in living it, he had a major revelation. He realized that if you want to escape from suffering through the relinquishment of desire, which you could say is one of the main goals of both Taoism and Buddhism, living your life to extremes will often prevent clarity. Plus it doesn't really satisfy you anyway. Eventually he espoused "the middle road." In giving up asceticism, which he and his followers had lived for years, he explained you don't need to give up the world if it's not real. At the same time, you don't have to go crazy experiencing worldly pleasures and orgiastic attempts to make it more tolerable. In other words, be normal! It's from that place that it's the easiest to actually apply the truth to the illusion you're witnessing, because you can think more clearly and you have normal situations to apply the teachings to. Notice I didn't say *easy* situations, I said *normal*. Sometimes situations in life are very hard, such as the death of a loved one. Yet even then, be normal. If you need time to grieve, take the time to grieve. If you get hungry, eat. If you're sick, take your medicine or do whatever works for you.

You've got the level of the mind and the level of the dream. They're like apples and oranges. You don't have to change the dream world, just the way you're looking at it. That's the difference between being at *cause* and being at *effect*. Your job is to take care of the cause. If you do that, the effect will take care of itself.

ARTEN: Even though Lao-tzu wasn't always perfect in his teachings, he was a master himself, so let's be clear that he understood the trickery of the ego. For example, when you're young, it's like you're seeing everything for the first time, and you really believe you are. The veil of forgetfulness is so thick that it makes everything new, and certain things hold your interest and may even fascinate you. This is the ego's trick to make it seem important and suck you in. Of course, the script is written, as the Course that came later says, but you don't know that at the time. You just think it's real and amazing.

GARY: Yeah, I remember when I was around three years old, I went to my cousin's house and there were these shelves that were behind glass. There was this really bright blue balloon on the shelf, and I was so fascinated by that balloon and wanted to have it so much.

ARTEN: Isn't it amazing how such a simple thing can mean so much to you? And guess what: it never stops. The things just get more complex, and even if they're just hobbies they seem very important.

GARY: That's true. Like the first time my dad brought my brother Paul and me to Fenway Park. I was seven, we lived in New Hampshire, and we'd been watching the Red Sox for a couple of years on a black-and-white TV. I'd never seen them in person. Then we walked down the runway and saw Fenway for the first time, and I was absolutely amazed and fascinated at how *green* it was—the grass, the walls—and how colorful everything else was. I was hooked. I must have ended up going there a hundred times over the years, and I probably would have gone even more if I lived right in Boston.

ARTEN: Lifetime fascinations are scripted all the way through, Gary, and there are no accidents along the path. The question is, what are they for?

GARY: Well, I know the Red Sox never won a World Series from 1918 on until I forgave them.

ARTEN: I don't know if you can take credit for them winning the World Series, except on a macro level, but you can certainly get the benefits of forgiving them.

PURSAH: Because of the veil, the newness of experience will always be there from time to time, even when you get older. People always act like they're the first people to ever have a baby, and they don't realize that even if it's their first baby, it's not their first time having one. It's only the forgetfulness that makes them block out the memory of all the other families they've had over thousands of dream lifetimes.

GARY: So the ego wants us to think special relationships are vital, and those relationships start with the family and continue to be introduced.

PURSAH: Absolutely. And in the lifetime we're talking about, J and Buddha had a relationship also, from the time they were children. But they weren't ordinary children. Because of their previous Shinto discipline, their minds were already more advanced than your average person who isn't particularly interested in the unseen. In fact, they were what you would call *psychic*, or *clairvoyant*.

GARY: When I was a kid I never felt like I was clairvoyant. I think I had clairavoidance.

PURSAH: As I was saying, they were unique—not special, but unique in their ability to save time. That led to being in the right places at the right times.

GARY: Wait. Quick question before we go on. How many lifetimes did these guys know each other in?

PURSAH: They weren't always guys, but it was about 40. We're going to mention only the six most relevant ones.

GARY: Forty! That's quite a bit, isn't it?

ARTEN: That's not really a high number at all. There are beings you've known several hundred times spread out over thousands of dream lifetimes. J and Buddha didn't have as many lifetimes as you because they didn't need them, and the reason their relationships will appear to be so important to you is that they knew people who were famous and were also spiritual masters. There's a good reason for that. Remember, they didn't believe in the dream as much as others. That's why they were ready to be with people who were ready to teach them.

GARY: So it's like when the student is ready, the teacher will appear.

ARTEN: Yes, and vice versa.

PURSAH: At this place and time, in China, life was more diverse than you might think, partly because China is so big. The things you read about in history books are just a small part of the story, and there's no sense in getting into it. For our purposes, what's important is the truth and using it to awaken from the dream.

From now on, when we're talking about Buddha we'll sometimes simply refer to him as B. And the names of J and B at the time we're talking about were Shao Li, who was female, and Wosan, who was male. They were neighbors who both exhibited psychic abilities. This was not a happy circumstance for their families, who worried that the children would be seen as different and made fun of, or worse. But the parents' attitude changed when word got out about the children, and wealthy families began to seek them out for advice. These families were able to pay with gold, and the parents, who were not rich, weren't about to turn down the opportunity. The children would tell the families things that the children couldn't possibly know, so the families could tell their ability was real. Then Shao Li and Wosan would tell them what actions they should take to get what they want.

GARY: So Shao Li was later J, and Wosan was later B?

PURSAH: That's right. Now, people haven't changed much in 2,600 years, only the scenery. What the children's questioners wanted was money, success, fame, and special love. And the children were actually quite good in guiding people to those things. If they wanted, Shao Li and Wosan would have "had it made," as you say, for the rest of their lives.

That, however, was not the end of the story. Friends as children, Shao Li and Wosan fell in love as teenagers. They also found themselves wanting more than the kind of life they had. Their parents may have been relatively happy, but they were not. They knew there was more, much more: more to learn, more to experience, and something more important than what the physical world had to offer. They planned their escape for months; then one night, they took what they could with them, including gold, and ran away, eventually a long distance away.

The two of them got married and stayed on the move. At first they were like fish out of water, taking tentative steps and trying to blend into whatever town they found themselves in. But after a year or so, they heard of a teacher, one who knew "the secrets of life" and could lead one to salvation. Shao Li and Wosan began to get excited. Their advanced intuition told them they should go to this man and learn from him.

The man was Lao-tzu. Most teachers and traditions didn't accept female students at the time, but Lao-tzu was different. He took the two new arrivals aside and spoke with them. He told them that to follow him they must give up worldly possessions and any attachment to old beliefs, and that eventually they would be asked to give up desire. Were they ready to accept this kind of a life?

They were. They trusted their own innate wisdom, but they didn't know if this would be a permanent way of life for them. Even though Lao-tzu was looking for commitment, Shao Li and Wosan were experimenting, wanting to see if this was really what they were looking for. They had already spent years in discontent and were not willing to do it again. So if Lao-tzu didn't work out, they'd move on. They did show some commitment, however, by quietly giving away the gold they had left to people begging in the streets. They would take some of the beggars aside and slip them small amounts, so as to not cause a scene or a riot.

ARTEN: It takes time to get used to being an ascetic. If one is used to eating regularly, the hunger can be great at first. In the beginning, Shao Li and Wosan missed abundant, tasty food as well as the many conveniences they'd been able to pay for. But the master taught them much about the nature of the world, which he said was completely illusory. He didn't make any bones about the fact that it was *all* a result of the trickery of the ego.

Occasionally Lao-tzu would take one of them aside to talk. Any student who got this opportunity considered it a privilege. Here's an example of an exchange he had with Shao Li, translated into English. You can also find some things Lao-tzu said in the Tao Te Ching. Of course, the Tao Te Ching has always been reinterpreted and changed, just like other traditions and teachings.

LAO-TZU: What a human being sees is coming from the self, which is mind, and is not being done to a person, the way most people experience it. Almost all beings see themselves as victims of a world outside of them. And if the world was outside of them they *would* be victims. But the thought of the world of multiplicity is not without but within, and then is seen as being without. The idea has not left the mind, where it has always remained. And this is the only place the thought can be changed and the problem truly dealt with.

The truth is the Tao, and the Tao is One. It has no parts. It does not collide with other things or make noises. It simply is. It needs only to be. And you need only to be.

SHAO LI: Master, why does the illusion seem so real if it's not true?

LAO-TZU: It seems real indeed, but so do the dreams you have in your mind at night. Yet does the fact that they seem real make them real? No. It's your allegiance to them that makes them real: your steadfast belief in the trickery of the ego, and its resulting mockery of life. Everyone's time comes to return to the Oneness, but you will not be able to stay there until you yourself have achieved the condition of Oneness.

The Way is empty, yet contains all. Words cannot describe it. Better that one should look for it within. The answer waits for those who have no desire.

SHAO LI: But master, how can I have no desire?

LAO-TZU: There is no "but." Without your belief in it, the world could not tempt you with desire. Practice the way of renunciation and you will find your beliefs being altered.

SHAO LI: If this is all in my mind, then why change my behavior? Why not just change my mind?

LAO-TZU: That's an excellent question, bright one, but beware of too much cleverness. *Can* you just change your mind? That is something that cannot take place without discipline. And discipline of the mind is made easier by discipline in your behavior. Discipline in worldly behavior is born of habits, and so is mental discipline. You must get into the right habits. Giving up the world in your actions will help you give up your belief in it. That in turn will help you become free of desire, and of suffering. When you are free of suffering you will be at peace. The Oneness is peace, and you'll be more prepared to rejoin with it. The world and its illusion of conflict will no longer have a hold on you.

ARTEN: You can see Lao-tzu's logic here, but at the same time he's making his students go through a stage where they think they have to give things up in order to be free of them. Yet in thinking they have to give things up, it makes those very things real in the mind and blocks the relinquishment of belief.

GARY: And that's why Buddha eventually recommended the middle way, not too worldly but not renunciation either?

ARTEN: Exactly. Besides, I'm sure you know it wouldn't be easy to give up the world completely.

GARY: No it wouldn't, but it would be cheaper.

ARTEN: In any case, the goal was eventually to give up mental attachment to the world. According to Lao-tzu, giving it up physically was just a stepping-stone. So let's give credit where credit is due. Lao-tzu was a big influence on Buddha and everything that came after Taoism, starting with our friend Wosan and including Buddhism, Platonism, J, Gnosticism, and even Christianity to a certain degree, before it was turned into a Roman farce. Lao-tzu understood and taught nondualism, even though not everybody picked up on it.

PURSAH: Lao-tzu and some of his parts in the Tao Te Ching emphasized ethics, but it should be understood that the purpose of this was to tame the ego. Because of that, humility was considered by him to be the cornerstone of true ethics.

Here's an exchange between Lao-tzu and Wosan.

LAO-TZU: You must have the humility that would bow its head before a child. Renounce respect. You do not need it. Do not think you need anything. To need something is to be a prisoner of it. To need nothing is to be rich, for you already have everything you need.

WOSAN: Then how will I know what to do?

LAO-TZU: You don't have to do anything. The Tao is emptiness. In your illusory life, to be empty is to have no agenda. The illusion is meaningless. Why would you have an agenda for something that is meaningless?

WOSAN: Then why try to be free of it?

LAO-TZU: Exactly.

GARY: A bit of a *koan* there?

ARTEN: Yes, and that was before there was anything called Zen. And Lao-tzu knew that every student goes through many stages, all of them temporary. You've been through many phases in this dream lifetime alone. Have any of them lasted?

GARY: No. In my experience, different phases on the path seem to last from six to nine months, seldom more than a year and a half. Never two years. Some of them are good stages, even fun, but some of them are hard.

ARTEN: Good. In this lifetime Shao Li and Wosan went through several phases, and they also had some of what you might call peak experiences. You've had those too, right?

GARY: Yeah, but I think I peaked too early.

PURSAH: Meditation was part of the daily discipline for every student of Lao-tzu. The idea was to achieve absolute stillness of the mind; to eventually have no interfering thoughts of any kind. Thus the mind becomes more peaceful.

GARY: My understanding is that one cannot be enlightened through meditation alone. Is that right?

ARTEN: Yes, but let's not get too far ahead of ourselves. It *is* helpful to quiet the mind. It helps prepare the mind for training. But the most important training is done through a thought system. Lao-tzu's thought system, like most, didn't go all the way home, even though it was a good one. We'll get into more detail about the importance of having a thought system later.

PURSAH: One day, Wosan was meditating on a hill. As you know, China is a hilly country. It doesn't have the abundance of farmland that America does.

GARY: That's why they make food out of anything they can. I had chicken feet, duck tongue, and pig's blood. I'll try anything once, except monkey brain. I have ethics too, you know.

PURSAH: Wosan began to lose awareness of his body. It started to disappear. Then he was invisible. His awareness began to expand, and he was no longer limited to the space he had occupied before. He could still view the world, but it no longer seemed like anything in it was bigger than him. It was coming from him, not at him. He was no longer a body but mind, and it was mind that he was seeing with, not a body's eyes. He was weightless, and the experience was ecstatic. As he continued to expand, he knew that this was a state that was more true to himself. The reason he had felt so small was that he believed that the body was him, but now he knew he could never really believe that again.

GARY: That's a great experience. I imagine he had trouble putting it into words?

ARTEN: Oh yes. Peak experiences are beyond words, just as the truth is beyond words. I make a distinction between those two things because the real truth, as we will see, is a whole level beyond Wosan's experience. But it was certainly a step in the right direction.

PURSAH: Wosan did his best to explain his experience to Shao Li and Lao-tzu. They could see his sincerity and they were excited for him. Shao Li and Wosan were very much in love, and encouraged each other whenever they could.

GARY: Did they have sex?

PURSAH: Yes, they had a normal relationship, but they weren't obsessive about it. It was a way of showing love. However, they had to hide this from Lao-tzu, who demanded that his students be ascetics in order to be a part of his following.

ARTEN: Wosan had other peak experiences, and Shao Li had her own. Once, the two of them were sleeping outside under the stars when she woke up. She looked up and began to embrace the moon, the stars, and all of the sounds in the darkness. She didn't feel apart from anything in the universe, but rather like she *was* the universe.

She was everywhere. The limitations of time and space were broken through, and she felt the Oneness of all that is. Nothing was solid; everything was interchangeable. Even after the experience faded away, she would never think of the universe the same way again.

PURSAH: These are the kinds of experiences every seeker has at some time, in some lifetime. That time may not be in the lifetime you are experiencing, even if you are on the path. You may have already had such experiences in another lifetime, and are supposed to focus on discipline more in this lifetime without repeating experiences you've already had. That's why no one should compare their experiences to someone else's. No step along the way is by accident, and neither are any of the experiences you have, or don't appear to have, along the way.

GARY: Did our two friends spend the rest of their lives with Lao-tzu?

ARTEN: No, they didn't. They followed him, mostly on the road, for about six years. Then, after very careful consideration, they decided to leave. They worked up the courage to tell him. They didn't want to run away. In fact, they wanted to thank him, which they did. They had learned much in a short time, but they felt they could continue to make good progress on their own. He had introduced them to nonduality, and they were ready to take the ball and run with it. They also had decided they wanted to have children.

GARY: Did they?

ARTEN: Yes, four, though one of the children died as an infant.

PURSAH: Our two friends had gone from semidualism as Shintos to nondualism with Taoism. But it's not easy to pass through the eye of the needle. All must be forgiven, and much of a human being's repeated experiences are merely setting up the classroom to learn, through repeated opportunities, to completely forgive the ones they keep coming into contact with again and again.

Although later J would be the one to completely teach forgiveness, he would not be understood by most. Today, more people are understanding his deeper explanations.

ARTEN: We'll continue to examine nondualism until we get to pure nondualism. In the meantime, we trust you'll continue to talk to J in your mind and learn from him. You really do have a close relationship with him, don't you?

GARY: Sure. If it wasn't for Jesus I wouldn't have anybody to look up to.

PURSAH: When we return we're going to examine two different times that J and B knew each other as Hindus. Hinduism is a classic example of nondualism devolved into dualism. Yet some have still found their way home because of what they learned from it and, far more importantly, how they applied it. Be well. By the way, Luna's been good. Don't forget to give her a treat and some lovies.

And with that they were gone, although they were never really gone.

3

A Time as Hindus

There are two eternal paths. One is light, the other is dark. The first leads to freedom from the wheel of death and rebirth. The other leads you here again. The Real never is not. The unreal never is.

— THE BHAGAVAD GITA

Many years ago, when I first heard the above quote from the Bhagavad Gita spoken at a spiritual conference, I couldn't help but notice it was saying there are only two things to choose between, not many. There are only two paths, and each one leads to a very specific result. I liked the simplicity of that. I had also heard that the ancient Hindu Advaita Vedanta was so named because the words mean "the end of knowledge." I thought that was pretty cool. Most Western approaches pride themselves on their abundance of knowledge, and here's something that sees the end of knowledge as a good thing! I was interested.

It wasn't until many years later that I would find out these ideas were associated with something called nondualism. Early on my spiritual journey, I didn't even know what that was.

The words Lao-tzu had spoken reminded me of something Cindy once said: "I have nothing to do, but everything to be." I thought that was brilliant. But Cindy herself would be the first one to say it doesn't necessarily mean you don't do anything. At one point, *A Course in Miracles* says, "I need do nothing."[1] Many students misinterpret that to mean you're not supposed to do anything, which is what the Course would call *level confusion*. The important part is that you *need* do nothing. You don't have to. If you think you have to, it involves bodily identification, so one must put the entire quote in context, and also bring in the Course's essential time-saving aspect of forgiveness:

When peace comes at last to those who wrestle with temptation and fight against the giving in to sin; when the light comes at last into the mind given to contemplation; or when the goal is finally achieved by anyone, it always comes with just one happy realization; *"I need do nothing."*

Here is the ultimate release which everyone will one day find, in his own way, at his own time. You do not need this time. Time has been saved for you because you and your brother are together. This is the special means this course is using to save you time. You are not making use of this course if you insist on using means which have served others well, neglecting what was made for *you.* Save time for me by only this one preparation, and practice doing nothing else. "I need do nothing" is a statement of allegiance, a truly undivided loyalty. Believe it for just one instant, and you will accomplish more than is given to a century of contemplation, or of struggle against temptation.

To do anything involves the body. And if you recognize you need do nothing, you have withdrawn the body's value from your mind. Here is the quick and open door through which you slip past centuries of effort, and escape from time.[2]

It goes on to say:

To do nothing is to rest, and make a place within you where the activity of the body ceases to demand attention. Into this place the Holy Spirit comes, and there abides. He will remain when you forget, and the body's activities return to occupy your conscious mind.

Yet there will always be this place of rest to which you can return. And you will be more aware of this quiet center of the storm than all its raging activity. This quiet center, in which you do nothing, will remain with you, giving you rest in the midst of every busy doing on which you are sent.[3]

In a state of nondualism, which Lao-tzu understood, no part of the illusion was accorded reality, nor did the Truth include any illusion. The truth and illusions were mutually exclusive, a fact that is lost on almost everyone. Instead, as my teachers said, people always tried to make the illusion, or at least part of it, true. This would also involve the attempt to bring whoever people thought was the Creator or Creators of the universe into the illusion by making that deity responsible for it.

One of the most common New Age beliefs is that God created the dualistic universe so He could experience Himself. The insanity of that idea is almost never questioned. It's like saying that in order to enjoy, appreciate, and experience the orgasmic joy of sex you have to shoot yourself in the stomach so you'll have a dualistic experience to compare it to. But God is not insane. The truth is a constant state, and as both the Course and the Bible have said, God is still perfect love. This dream world is the opposite of perfect, but the reality of God gives us a perfect home to go home to. To go home to that real world, however, one has to wake up from this one. There are not two real worlds. The math of nondualism is very simple. It always comes out to one.

Since the fall of 2013, when my third book, *Love Has Forgotten No One*, was published, I had continued to travel all over the world teaching the Course, most of the time with Cindy as my co-presenter. I noticed an interesting phenomenon involving my dreams in bed at night. I knew ACIM was saying that all minds are joined. That's true because ultimately there is only one mind, really just one of us that thinks it's here. That's why psychic phenomena are possible. A good psychic or medium has the ability to "tap in" to seemingly split-off parts of the mind and receive messages and information.

As the years of traveling went on, I noticed my dreams at night could be influenced by the number of people in the area. If I was in a quiet place—like Cedar Rapids, Iowa—my dreams were usually very peaceful and tranquil, except in the rare event there was someone close by in a condition of great conflict. On the other hand, if I was in a big city—like Guangzhou, China, which has 13 million people—I'd often have active, chaotic dreams that sometimes included violence. As I slept, my mind was actually tuning in to the minds of others in the area.

A happy corollary of that is that, because minds are joined, if your mind is becoming more peaceful and is having right-minded thoughts with the Holy Spirit, you cannot help but be some kind of a helpful influence on those around you. The Course teaches that the simple presence of a teacher of God acts as a reminder. At some level, you're getting through to people's minds whether you realize it or not. That doesn't mean you can do their forgiveness work for them; they still have to do their part, but you *can* point them in the right direction.

Many students in history have thought they could become enlightened simply by living in the presence of a master; that somehow his or her enlightenment would rub off on them, like catching a virus or something. That would be nice. Unfortunately, it doesn't work that way, whether 2,600 years ago or today. The ego must be undone, and that takes discipline.

The next time my ascended friends showed up, I'd been watching some news shows on CNN and MSNBC and trying to forgive what I saw. That effort was helped by the fact that the news had become more comical, almost cartoonlike. Yes, there's tremendous tragedy in the movie-illusion we call life, but it's making it real that makes it painful. Arten began the conversation.

ARTEN: I see you've been entertaining yourself with the news. That's fine, as long as you remember what it's for. After all, everybody loves a circus.

GARY: I know. I can't believe Donald Trump is doing good.

ARTEN: Then don't believe it.

GARY: Oh, yeah.

PURSAH: Today we're going to give you a glimpse of a very interesting part of J and B's history together, a time they spent as Hindus. This was a leap forward for them. Later they'd also know each other as Buddhists at the very beginning of what would become Buddhism. So you should realize that Buddhism is kind of like Hinduism without all the Gods. Monotheism, the belief that there's only one God, wasn't popularized until Judaism, then later Christianity and Islam. By the way, all three of those faiths have the same God: the God of Abraham. But before those religions, you usually had at least a few Gods for different purposes.

GARY: Like the Greek Gods.

PURSAH: Yes. The Hindus and the Greeks probably had the most Gods, and Buddhism focused on the mind. By the way, we'll be talking a little about Buddhism later, but you should realize, since we're going to be talking about Hinduism now, that at first Buddhism was considered to be part of Hinduism, like a sect, just as Christianity originally considered itself to still be part of Judaism, not something separate from it. Also, Buddhism never really caught on very much in India. It was only when it spread to China that it took off, as you would say.

GARY: Yeah, it's hard to have a hit.

ARTEN: One accurate thing you could say about Hinduism and its history is that it's complicated, so we're not going to be getting into all the different books and schools of thought. Hindus believe that many of their Gods, including Krishna, can be traced back at least 3,200 years. That can't be confirmed, but that's the belief. Some of the philosophy in the Advaita Vedanta also goes back before recorded history. You may recall we told you a long time ago that even though the original idea behind it was nondualistic, it was incorrectly interpreted by some of Shankara's followers as being dualistic, and that's how a large segment of Hindus eventually came to think of it. That's par for the course. By the way, you said it was Shankara who misinterpreted it, but that was a mistake: it was some of his students who got it wrong and passed it along.

We want to tell you a little about J and B and a lifetime they shared around 500 B.C. That was about a hundred years after their experience with Lao-tzu. Their names were Harish and Padmaj. No need to give their full names. They were cousins and neighbors in a fairly large village. They were raised to be devout Hindus, but Harish felt the temptation to have worldly experiences.

This is where you want to realize that people are *thrown by the ego* to be a certain way. They are the way that they are because that's the way they're supposed to be in order to have the experiences they've been set up for, and they don't know why because it's all unconscious.

Let's say you were born today in Canada, and when you're six years old, you start playing the game of hockey. Of course you don't know why, you just love it. You keep playing, and over the years you get really good at it, good enough that one day you become a professional player. Nothing in the world interests you as much as the game. Yes, you have a personal life, but it's the sport that enthralls you. This happens because it's supposed to, and this is the way it is with all people, their professions, and the things they're most interested in. They are thrown to live out a script, and nothing can stop it.

PURSAH: Do you remember when you were 12, you were at a friend's house, and he took you into his father's room and opened up a case that had a gun in it?

GARY: Oh my God. I haven't thought about that in ages.

PURSAH: How did you feel when you saw the gun?

GARY: I was scared, really scared. I didn't want to have anything to do with it. My friend, I won't say his name, probably thought I'd be fascinated with it like him and that I'd want to play with it, but I got the hell out of there as fast as I could.

PURSAH: Why do you think you felt that way?

GARY: I don't know. I guess it was unconscious.

PURSAH: Precisely. So there are two things you should know about that. First, in your previous dream lifetime you were killed fighting in World War II. The horror of war was deeply imprinted in your unconscious, and a gun was the last thing you wanted to see. Second, it was because of your experience of war in your previous lifetime that you didn't have to go to war in this lifetime. That wasn't an experience you had to have again right away.

GARY: You mean that's why when I was 19 they switched over to the draft lottery, and my number was so high that I didn't get drafted and sent to Vietnam?

PURSAH: Yes. Come to think of it, have you ever fired a gun in your life?

GARY: No. I never have.

PURSAH: And you never will. It's not something you're supposed to do this time. On the other hand, your friend who showed you the weapon remained fascinated with guns and practiced using them whenever he could. Eventually he decided to make the military his career. However, he ended up getting killed in Vietnam.

GARY: I didn't know that. I didn't stay in touch with him after that gun episode.

PURSAH: You weren't supposed to. Eventually, because of the path you've chosen, you'll remember that World War II experience of being killed and be able to forgive it. Then you'll be free of it.

GARY: You're saying that what happens is already predetermined, but I still have the power to practice forgiveness at the level of the mind, and be free of feeling the uncomfortable effects of whatever happens.

PURSAH: Excellent. And even though the purpose of forgiveness is not to change the script, but instead to be free of its effects, it's also possible, within a fixed system, for the Holy Spirit to adjust time and space for you. You may then have a different experience than you would have. But that's up to the Holy Spirit. Your job is to do the forgiveness work. The Holy Spirit knows if it's appropriate for you to change dimensions of time.

ARTEN: We say all this so you'll understand why Harish had a certain kind of personality, and potentially harmful situations he felt drawn to, but his cousin Padmaj was different. Padmaj wasn't as interested in the temporal experiences of the world, and wanted to attain enlightenment.

They were born to be this way because of the ego's plan to divide and separate them. They'd already learned a great deal together at other times, and the ego, at the level of the unconscious, felt very threatened and planned to get them to part ways. When he was old enough, Harish would go into the town that was about an hour's walking distance from the village. He liked to have a good time, drinking rice wine, gambling, and flirting with women. He always asked Padmaj to come with him. Padmaj wasn't very interested in fun and games, but Harish was his only friend as well as his cousin, and he wanted to be with him rather than feeling left out and lonely. So in the illusion you have the duality of Padmaj, seeking to be holy, and Harish, seeking to be worldly. You can add to that the complication that because of their studies at a young age, as well as their Lao-tzu experience, they both already knew a basic truth.

As Hindus who believed in Advaita Vedanta, they saw the absolute Reality, which they called *Brahman*, as having nothing to do with the physical world. *Atman*, which means soul, was thus understood in two ways by them. One was illusory; the other was real. The illusory

Atman was the individual soul, the one that seemed to be separate from everyone and every illusory thing. Then there was the Atman of Brahman, or *Reality*, and the absolute Reality was only Oneness. But at the same time, many Eastern thinkers, even though they considered the phenomenal world to be illusory, still saw it as being a reflection of their Gods. This helped perpetuate the popular confusion that a God or Gods made the illusion, which a perfect Being would actually have nothing to do with! The projection of the universe of multiplicity is a product of the ego, based on the idea of individuality and separation.

GARY: I like the way they put it in the movie *The Matrix*. The world you see is an illusion to pull the wool over your eyes and prevent you from seeing the real world.

ARTEN: Yes, but the real world they were talking about had nothing to do with God. Still, what the movie was saying there was a step in the right direction.

GARY: By the way, I'm sorry about the mistake I made regarding Shankara.

ARTEN: No problem, my brother. Considering all the information we give you, you've made very few mistakes. Just a couple of minor ones. For example, you told the same joke in two different books, which Mikey pointed out to you.

NOTE: Mike Lemieux, also known as "Giddyup Mikey," is a good friend of mine who knows my books extremely well, maybe better than I do. He's the author of *Dude, Where's My Jesus Fish?* He also facilitates my fan page at Facebook and writes many excellent observations.

GARY: What other mistakes did I make?

ARTEN: In DU you had us saying there was an earthquake in China in the 1960s that killed over a half million people. Actually it was the 1970s. No big deal; the recording we allowed you to make at that time wasn't very clear, and you couldn't channel us as well in between visits back then. Also, you got the length of J and Mary Magdalene's marriage right, 15 years, in DU, but in *Love Has Forgotten No One* you made a mistake taking your notes and listening to us at the same time and you said they got married when they were in their 20s. Actually, it was when they were in their teens. J was 18 and Mary was 15. Then they were married for 15 years, up until the crucifixion. That's about it. Nothing fatal.

PURSAH: Getting back to our two friends, Harish and Padmaj, they had done their homework when it came to studying the ancient Texts that had been handed down through the generations. They understood the kinds of things we're talking about *intellectually*, but they were not experiencing it. They hadn't yet developed the discipline in that lifetime to engage in the kind of practice that trains the mind.

One night, the two of them went to a drinking and gambling house, and Harish was having a good night, winning a fairly large amount of money. Then an intoxicated man who was losing suggested that Harish was cheating. He wasn't cheating, but it was a serious accusation that Harish didn't take kindly to. Voices were raised, and soon a fight broke out. Padmaj came to help his friend, but during the fight he was stabbed with a knife in the abdomen. Harish was horrified, realizing immediately that his foolish ways may have just resulted in his best friend and cousin dying.

Fortunately, people who worked at the place managed to break up the fight. Harish and a couple of the gamblers took Padmaj to a nearby doctor, who practiced what you today would call Ayurvedic medicine. The wound wasn't that deep, and the doctor knew what to do. Padmaj survived and was back to normal health in a few weeks.

This, however, was a jolting wake-up call for Harish. He hadn't felt like his way of life was a sin, and he still didn't. But he did have the realization that it was a waste of time, which he felt could be even worse. Also, and this is where you'll remember there's no such thing as an accident, the doctor, whose name was Sabal, had time to talk to both Harish and Padmaj in the weeks he would visit their village for Padmaj's treatments. He told them about a Holy Man who they should visit; and even before Padmaj was completely healed, the two made a decision to go and find out if this man had something to offer them.

They left the village to find the Holy Man, who Sabal said had no name. The Holy Man had once told Sabal that to have a name would limit him to being a human being, which he did not consider himself to be. Intrigued, Harish and Padmaj went to the area they were told the man with no name would probably be.

On the way there, they came across a group of people who were following a different man who they saw as being holy. They were invited to camp out with the group, which today you would call a cult. They were given a small amount of food and then asked if they'd like to take part in one of the group's ceremonies. There didn't seem to be anything going on that would be harmful, and they agreed.

The ceremony consisted of drinking liquid from a bowl that was being handed around by the leader. The liquid was very similar to what you today would call *ayahuasca*. The two visitors just saw the drinking as a social thing, part of a ceremony, but they soon found out that the people there were beginning to have unique experiences. At first they would purge, which is a nice word for vomit, and then they'd begin to hallucinate.

GARY: I've talked with several people the last few years who've told me they've had interesting experiences with ayahuasca. Some of them just call it "the plant." As you know, since you're always aware of what I'm doing, I've never taken it. But some of these people describe deep intuitions about their childhood, and spiritual realizations they seem to think are valuable. What do you think about that kind of stuff?

ARTEN: Gary, at the end of the day you've got to remember that even though people may report beneficial experiences from taking ayahuasca, we're still talking about a drug, a hallucinogen. And the truth is you never really know how someone is going to react to a hallucinogen. Every ego mind and brain is different, which the ego would have no other way, and it's possible for someone to have a bad reaction, one that could scar them. So despite the good reports you've heard, we simply can't recommend to people that they take a drug.

PURSAH: Remember, what you experience under the influence of a hallucinogen is not real. Yes, you could argue that none of this is real either, and you'd be right. But it's possible to come to the exact same realizations people have while taking ayahuasca *without* taking the drug. And that's the path we recommend.

ARTEN: Our friends did indeed have some revelations that evening. In Harish's case it was in regard to how deeply he loved his parents, which was something he'd forgotten and hadn't experienced for a long time. And Padmaj remembered Lao-tzu and was suddenly full of the awareness of all he'd learned from him. By the morning they both felt a renewed desire to move on and find the fulfillment they were looking for. Drinking the bitter nectar of the plant was fine, but it didn't strike them as a way of life.

The one who the people there saw as a Holy One wanted them to stay. He told them there was no other path that could offer them more, because he could explain to them the many experiences they would have while living with the group, meditating, learning his teachings, and partaking of the liquid. But they sensed this wasn't the place they should be staying, and they left, despite a few threatening looks from certain members of the group.

After a couple of weeks on foot, Harish and Padmaj found who they were looking for. They approached the one with no name and introduced themselves.

GARY: Okay. So I don't get lost, B and J were in a state of dualism as Shintos, although you could call it an advanced state of dualism, kind of like semidualism, because they didn't buy into the dream as much as others. But it was still dualism in the sense that it was real to them, especially the reincarnation thing and the respect they had for their ancestors, which were extremely strong parts of the culture. And if something is real, it means there's something outside of you, so you've got a subject and an object, something else to be conscious of, which is not the oneness of nondualism.

Then with Lao-tzu, even though he was teaching nondualism, the experience of J and B in that lifetime was also like what you would call semidualism, because the resistance to the world they were being taught as ascetics was still making it real to them in their minds and thus their experience.

Now, since you're talking about a teacher with no name, I suspect our friends were moving toward not just a theory that says nothing in the illusion is real, but something they could actually feel.

PURSAH: Very succinct, although I can't say they experienced nondualism all the time in that lifetime. With these different levels of learning, students will go in and out of them at first, moving forward and slipping back in their experience. So you'll have an experience of oneness, and it will blow your mind, but then you'll go back to twoness. You have to get used to the new level, and even then the only way to maintain it on a permanent basis is through the process of undoing the ego. The teacher our friends were about to meet was the first to start teaching them how to do that and eventually accelerate the process.

ARTEN: When Harish and Padmaj introduced themselves to the one with no name, who we'll simply refer to as O, he asked them to sit on the ground in the back of the group and listen. He told them they could decide for themselves if what he was teaching was something they'd be interested in. They could feel free to leave at any time, but he would be the one to let them know when it was time for them to speak to him.

It would be three months before O sent word to them to come and meet with him. In the meantime, while they were part of the group, he had taught them much. He explained how the most important bodies in the story they thought of as their lives were completely unreal. Their parents were never really there. They were false images the ego had created to draw them into the illusion of multiplicity. They, as well as their parents, were never really born. They didn't exist. It was all made up. The physical wasn't true. It was all a lie, and their lives were a lie. And if they had children, that would be a lie too, because everything they see that has a shape to it isn't true.

He had them do a visualization in which they floated high above the Earth and then saw all of the bodies of humanity below them. They were instructed to see part of that mass of people disappearing, as tens of thousands of people passed away each day, to be replaced by more bodies who dreamed they were being born, all the while none of it being real. The bodies were just veils and not something to be valued.

GARY: That reminds me of something it says in the Course about death: "What seems to die has but been misperceived and carried to illusion."[4]

ARTEN: Yes, and our two friends were having some experiences of nondualism. When O spoke with them in private, he told them it was time for them to practice a certain kind of mind discipline in order to consistently think along the lines he had been teaching them. He told them to practice each day by thinking of people not as the bodies they were seeing, which are merely false images, but as the oneness that was beyond the veil. When Harish and Padmaj found themselves making anything in the world real in their minds, he admonished them to stop it and instead think of everything—not just human bodies but anything—as being a thin veil covering the oneness of Brahman.

PURSAH: If people did something they didn't like, O told them to pardon them in their minds, not because those people had really done something, but because they hadn't really done anything.

ARTEN: As you can see, this was their introduction to a certain kind of forgiveness, and it included an important element of the advanced kind of forgiveness they would learn later. There was an essential part of it being left out, which we'll get to, but what they were doing with O was a vital step forward in their spiritual progress. PURSAH: These two students of O were very dedicated, as well as steadfast in their determination to undo whatever it was in their minds that was making them believe in the world of multiplicity, instead of the truth of oneness that existed just beyond it. For years, they reinterpreted everything they saw, as well as everything they remembered in their lives. Much progress was made.

Harish and Padmaj didn't live long lives. Their determination to not make the world or bodies real caused them to neglect taking care of their own bodies, which is a typical mistake that spiritual students make. This is because of level confusion. Just because the world isn't real, it doesn't mean you don't live as though you're in it; and just because your body isn't real, it doesn't mean you don't take the necessary steps to keep it healthy. You wouldn't not put oil in your car. If you didn't, it would break down. Well, until you're a master on the level of J or B and know how to use the power of your mind to overcome the world entirely, your body will break down if you don't give it what it needs. Our friends didn't eat well. They also didn't usually have good water to drink, which was part of the ego's screenplay. They both lived to be around 27 years old. As Shakespeare would later write in *As You Like It*:

All the world's a stage,
And all the men and women merely players;
They have their exits and their entrances,
And one man in his time plays many parts.

ARTEN: The good news is Harish and Padmaj not only learned a great deal, they practiced a great deal. Much healing took place in their minds, opening up the possibility of completing the job of undoing the ego before other people would be ready to.

PURSAH: The next time we come, we're going to let you know even more about the difference between philosophy, which can be fine, and the mental practicing of philosophy, which is essential. Keep forgiving, and we'll be back very soon.

I was happy to hear about Harish and Padmaj, and found myself identifying with them and their brief but important lives. I couldn't wait to hear more about J and B. I felt encouraged knowing that their examples could help us all to follow their lead.

4

Plato and Friends

We must, in my opinion, begin by distinguishing between
that which always is and never becomes, and that
which is always becoming but never is.[1]

— P L A T O

$\mathcal{D}$uring the next few weeks, I reviewed what my ascended visitors
had been telling me about J and B and their learning adventures.
My knowledge of Hinduism was almost nonexistent. I got what Arten
and Pursah were saying about nondualism, but I didn't follow the
lingo of the religion. Also, my teachers had already taught me that
the idea of the world being an illusion is of very limited value. You
can't stop there or, because of the way the mind works, you'll end
up thinking that you're an illusion, which will leave you feeling empty
and meaningless. You've got to replace the idea with something else.
It seemed to me, looking from the outside in, that spirituality in India
had become too much about the illusion and not enough about the
reality that must replace it. Then, of course, I found myself wondering
if that was too much of a judgment.

Indeed, I'd met people in America who I respected who were very
enthusiastic about Hindu teachers. A chiropractor named Bruce, who
I've written about before and who made a big difference in my life
in the 1980s, was a big believer in Babaji, the immortal Indian avatar
who brought the world an advanced style of Kriya Yoga. In fact, Bruce
took his son to India every year to study it and practice with him.

Cindy and I loved to go to Lake Shrine, the beautiful home of Self-
Realization Fellowship, founded by Paramahansa Yogananda. Lake
Shrine is only 15 minutes from where we live, and it's a great getaway
place to walk and meditate. The swans and ducks that occupy the
peaceful pond are a pleasure to watch. If we're in the area, we also
like to visit Yogananda's other beautiful hangout, the Self-Realization

Fellowship in Encinitas. Walking around the lovely grounds, one gets the feeling of being in South Asia, because there are many trees and flowers there that are usually found only in India. I had tried to read Yogananda's book, *Autobiography of a Yogi*, but found it too long for my taste. I figured I'd get back to it someday. But walking around Yogananda's places, I somehow felt like a Hindu. Perhaps ancient memories were being triggered in my unconscious mind, but I couldn't quite put my finger on them.

One day Cindy and I were walking around one of the many cool shopping malls in Los Angeles when a gentleman recognized me. He came up and told me he was a reader of mine, and that he was also the grandson of Yogananda. (It is generally believed that Yogananda did not have any children, however, so the truth of this is a point of controversy.) I knew we would be friends. I'm always fascinated by the many connections that are made with others on a spiritual path.

My only other connection to Hinduism was my cousin Bobby, who back in Massachusetts in the 1970s gave me a copy of the book *Be Here Now* by Ram Dass. I enjoyed the philosophy in the book as well as the irreverent style, but I was still a few years away from getting on a spiritual path. Still, books like that and *Siddhartha* had awakened an interest in me.

I was struck by the fact that Harish and Padmaj had lived lives that were at first dominated by the ego, but still managed to go on and learn so much on a spiritual path. And they did so despite the fact that they didn't live a long time. But then I can look back and see all of the phases I've gone through, and all the corresponding phases that the society I've lived in has gone through with me.

As an 18-year-old musician, I intended going to Woodstock. Then I couldn't go because my band got a gig for that weekend. Gigs *always* came before everything else, even girlfriends. One of our slogans was "a girl is here today, but the band is here to stay." Later, of course, when wives came along, the band no longer held the position of top spot in the universe.

One of the things I remember very well is the Woodstock spirit that prevailed for almost two years, from the summer of 1969 until the spring of 1971. For me and my friends and fellow musicians, it was all about peace, love, and music. We were brothers and sisters. Money wasn't important. We were going to change the world with love and passive resistance to the powers that be.

By the spring of '71 I could feel that things had changed. I remember going to a concert at Salem State College in May of that year where the bands Spirit and Sha Na Na were playing. Many in the crowd of ten thousand people behaved like animals. It wasn't uncommon for someone in the group who had finished a bottle of wine to then throw it up in the air. They didn't seem the slightest bit concerned about whether or not it would come down on somebody's head. I remember a fellow musician in the crowd saying, "The Woodstock spirit is dead, man." He was right.

The devolution of the peaceful spirit had really started just three months after Woodstock, with the ultrarowdy Rolling Stones concert for hundreds of thousands of people at Altamont in California. The Hell's Angels, acting as security, actually killed a person in the crowd. The stabbing was caught on camera and later shown in the documentary movie *Gimme Shelter*. It appeared the slain concertgoer had a gun and was pointing it in the direction of Mick Jagger. Nothing is simple with the ego.

The summer of 1970 still had a great vibe though, partly because of the release of the movie and soon-to-be-classic music album *Woodstock*. But it would be only a matter of time before the Woodstock spirit would give way to the ego.

As for the Rolling Stones, I had seen them play one of their first American concerts in the mid-1960s at a football stadium called Manning Bowl in Lynn, Massachusetts. The concert ended in a riot, which was a bit of a tradition during the first part of the Stones's career. The goalposts at the stadium were torn down, even though there was no game. One of the goalposts was then used to try to destroy the Stones's limousine, which was leaving with them inside. When people freak out, they freak out.

Little did I know I would see the Stones once again, almost 50 years later in 2013, at the Staples Center in Los Angeles. If you told me that could happen when I was a skinny kid in the mid-'60s, I'd have been astonished. First of all, the idea of being 62 years old would seem unlikely, and perhaps not even desirable. Second, California seemed so far away at the time it might as well have been Mars. But it happened. And because of the Course, I still felt young, as if I hadn't aged one day in the 23 years since I started doing it. Also, to help make it a real celebration, the Stones were still great, and Mick Jagger moved and sang like he didn't know anything about time.

The Woodstock spirit was inspired by the Holy Spirit, and the ego then reasserted itself, as it always does. The spring of 1971 saw music become a lot about making money. Bill Graham (not to be confused with the evangelist Billy Graham) had to close the two premier music venues in the country, the Fillmore in San Francisco and the Fillmore East in New York City, both of which he owned, simply because the bands had started charging too much money for him to make ends meet. Everybody was selling out. Selfishness had won the day, and peace went underground. But a fresh movement with a higher purpose, one that was based on the idea of being "spiritual but not religious," was waiting in the wings. Although I wasn't expecting it, by the later part of that decade I would be on a personal spiritual path, just like millions of other seekers.

I'd just gotten back from a trip with Cindy to Rio de Janeiro, where we did a weekend ACIM workshop. It was an enriching experience, filled with warm, friendly people like our friend Nadja, who showed us all over the area. And the views from the famous "Christ the Redeemer" statue were breathtaking. When I was back home, enjoying the memories of a great trip, Arten and Pursah were suddenly there with me.

ARTEN: Hello, Gary. What do you say we get right to it? From what we've discussed so far, you know more about the personal experiences of dualism and semidualism as experienced by J and B. And, of course, you have your own experiences. Plus there's what we've taught you in other conversations, like the four attitudes of learning we explained to you during the first series of visits. As a way of reviewing, do you recall how we explained the first two to you back in the '90s?

GARY: Does a bear—never mind, I won't say it. Anyway, as we've been discussing, the first attitude, or level, is dualism, which is the way 99.9 percent of all people think. It's the world people take for granted, along with the experience of consciousness, which is the domain of the ego. In order to have consciousness, you have to have something else to be conscious of. So it's not the oneness of spirit. You think the world is outside of you, and it's real, period. The New Age crowd thinks consciousness is very important, and then they try to spiritualize it; but it's not spirit. Real spirit is perfect oneness. However, you can learn how to train the mind and *use* consciousness to make your choices with the Holy Spirit instead of the ego.

Then you have semidualism, which is a move in the direction of spirit and slowly away from dualism. By the way, I should mention that people don't even realize they're in a temporary stage. They just think things are the way that they are and that they're right about their interpretation of everything. But along with the attitude of semi-dualism would come gentler beliefs, like the idea that God is love. That idea might start to make you think and ask questions, like Saka and Hiroji did when they were shifting from dualism to semidualism. For example, if God is really love, can He also be hateful? You may start to suspect the answer is no, and your mind will start to lose some of the unconscious fear you had of God, even though you may not even know you had it.

PURSAH: Good, and even when you're on various spiritual paths it can take centuries for you to maintain the progress you've made and not slip back from it.

GARY: And why is that, my mysterious flower?

PURSAH: You know why, Gary. It's because there's tremendous unconscious resistance to the truth. The ego will do anything to keep you away from the truth, from the beginning to its very end. The truth is oneness, not the separation fostered by the ego. So this is the beginning of the end for the ego, and the ego senses it.

ARTEN: We'd like to talk a little about Plato and some of his associates.

GARY: Is this where J and B get to actually experience nondualism in a permanent way, as opposed to just temporarily like when they were Shao Li and Wosan, or Harish and Padmaj?

ARTEN: Ah, no, but it was an important learning time for them just the same, because it was a necessary step toward oneness. Also, they ended up coming to an important conclusion, as you'll see.

In the illusory lifetime we're going to talk about, J and B became students of Plato at his Academy in Athens.

GARY: Of course! I should have known. And did you know I used to hang with Aristotle?

ARTEN: How do you know you didn't? You don't remember everything, buddy, although you do have access to more memories than most people do. But I'm serious. At the Academy, J was a student named Takis, and B was a student named Ikaros. They were both brilliant young men, and they were expected to take leadership roles of some kind. One of the ideas behind the Academy, which was the first higher-learning institute, was that it would train people in ethics and develop its students' intellects in such a way that they could produce a better world. A lofty ambition of course, but Plato meant it. He was also arguably the greatest philosophical writer who ever lived. Of course, it doesn't hurt that, unlike other ancient teachers, most of his writings survived.

GARY: I remember we talked about his Allegory of the Cave a long time ago. That was really cool.

PURSAH: Your mom used to plant seeds in your mind by reading it to you when you were a child. From that allegory, it's very clear Plato understood that what you're seeing in this world is not real. The prisoners in the cave are bound in chains so hard they can't even move their heads to get a different view. And they've been there so long they've forgotten what reality is like. They think the shadows they see on the wall in front of them are reality, and they don't understand they are merely the shadows of those walking by outside. When one of the prisoners escapes, he eventually can stand to look at the light again and sees where the images are really coming from. He runs back into the cave to tell the prisoners the truth, but none of them want to hear it. They're stuck in the doldrums of being the way they are. It's what they're used to, and the returning escaped prisoner is hated by them.

ARTEN: There's a parallel saying to that in the Course. This quotation is also an obvious tip of the hat to Plato. "Prisoners bound with heavy chains for years, starved and emaciated, weak and exhausted, and with eyes so long cast down in darkness they remember not the light, do not leap up in joy the instant they are made free. It takes a while for them to understand what freedom is."[2]

Most people aren't ready for the truth. People are comfortable in their cages, and the truth isn't welcome to them at first. They're fixated on making their lives work, forgetting that the ending is always going to be the same for every human body, and that it would be wiser to build their lives on something permanent rather than on the cheap imitation of life they are being shown by the ego. Still, you can't blame them, because it's all they know. The truth is like the Course, Gary. It may be simple, but it's not easy.

Plato wrote, "We can easily forgive a child who is afraid of the dark. The real tragedy of life is when men are afraid of the light."

GARY: I had a good friend named Chaitanya in a study group back in Maine, and he used to say, "The truth will set you free, but first it will piss you off."

ARTEN: Very appropriate. The escaped prisoner in the story, by the way, was based on Plato's teacher Socrates, who was the greatest influence on Plato. In Plato's dialogues he has Socrates asking leading questions; this technique, known today as the Socratic method, was what Socrates did with Plato in their teacher-student relationship. And in Plato's *Republic,* as well as in the other dialogues he created, Plato presents his philosophy in that way. In fact, he originated the dialogue as a teaching form.

GARY: Doesn't the word *platonic* come from Plato?

PURSAH: No, it was made up later by his students and readers. It was supposed to refer to denying the reality of the material world. Later, people started to use it to describe a "platonic" relationship, which of course means the denial of sex. But the original idea behind it was that Plato himself denied the reality of anything that wasn't the source of everything, which he simply called "The Good."

GARY: So Plato was nondualistic?

PURSAH: No. You'll see that mentioned in this brief exchange between Takis and Ikaros after having a class with Plato.

GARY: They were J and B in that lifetime?

PURSAH: Yes. No need to go into the details of how they knew each other. Just like schools of fish swim together in the ocean, people travel together in different dream lifetimes. They are destined to come into contact with each other over and over. Here's a little of what they said. Of course this is a translation. As with other past conversations we've told you about, they were not speaking English at the time.

TAKIS: Plato has a dilemma. In his philosophy all things come from The Good. And all the objects in the material universe are symbolic of an idea. So, like with the cave, the images the prisoners are seeing are symbols, or shadows of something else. They're not real. But here's the dilemma. Coming from The Good, Plato can't figure out why The Good would make something that isn't real, and he ends up compromising. He's come to the conclusion that the things he's seeing are *not* real, but that the *ideas* behind them are. And he has still ended up with dualism because he has the source making illusions. If the source is interacting with something else, that's dualism.

IKAROS: You're right. Plato is a brilliant philosopher, but the truth is that the symbols we're seeing are not real, and neither are the ideas behind them. They're coming from an illusory, seemingly separate mind. And this mind is not the source of real life, only an imitation of life.

ARTEN: Plato's Academy allowed for great intellects to come together and discuss ideas. Our two friends, with the cumulative experiences they had before, were able to learn from Plato yet think for themselves. They showed nothing but respect for Plato in the discussions that took place in class, but in private they came to another conclusion—something that would come back to them and influence their final two lifetimes.

IKAROS: This life is a hoax. It's all a distraction to keep us from experiencing the truth, from knowing real life. Philosophical speculation is fine, but where does it get you? We have to get to a place where there's no compromise, where we're making a firm decision between the real and the unreal, and empowering that decision with belief.

TAKIS: So we can't have it both ways. The truth is true and nothing else is true. We have to choose once and for all. There's a formless oneness just beyond the hoax. It's nondualistic. It's perfect, and only that perfection is true. We've both had lovely glimpses of it, but there must be a way to remove the barriers to it and experience it on a permanent basis.

PURSAH: As you can see, their journeys had led them to a place where they knew that salvation, as some called it, or enlightenment, as others called it, depended on making an uncompromising decision. Plato believed in logic, and that intellectual development would lead to self-fulfillment. But Takis and Ikaros had enough experience to know enlightenment had nothing to do with individuality. Indeed, it's the *relinquishment* of individuality—psychologically that is, not physically—that leads to real fulfillment. That fulfillment can be found only in oneness.

Remember, even though Plato's systems weren't perfect, his teachings and writings helped many people develop their minds to the point where they *could* make better decisions. For them, he was an important step along the way.

GARY: What time period did Plato live in?

PURSAH: People will argue about that, but it was actually about 500 B.C. to about 450 B.C.

GARY: Let me see what Wikipedia says.

[After a short delay.] Hmm, one of the things it says is, "The exact time and place of Plato's birth are unknown, but it is certain that he belonged to an aristocratic and influential family."

ARTEN: Let's just say he didn't have to work for a living.

GARY: Wasn't Plato the first one to talk about Atlantis?

PURSAH: Yes. He heard about it from Socrates and brought it up later in the dialogue he wrote called *Timaeus*. He wrote it as though an Egyptian named Solon was telling it to someone named Critias. That doesn't matter. But what the dialogue said was true. There was indeed an Atlantis, in the dream, and the people who came together at Plato's Academy had also been together there. That's why Socrates remembered it. He lived there, as did his student Plato and Plato's student Aristotle, along with Takis and Ikaros. They all knew each other at the time of Atlantis. Plotinus, a student of Plato's writings a couple of hundred years after Plato's time, was also there. As you may recall, Plotinus was the one who came up with the idea that the Good, Plato's Source, was One.

GARY: Yeah. "The Good is One." Boy, those guys had some pretty cool lifetimes.

ARTEN: Sometimes they were good times and sometimes they weren't. That's the nature of the dualistic dream. Atlantis ended in violence and tragedy. Not such a cool lifetime after all.

What today are the Canary Islands—which you'd like, by the way, because they're similar to Hawaii—are part of the remnants of Atlantis. But some of the remnants extend all the way to the Bermuda Triangle. Plato wrote that Atlantis was out beyond the Pillars of Hercules, which today would mean beyond the Strait of Gibraltar.

GARY: And what exactly happened to Atlantis?

ARTEN: Although Atlantis was an extremely intelligent society, originally founded by your ancestors who were not from this planet, they made the same mistake your civilization is making today. Despite there being a very spiritual and sophisticated minority, the majority chose the duality of the physical, or materialistic, instead of the pure nonduality of spirit. Remember, just because beings are intelligent and technologically advanced, it doesn't necessarily mean they're spiritually advanced.

GARY: Just because they're intelligent, it doesn't necessarily make them smart either. I could name a few Ph.D.'s I've met who use intelligent-sounding words, but they're not very bright. I like Einstein's quote: "The difference between stupidity and genius is that genius has its limits."

ARTEN: Unfortunate but true, in the illusory sense of the words. In any case, we're not going to give you a big song and dance about Atlantis. The point about it is—and this is also the point of this series of visits—that the majority of people find it impossible to stick to nondualism, especially pure nondualism. You even see it today with *A Course in Miracles*. It seems that people will do *anything* to not stick to the message, even though they'd be happier if they did. For them, this is a reminder, a tap on the shoulder.

When it comes to Atlantis, the beings in power made a form of free energy that was limitless and could have been used for good. Instead, a deranged group of people found a way to make it into a weapon. They thought it would shift all the power to them.

GARY: You mean like we did with nuclear energy?

PURSAH: Yes. Instead of using it for good, people used it to further prove the insanity of the species. It was used to make weapons that could destroy the planet, and still could today.

GARY: Are you making a prediction?

PURSAH: No. We're not going to make predictions right now, except for this one, and it's the same thing we said to you back in the '90s: The ego's script in the future will be more of the same, except it will be bigger, faster, and scarier. It has to be bigger. That's what the ego craves. It has to seem more important than what's come before so you'll be tricked into believing in it. Without your belief, the ego is nothing! The difference between most people and people like J and B, even in Plato's time when they were Ikaros and Takis, is that they weren't taken in by appearances. They saw right through appearances, recognizing them as the hoax that they were.

Atlantis was destroyed by ignorance, greed, and the resulting violence. The ego's goal is always murder. Why? Because if you can be hurt or destroyed, it means that you're a body; and if you're a body, the whole ego thought system of separation is true. Then, even when you're seemingly born again into a different body, you still think that body is you! It's a gloomy cycle that can be ended *only* by undoing, not by redoing.

GARY: Quick question before I forget. You explained the 9/11 conspiracy in the third book, and how the planes that went into the towers weren't the real planes with the people on them, and also how the buildings were imploded. But since then people have asked me, what happened to the people who were on the planes?

PURSAH: First of all, there weren't as many people as usual on the original planes, and one of those planes was seen landing in Minneapolis. Some of the passengers had been selected ahead of time. All of them were offered several million dollars and a place in the witness protection program. Some of them were happy to take it. Others were not. They were then convinced through intimidation and sometimes beatings that it would be a good idea for them to do so. Most eventually accepted, but about 20 percent were quietly taken away and disappeared, and I'm being polite. That was a long time ago now. A few tried to "come out," so to speak, and they were disposed of. The rest were slowly but surely killed off. They thought they'd have a long, rich life, but the CIA and the powers behind the scenes wouldn't take the chance.

GARY: So they're all gone now?

PURSAH: Yes. Do you remember how most of the witnesses to the JFK assassination were dead within a few years?

GARY: Sure do.

PURSAH: Same idea.

ARTEN: Moving on, in the coming weeks we want you to think about how uncompromising Ikaros and Takis were showing themselves to be, even in the presence of a great philosopher like Plato. To them, it became the truth that was important. They decided to put their belief where belief was justified, not in appearances. And after all these years with us and the Course, you know how relentlessly uncompromising the Course is.

Be well my friend, and give our love to Cindy. She's very dedicated to the Course. That's wonderful to see.

GARY: Do you mind if I ask you one more thing?

But they were gone. I've come to realize that my teachers know what's best for me, even when I don't. They would return exactly when they were supposed to, and I'd ask them exactly what the Holy Spirit wanted me to, not just for me, but for whoever else the ideas may be helpful to.

Later, on one gorgeous California Sunday, Cindy and I took a day to drive up and down a section of the coast. We went beach-hopping and town-hopping down to Huntington Beach and back up to Redondo Beach (which I call Redundant Beach for fun), Hermosa Beach, and Manhattan Beach. It was one of those perfect days when everything went right. From the people to the weather to the sights and experiences, it was perfect. We felt wonderful.

On the way home, we stopped in Marina del Rey, and we found a lovely place on the ocean to have dinner. It was early, so we were lucky and got a table right on the water where we could take in the sunset. We ordered our food and were enjoying the view. Then, for some reason, Cindy decided to check her phone messages.

As she listened to the messages, I saw the gentle smile on her face replaced with a look of horror. Cindy's stepbrother, Jeff, whom she grew up with and was very close to, had been killed in an accident. While Cindy tried to contact her dad and her stepmother, Alice, it seemed like life had stopped. It's a hopeless, gut-wrenching feeling to be confronted with the death of a loved one.

Looking back on that day, it was an extreme lesson in duality. One second you're enjoying a fantastic day; the next second the ego's dream of death kicks you in the face. We did everything we could to deal with the situation, but it never feels like enough. So we did the best we could.

Jeff was someone I was just getting to know. It was strange to have him go so soon, because I really felt like I'd get to know him a lot better. We were both guitar players—in fact he was probably the most sought-after guitar player in Las Vegas—and I looked forward to jamming with him.

Sometime after Jeff and I met, something happened that was a joyful surprise to all of us. Jeff had read my first book and was starting to study the Course. Jeff's mom, Alice, after visiting with him one day, called and emotionally expressed her gratitude to me. She had never heard Jeff so peaceful. A mother knows her son. She knew a transformation had occurred.

I was really struck by this huge lesson in duality, but not just by the negative part of it. As the weeks after Jeff's death went on, there was a tribute to him in Las Vegas that we attended. Most of the entertainment community in Vegas showed up and paid tribute by doing what they do best: performing. It was probably one of the best concerts of the year. Cindy was a featured singer, and she spoke poignantly about her and Jeff's childhood. Many of the performers present said the tribute was the best thing that ever happened to the entertainment community in Vegas. People who hadn't spoken to each other in years reunited and renewed their friendships; others got to meet each other and become friends. There were a couple of people in Jeff's family who also hadn't spoken in years who ended the day hugging each other. It seemed that Jeff was still helping his friends and family, even though his body wasn't present.

About a year later, I realized that the same experience I had with my parents was repeating itself with Jeff and his friends and family.

Yes, we grieve, and we should. It's best to be normal when that's what's called for. But there was something else.

Eventually, the pain you feel for the one you appear to have lost goes away, but the love doesn't. It will always be there. The love is real, the pain isn't. And isn't it interesting that the most real thing we have in our lives is something that you can't see? You can't see love. You can see love in action, but you can't see the love behind it.

This is also true of the Kingdom of Heaven. You can't see it with the body's eyes, yet it's the most real thing that there is. We will return to a world we can't presently see, although it can be temporarily experienced, even while we appear to be here. Then a permanent experience will come where there will be only reality, an awareness of a constant state of oneness, and the only thing that is real—love—will be all that there is.

5

Siddhartha and His Son

In the sky, there is no distinction between east and west.
People make up differences in their own minds,
and then believe them to be true.

— BUDDHA

In the 1980s, I heard a Buddhist monk speak at a Unity church. Something he said caught my attention: "Being angry at another person is like drinking poison and then waiting for somebody else to die." He knew there's only one of us, so your thoughts really just go to you. My Teachers had repeated that thought later, and I got it on an even deeper level, which is how the undoing of the ego works. But back in the 80s, through my forays into various spiritual approaches, I was starting to get a hint about nondualism, even though I'd been on a spiritual path for only a few years. Of course I didn't have an inkling as to how to *experience* it, but I felt interested in it nonetheless.

During their first series of visits, Arten and Pursah told me, "The Vedanta is a nondualistic spiritual document that teaches that the truth of Braham is all that there really is, and *anything* else is illusion—untrue, nothing, zilch—period. The Vedanta was wisely interpreted by Shankara as Advaita, or nondualistic." In other words, reality is *completely unrelated* to the phenomenal world and universe.

This information was given to me during the second visit of my teachers, just before I bought my first copy of *A Course in Miracles*. I'd soon go on to learn that the God of the Course was also completely unrelated to the ego's world and universe. There was one more form of nonduality I'd learn about later, but I was already starting to genuinely believe in the distinction between the real and the unreal.

Many years later, on a warm June night in 2014, Cindy and I had gone to the beautiful Greek Theatre in Hollywood, near the Griffith Park Observatory, to see one of Cindy's favorite musicians, Sarah McLachlan. "The Greek" is an outside venue with great acoustics, the perfect place to see a summer concert. We were walking around during the intermission, when just as we turned to go back to our seats, standing right in front of us was Marianne Williamson. I thought it was really nice of her to come up and say hello to us. The show was about to start again and we didn't say too much, just things like "good concert." But we all hugged and had a moment.

Interestingly, we had just voted for Marianne three days before that in the primary election for Congress. She was running in our district, and even though she didn't win, I think it was worth it for her to run. She ran as an Independent, and I thought she might have done better if she had run as a Democrat. But that was her call, and besides, there's more to life than just winning.

That night Cindy went to bed before me, as she sometimes does. I've always been a night owl, and she's used to more normal hours. I was sitting in my chair in front of the television, dozing off. When I opened my eyes I was shocked to see Arten and Pursah sitting on the couch, apparently ready to have a conversation. With the door to the bedroom closed, Pursah began to speak.

PURSAH: Hey, music lover. Did you have a good time tonight?

GARY: I sure did, and Cindy loved it. But hey, won't we wake her up? She might come out here and see you for the first time!

PURSAH: Actually she won't. We joined with her at the level of the mind and gave her the suggestion to sleep deeply and dream happily. If she does hear anything, she'll just think it's the television.

GARY: Wow. This is the first time there's been someone else in the house when I talked with you. Feels different.

PURSAH: We'll appear to Cindy if the time is right. That depends on her too, you know. Because we're the Holy Spirit taking on a form in order to communicate, we're aware of the readiness of all people to have appropriate mystical experiences. Some people don't need them right now. And some people need them as a way of encouragement.

ARTEN: Do you know that back in the late '80s and early '90s we'd sometimes show up and be with you when you were meditating? We'd be sitting there, but just as you were opening your eyes, we'd disappear so you wouldn't see us. We were evaluating your readiness, waiting for the right moment, which didn't come until that day in Maine.

GARY: The feast day for St. Thomas!

PURSAH: Yes. No coincidence. But if you'd been ready sooner, we would have shown ourselves to you. Before that there were about a half-dozen times we were there and you didn't even know it.

GARY: You're kidding! But it kind of makes me feel good you were there for me. It's nice you'd take the time to do that.

PURSAH: We didn't have anything better to do. Just joking.

GARY: Hey, doesn't that contradict the idea that the script is written and all this is predetermined?

ARTEN: No. According to the Course, you do still have one power as a prisoner of this world, remember?

GARY: Oh yeah, I remember. The power of decision. I can choose with the Holy Spirit. I can decide to see everything right. That would mean watching this movie I used to think was real and listening to the Holy Spirit's interpretation of it instead of the ego's story. That in turn leads to a different experience. So you're saying it was my own progress that told you I was ready for a different experience. It's the same movie, but I was finally ready to listen to the right interpretation.

ARTEN: Yes, which is *not* your interpretation, but the Guidance of the Holy Spirit. People need to be willing to resign as their own teacher, for as the Course says, they were poorly taught. But that takes a certain amount of humility.

GARY: So at least I did *something* right.

PURSAH: You've done a lot of things right. You've made mistakes, yes. But all mistakes are overlooked. We told you from the start we'd never judge you. So, do you want to hear what we have to say tonight?

GARY: I don't know. I'm kind of tired. Can you just plant it in my mind like you did with Cindy?

PURSAH: Moving along, we're going to talk about Buddha and someone who was very close to him.

GARY: I take it you mean the J guy in that lifetime?

PURSAH: Good to know you're paying attention. The story of Buddha, or Siddhartha, which was his real name, is fairly well known by many spiritual students, including Westerners, and very well known by Buddhists. But it *is* a story, and just like the story of J, some of it is true and some of it is made up; it's partly religious myth. What we'll include in the story is not myth.

ARTEN: About 450 years before J, Siddhartha was born in eastern India to a life of privilege. His father was a king named Suddhodana. He was brought up by his mother's younger sister, Maha, and sheltered from the ways of the world. He was confined to the large palace and the enormous grounds, but because there was so much space to play in, he didn't feel confined. He was pampered by Maha, and his father made sure he was very well educated. So he did learn about the outside world as it was known at that time, but he wasn't allowed to see it.

At the age of 19, according to the wishes of Suddhodana, Maha introduced Siddhartha to a beautiful woman who would become his wife a year later. Her name was Yasodhara. For both of them, it was love at first sight, so they didn't feel put-upon by being urged to marry; they were very happy with the situation. The first few years of their marriage was a joyful, storybook existence. But Siddhartha's father very much wanted them to have children, and when that didn't happen after a few years he was very disappointed, and so were Siddhartha and Yasodhara.

As the years passed, Siddhartha grew restless. Although he loved his beautiful, intelligent wife, he began to feel more and more of a desire to see the world that had been hidden from him, despite the fact that his father had forbidden it. Yasodhara loved him, but she could tell he had wanderlust in his eyes, and did everything she could think of to coax him to stay.

Siddhartha began to have dreams and visions that told him he was going to be traveling and meeting many people, and that his salvation was awaiting him outside the walls of the palace and grounds. It was a difficult time for him, because he knew if he left it would hurt people. He was a kind, gentle man, and he wanted no one to suffer.

But Siddhartha himself was suffering. He felt like something was missing, and that he had to go out and find it. His dreams and visions also told him of other times—times when he had been on spiritual quests—and that there was a mysterious stranger who might help him find what he was looking for. After many years of doubt and questioning, Siddhartha felt impelled to act. Although he was emotionally torn, one night when everyone was asleep he snuck out through a secret exit he had accidentally discovered as a child, but which he'd never had the nerve to use.

Yasodhara was heartbroken. She told herself Siddhartha would come back and that he needed only to get over the desire to see some of the outside world. This was her prayer. But then another, almost forgotten prayer was answered instead. She found out that she was with child. She was so happy and yet so sad, because she desperately wanted Siddhartha to know they were going to have a baby.

It is known, but not widely, that Buddha, that is Siddhartha, had a son. His name was Rahula. This is not part of the accepted Buddhist story, but Buddhism is very diverse, and there are different versions of the story. In any case, Siddhartha didn't know about the child, and he spent his first couple of years of freedom wandering around the eastern part of India. In a way, his journey became a replay of his previous lifetimes we've told you about, like a review. But this time was a little different because he had already lived the life of a rich man at the palace, and he would be able to compare that to other things. He then decided to be an ascetic. After a couple of years of experiencing that, however, he came to the same conclusion he had come to in one of his lifetimes in China: asceticism wasn't necessary. He could not have fully realized that, however, if he hadn't been a rich man. He knew that having all the possessions and physical gratification he wanted didn't really satisfy him, and now he realized that giving up those things and the rest of the so-called good life was not satisfying him either.

GARY: So that's why he took up the middle way?

ARTEN: Yes, but for Siddhartha, there was another important breakthrough during this period. He became a master of meditation. He would learn that meditation by itself will not make you enlightened. That's because it doesn't undo the ego, which is 100 percent necessary in order to achieve enlightenment. But meditation *can*, if practiced diligently, both calm and strengthen the mind. This, in turn, makes it much easier for the mind to be trained and disciplined. When the mind is in that condition, you can use it more effectively to practice a thought system. You yourself found that out in Maine.

GARY: Yeah, I used to meditate every day. I still do, although I've done different styles over the years, mostly guided at first by what I thought was intuition, and then later I realized it was the Holy Spirit. I never studied it or anything; it was like I was remembering how to do it. Later, when I started doing the Course, I think I found it easier to do the lessons and watch my mind at work throughout the day because of the meditative practicing. Plus I noticed a lot of the lessons are very meditative, although they're not the same as traditional meditation because they involve specific thoughts, except for when the time comes in a lesson that you're supposed to still the mind. Also, later in the Workbook, some of the lessons involve an actual approach to God. Anyway, I definitely think I was able to do the Course more effectively because I had practiced meditation. But then, people could start getting some of the benefits of meditation simply by doing the lessons.

ARTEN: True, and with his meditations, Siddhartha started to have more memories of his past lifetimes and the things he had learned. He also remembered his friend J in his various forms, and realized J was the one he was searching for to help him attain his enlightenment, although he didn't know what form that would take. He couldn't yet see who his friend was in this particular lifetime, but he wanted to find out.

Everything he had learned in all his dream lifetimes came back to him and stayed with him. As you know, you never lose what you learn, but you do have to remember it, and his meditation helped.

Rather than extremes, Siddhartha lived a life of moderation and meditation. He had picked up followers during his practice of asceticism, and most of them left. But many people began to come and hear him share his wisdom. He began to be well known as a guru, although he didn't seem to care. His ideas of moderation also applied to how he reacted to people.

GARY: It reminds me of a saying we have, "All things in moderation, including moderation."

ARTEN: You got it. And that's why Ken Wapnick used to tell his students, "Don't forget how to be normal."

NOTE: In Chapter 7, we discuss more about who Ken Wapnick is.

PURSAH: So, our friend had come to believe that it's not what you do that matters, but how you think. Of course, what you do is a result of what you think, but now Siddhartha was putting the horse before the cart. He had been schooled at the palace and understood the Vedas and the Upanishads. He knew well the difference between Brahman and the world. As the Bhagavad Gita puts it, "The unreal never is. The Real never is not." But until now, he hadn't experienced it, so he decided to find a way to live it. His goal became to actually experience the truth all the time. That's a pretty tall order, but he was determined.

He practiced lucid dreaming, something he had experimented with at the time of Lao-tzu. Eventually his students would also practice lucid dreaming, thinking that if they could control the decision-making process in their dreams, then when they died they could continue that ability and choose not to reincarnate. That doesn't work, by the way, unless the ego has been completely undone. But it can be helpful, as lucid dreaming in your sleep at night can help you realize you're also dreaming when you appear to wake up.

Although Siddhartha had not suffered greatly in his life, he missed Yasodhara. He briefly considered visiting home, but then had another idea. He realized that missing her and feeling like he had to perform certain acts was a form of suffering, of being chained to the world. And if you're chained to it, you're dependent upon it, which makes you a slave to it. He wanted to be free—free of the world and free of any form of suffering, which the Hindus called *dukkha*. (Later, Buddhists would also call it dukkha.) It was then he had another great revelation: suffering is caused by *desire*. What if you didn't need anything? Then you wouldn't suffer when you didn't have it. And why would you need it if it's not real? And if you didn't have to get anything from anyone, then you could have an authentic relationship with them. You didn't have to be an ascetic and physically give up the world in order to do this. It was something that could and should be done with the mind.

GARY: The Course would say it's not desire, but the seeming separation from God that causes suffering and the feeling of lack. In fact, the desire is just a symptom of lack, and the solution is undoing the sense of being apart from your Source.

ARTEN: That's true, Gary, but desire makes it real. So let's stick with Siddhartha for now. We'll get to the one thing his approach missed later. But the most important realization he had, as a result of all his other realizations, was that it was possible to undo the thing that was causing the illusion in the first place, which was the ego. The Hindus not only knew about the ego, they also knew there was only one ego, or what they would call the one appearing as many. That's what makes the world of multiplicity, or all that you see. If you find a way to undo the ego, then you have found the way to undo the *cause* of the illusion!

It was during this phase that he discovered the synergy of thought and belief. So let's be clear that even though Siddhartha believed in the Hindu Gods, he didn't crystalize that belief because the focus was scattered. Many Hindus tend to single out one of the Gods, like Shiva or Vishnu, and focus their worship on the one they choose. Monotheism taking hold in the world was just a matter of time, and by the time Siddhartha came along there was already one of what is now three major monotheistic religions, Judaism. But Siddhartha, not being psychologically committed to one God, chose to focus on what he called "the Higher Self" of Braham, which was reality. This is where the power of belief comes in. What have you learned about the power of belief?

GARY: It's simple. *What you choose to believe in is eventually what affects you.*

PURSAH: Excellent. What you choose to believe in is what you will think is real, and you will come to experience it that way. Knowing this, Siddhartha withdrew his belief from the world, and after years of practice he had no belief in it. Instead, he put that belief where he knew it belonged, in reality, Braham.

But there's more. As he stopped believing in the world and it had less of an effect on him, he began to actually experience his life more and more like the dream that it was. He hadn't yet completely found the way out of suffering, but he was making great progress.

Siddhartha continued to travel around eastern India, teach his wisdom, and undo his ego. Instead of denying himself the world physically, he denied it psychologically, refusing to believe in it, overlooking it, and putting his faith in the reality he could sense just beyond the veil of illusion.

He had been 27 years old when he left the palace. It was 20 years later, when Siddhartha was teaching a group of students about the way out of dukkha and to salvation, that a man standing behind the sitting students was surprised to see this teacher. Because he had been denied the world by his father, Siddhartha was not well known when he was at the palace, except by the people who worked there. But this man in the crowd thought he recognized him. When the gathering was over, the man walked up to Siddhartha to get a better look at him. Upon doing so, the visitor asked Siddhartha if he remembered him. He told him his name was Vadmer, and he worked on the grounds when they were both at the palace. He also said everyone there was very sad to hear Siddhartha had left.

Siddhartha was surprised and interested. He asked the man how long ago he had left the palace, and the man told him about two years. Then Siddhartha asked Vadmer how Yasodhara was doing. Vadmer bowed his head and said he was very sorry Siddhartha didn't know, but that Yasodhara had passed away as the result of a fever three years before. Tears began to form in Siddhartha's eyes. He thought he had overcome being at the effect of the world, but obviously that wasn't total yet. His tears did not last long, however, because of what was said next.

Vadmer asked Siddhartha if his son had found him. Siddhartha couldn't believe what he was hearing. A son! He was both shocked and overjoyed. The duality of the sadness over Yasodhara and the news of a son was disconcerting, but he asked Vadmer what the boy's name was. Vadmer said that his name was Rahula, and that about a year after his mother died he left the palace to search for his father, Siddhartha.

This changed everything for Siddhartha. From that moment on, he was intent on one thing: finding Rahula. He got a good description of him from Vadmer. The next day he began walking in the direction of his former home, asking anyone he could along the way if they had seen a boy, about 20 years old, tall and slim with black hair, who may be saying he was looking for his father.

GARY: Wow. So Siddhartha wasn't completely enlightened, but obviously he had learned and experienced enough to almost be there, and then he went looking for his son.

ARTEN: No one would blame him for doing that and for wanting to find him. We just want you to notice that now he's looking for something that seems to be outside of him. And if something is outside of you and you're making it real, then you're not in a condition of oneness, you're in a condition of separation. This change of events has once again brought up desire in Siddhartha: the desire to find his son. And desire leads to suffering. It's a circular condition.

PURSAH: Which brings up an uncompromising principle that few are ready for: *The instant that you think anyone is a real human being, you are practicing separation.*

GARY: Great, I'll start off my talks with that. Just kidding. I understand what you're saying. It reminds me of something J said to Helen in a message that was meant for her personally at first but which she shared later. It was about her not being able to say no. He said if you cannot say no to the requests of others, you have not yet overcome egocentricity.

PURSAH: Yes, Gary, because if you can't say no then you're making it real. You're saying this is a real person with a real problem that you really have to do something about. Now, that doesn't mean you don't ever say yes and help people. What it means is that you don't *have* to.

GARY: I get it. And when you get used to working with the Holy Spirit you can get Guidance as to what to do anyway. Oh my God. I just thought of something. You said Siddhartha thought there was someone who would help him, someone he was searching for, and that at some point they would find each other. Was that person his son?

PURSAH: Yes.

GARY: And was his son J in that lifetime?

PURSAH: Yes.

GARY: Are you telling me that the one who people would later call Jesus was the son of Buddha?

PURSAH: Absolutely.

GARY: No freakin' way! But, well, I have to admit it makes sense. I mean these guys have been with each other, and had the other's back, all the way through.

ARTEN: But they haven't yet remembered each other in that lifetime because at this point they haven't found each other. And Siddhartha started suffering for the first time in a long time, because he was missing his son. He went from village to village and across the country with a longing in his heart, yet after a year they still hadn't found each other.

Fortunately, during his evenings of rest and reflection, Siddhartha's training and discipline slowly but surely came back to him. Soon, a calmness began to take its rightful place in his mind. Remember, everything you learn stays with you. If you temporarily forget what you've learned, it will eventually return to your awareness. That is the way of enlightenment. You forget the truth but then you remember, and eventually you will not forget.

PURSAH: Rahula, being who he was, also knew very much about different forms of spirituality. The many things he had learned at other times were also returning to his awareness.

Both Siddhartha and Rahula possessed the quality of perseverance, which as you know is the most essential trait for anyone on a spiritual path. As a result, they were determined to find each other, even though at this point Rahula had been searching for three years. Then one day, in a small watering place, Rahula had a feeling of excitement: a recognition of great familiarity filled his consciousness. He turned around and there, standing right in front of him, was Siddhartha. They knew each other instantly. They didn't hug each other or jump up and down. Such behavior at that time would have been undignified. What they did was bow to each other, and a tear of joy formed in Siddhartha's eye.

They found a place to sit and talk. For hours they caught up on the story of their lives, which they both knew was just that, a story. In the next few weeks, they remembered everything from the past and all they had learned. They knew who they had been to each other through the ages, and they also made a decision: They agreed they would spend the rest of their days together, learning whatever it was they might still have to learn and applying it to whatever came up in their dream. They would attain salvation together.

This led to an acceleration of learning by which they eventually knew everything they had to know in order to be enlightened, and were also able to apply it. Knowing that their egos needed to be completely undone, they practiced not making the dream real. Siddhartha's suffering was soon healed. One of the pieces of the puzzle is that if the dream isn't real, there's no need to desire it, and without desire there is no suffering. But they took that tenet of Buddhism even further. If the body is just part of a dream, then it's not real, which means the pain you feel is not real either. You're not feeling real pain. You're having a *dream* of pain. And because a dream is in your mind, you can change your mind about it.

When you're in a dream in bed at night, your physical body is not there, only your mind. It's the same with this dream you call your life and your so-called awake time. Your physical body is not here; it's just a part of the projection like everything else.

Siddhartha and Rahula forgave their lives. They forgave the isolation they felt in the palace. They let go of the hurt of missing Yasodhara. It's not that they didn't remember. Some people mistakenly think that if you completely forgive something, then it disappears from your mind and you never think of it again. That's not true. The difference is that when you remember something that was painful in the past, it no longer has any *effect* on you. It doesn't hurt any more. It becomes neutral instead of painful. That's how you know you've forgiven it. And they didn't think in terms of forgiveness back then; they simply thought of it as not making it real because it's just a dream, which is one of the most essential realizations of forgiveness. There was still one step they had left out, and they realized this naturally because their awareness had been so expanded. That step would become one of the most important focuses of their final lifetime.

GARY: When I looked into Buddhism a long time ago I learned the four Noble Truths. Were they into that?

PURSAH: They certainly would have understood those things, including the eightfold path; but remember, Buddhism didn't become a religion until later. Siddhartha, who was Buddha, wasn't a Buddhist. The religion came from others who tried to follow him. And yes, Siddhartha did have some students again in the later part of his life, but these students had a very difficult time sticking with nonduality, as most people do. Still, all things considered, Buddhism contains many great truths that help people to be mindful instead of mindless.

Our two friends practiced until their minds could tell their bodies what to feel, instead of their bodies telling them what to feel. They went to a total place of cause instead of effect. The world was coming from them. They had attained the state of Brahman. They had become nondualistic beings.

Siddhartha lived to be 82 years old, Rahula only 52. It didn't matter by then. They had almost 30 years together. They had mastered the world, except for one thing. One day Rahula said to Siddhartha, "There's still something missing, and I think you know what it is." Siddhartha replied, "Yes. We've come this far together. I want us to awaken in God together: the One God, with us as One with each other and with God." Then he added, humorously, "Next time you be the teacher."

They knew they had one more lifetime to live, not necessarily because they needed it, but because others needed them. They could have chosen to complete their lessons in that lifetime. But they came to realize that the script is written, and that there was a greater plan in which they each had to play their part. Sometimes a master has to be there, if only to point people in the right direction, and perhaps to teach one or two seemingly big lessons in order to act as an example for others. They both knew that during this last seeming lifetime on Earth they would experience their destiny; that God would take the final step in their return to the Oneness of their Source.

As Rahula let his body slip away as a result of the same kind of illness that had come to his mother, he knew that the most interesting of all lifetimes was about to begin. He was happy; he was ready to go on and finish the job. And as *A Course in Miracles* would later say, "when he is ready to go on, he goes with mighty companions beside him."[1]

Part II

A.D.

6

The Final Times of
J and Buddha

*I said to Him, "Lord, what allows one to see a vision?
Do we see it with the soul or with the spirit?"
He answered and said to me, "One sees not through
the soul or the spirit, but through the mind,
which is between these two."*

— THE GOSPEL OF MARY MAGDALENE

$\mathcal{J}$ was excited at the prospect of hearing about the final times of J and Buddha. According to my teachers, he and J would have one more go-round, not so much for themselves, but to play their part in helping others. I played a guessing game about who Buddha was that final illusory time. Then I decided to just let the conversation with Arten and Pursah play out.

I was intrigued by Buddha, or Siddhartha, and by the role J had played with him as his son, Rahula. I was also fascinated with the path that Buddhism had taken, even though Buddha wasn't there. The religion never really caught on in India, where Hinduism still thrived. In the 2nd century A.D.—OR C.E., as it's also called—Buddhism found its way over the Himalayan Mountains to Tibet and China. Then some Buddhists mixed in with Taoists, and the resulting discipline began to be known as *Chan*. Chan migrated to Japan about nine hundred years ago and evolved into Zen, combining itself with Shintoism, which J and Buddha were trained in during their first important lifetime together. Zen brought with it the concept of the world being nothing but *maya*, or illusion. Although Zen was very meditative, it also took on a tradition of irreverence, rather than a belief in religious trappings. I recognized some of this irreverence in *est*, a fusion of East and

West which was my own introduction to spirituality in this lifetime. *Est* replaced the Zen meditations with what were called *processes*, or guided meditations that eventually led to silence.

Although I wasn't a Zen Buddhist in this lifetime, I knew by the time I was in my early 40s and living in Maine that I must have been one at another place and time. I started to focus more on meditation and found that I was very good at it without ever having been trained. I was remembering my training from long ago. I soon got to the point where I could achieve absolute stillness, where no interfering thoughts intruded, both resting my mind and making it more peaceful. Although meditation itself is not a part of *A Course in Miracles,* many of the later Workbook lessons are quite meditative, and involve an actual approach to God. I found my ability to quiet my mind to be very helpful in my practice of the Course.

I knew the story of Jesus, or J, very well, not only from the Bible but also from some of the alternative Gospels that had survived the rise of Christianity, though not in their original form. Then there were the many things J said about himself in *A Course in Miracles,* which my guidance and intuition told me were the most authentic statements of all.

Still, I couldn't wait to hear Arten and Pursah talk about the two masters. When my friends—who I had come to understand were the Holy Spirit taking on a form and *showing up* as Arten and Pursah—returned for their next visit, they didn't waste any time.

ARTEN: We're going to tell you a story. Some of it you're familiar with, and some of it you're not. It's not the whole story. That would require you to write an entire book by itself. But it will be sufficient for the purposes of *this* book.

PURSAH: A little over two thousand years ago there was a town called Nazareth. It's still there today, but it's nothing like it was back then. The world's population has grown exponentially, and it's hard to imagine that at the time of our story, Nazareth, which was considered to be a big town, only had about five hundred people. There were a few people who were born at the time who would get to know each other and become very close. Around the same time, a few other people were born in and around Jerusalem who would become very connected with their counterparts in Nazareth. People, who are not really people but appear to be, travel through space and time in groups.

GARY: You told me once that some people are in each other's orbit; that even though they may appear to go apart, because they're in each other's orbit, they're destined to come back together again.

PURSAH: That's true. You could also think of groups of people as being like schools of fish. They tend to travel through what the world calls life together. And at the time in Nazareth you had three people who were born within a couple of years of each other who would be together a lot. Their names were Y'shua, Mary, and Nadav. We'll simply refer to Y'shua, who is known to the West as Jesus, as J, like we always do. Mary was Mary Magdalene, not to be confused with J's mother Mary; and Nadav was the person who was Siddhartha, or Buddha, in the lifetime we just discussed with you. Eventually J and Mary would be very public people. Nadav, on the other hand, would be more of a behind-the-scenes person. He was one of the disciples though, and he also wrote a Gospel, which we'll talk a little about. Other than that, he was pretty quiet.

The three of them met as children, played together, grew up together, and would be lifelong friends. (Incidentally, Mary was also Megumi, the woman whom both Saka and Hiroji loved when they were Shintos.) And in Jerusalem you had four more people—Thomas, Thaddaeus, Andrew, and Stephen—who were all born within a few years of one another and would become lifelong friends. Thomas and Thaddaeus would meet as teenagers. As you know, I was Thomas at the time, and Thaddaeus, who you know as Arten, would become my best friend. Thaddaeus was gay, and he had a significant other, Andrew, who was also gay. These four people from Jerusalem would eventually meet the three people from Nazareth when they were, on average, 20 years old.

GARY: And from what I recall it was against the Jewish law to be gay at the time, punishable by death?

PURSAH: Ah yes, the old Book of Leviticus. You're making me nostalgic. Just kidding. But you're right, Thaddaeus and Andrew couldn't exactly advertise their sexual preferences. Of course the Romans would have had no problem with it at all, those silly savages, but it was against our laws.

ARTEN: J, Mary, and Nadav could tell early on they were different from other people. By the time they were 10 years old they could read each other's minds. They'd joke, "I know what you're thinking! I know what you're thinking!" And they did. Their egos had been so much undone by all of their learning and application in other lifetimes that there was no ego interference restricting their joining with other seemingly separate minds. Of course no mind is really separate because there's only one mind, but most people don't experience that yet.

By the time they were teenagers, they could see the future. They'd had some experience of this at other times, but this time it was absolute. And all three of them remembered everything, all of their learning that they needed to remember. No one remembers everything all at once. It would be too much information, resulting in system overload, so it has to be spread out a little. You've got to be aware of the present and able to deal with your surroundings right now. That's why we called one of your chapters in the second book, "It's This Lifetime, Stupid." But unlike you at that time, our three protagonists didn't have things to learn. When a master comes back for the final time, they don't have a learning curve. They already know everything they need to know in order to be enlightened. So why are they there? Usually to point people in the right direction. Every now and then, there has to be someone who is able to point people in the right direction because they actually *know* the right direction, which is rare. The Holy Spirit included that fact in His plan for salvation.

GARY: How did Mary get to be so advanced? And did she know J and Nadav in other lifetimes?

PURSAH: Oh yes. She taught them at various times. She wasn't as close to them personally as they were to each other in those lifetimes. That experience was reserved for J and Mary the last time around. This was how they could tell they had successfully learned how to not make the body real. If you can forgive someone who you love physically as well as mentally, and realize that all of it is only a dream, then you have finally overcome the ties that bind you to the Earth. And Mary, aside from learning the same things J and Nadav had learned, had her own personal experiences as both men and women in other lifetimes, which brought her to the same awakening they had achieved. Do you remember Saying number 22 from the Gospel of Thomas? Part of it says, "when you make male and female into a single one, so the male will not be male and the female will not be female . . . then you will enter the Kingdom."

To the three of them, all people were Spirit, exactly the same as their creator, not male or female. Of course the Gospel of Thomas was eventually corrupted by people who added dualistic Sayings onto it before it was buried in Nag Hammadi. That's why a while back I gave you the original version, or at least as close to that as you can get in English.

NOTE: For a corrected version of the Thomas Gospel, see Chapter 7 of my second book, *Your Immortal Reality*, "Pursah's Gospel of Thomas."

ARTEN: Also, during their teenage years, J, Mary, and Nadav would go to the Library of Alexandria in Egypt. They didn't need to learn, because they already knew everything that was important. But they truly enjoyed looking through the place and seeing what was there. They would then recommend that their friends go there and read certain works, if they could read. They knew which books would be the best for which people, and they would encourage them to learn. Once again, it was all part of the Holy Spirit's plan, which we'll talk about later. That plan was actually established looking back from the end of time.

They all knew the Scriptures well enough to quote them by heart. But they also knew which parts of the Scriptures came from the Holy Spirit and which parts came from the ego. As your awareness increases, you can tell the difference, and they would focus on the parts that came from the Holy Spirit and share them with others.

One of their favorites was the Psalm of David. It's interesting that that Psalm 23 is read at so many people's funerals, because it's not about death. "Yea, though I walk through the valley of the shadow of death, I will fear no evil: for thou art with me." That's about a fearless way of living, knowing that the Holy Spirit is with you, taking care of you.

By the time they were approaching their 20s, our three friends knew it was time to travel and share their knowledge with those who were supposed to hear it. They'd been to the Temple in Jerusalem many times, but they went there one more time before they set out on their travels. It was then that they spoke at length with Thomas, Thaddaeus, Andrew, and Stephen. Those four, who were spiritually advanced, but not yet on the same level of awareness as the three masters, got along very well with them. It was like a group of old friends having a reunion, even though it was their first time talking at length in that lifetime. Yet they had all met briefly during the trips of the Nazareth three to Jerusalem. And they had all been together, on and off, during the various lifetimes we've described to you: as parents, brothers and sisters, lovers, friends, and enemies. Now it was time for them to be together and travel to complete a mission.

GARY: Cool. It's like the Blues Brothers said: "We're on a mission from God."

PURSAH: Something like that.

GARY: Why didn't they all speak with each other before?

PURSAH: The four were somewhat in awe of and intimidated by the other three. They could feel the latter's advanced state of awareness. But now it was time for the seven of them to join.

This became part of what people today refer to as "The Lost Years" of J, from the time he was 12, where you have that story of him teaching the rabbis in the Temple, which was true, to the time he gets back to Jerusalem after his world travels with his friends, and begins his "formal" ministry. Those years weren't lost; they just aren't known by most people. I recorded a great deal of it, including many things J said from the time we met, when I was 20, to the time of the crucifixion, when I was 30 and he was 33. But almost everything I wrote was eventually destroyed by the church.

GARY: I'm sure they meant well, those bastards.

PURSAH: Don't be passive-aggressive.

GARY: Hey, passive-aggressive works for me.

ARTEN: It took about seven years for us to travel all of the places our three enlightened ones chose to go. One place was Egypt. We hadn't been to the Library like the three of them, and it was all new and exciting to us. We went down the Nile to the Temple of Luxor, and up to the pyramids. Wherever we went, the Jerusalem Four, as we thought of ourselves, would set up a time and place for J to speak to the people, and we would tell as many of them as we could about it, so they could be there to listen.

GARY: You were his organizers?

ARTEN: Yes, and it was easy most of the time. As we went along, people would be amazed at the clear authority of his teaching. And some people would volunteer to go on ahead and make sure we all had food and a place to sleep. It was actually a lot of fun, at least most of the time. And of course we'd sometimes run into hostility, but nothing fatal. Once in a while Nadav and Mary would discuss with J the things he was saying, and we'd get to listen. They were completely uncompromising about this world being nothing, and our real life being with God. Nadav would joke about J being the teacher and how he and Mary didn't have to say anything. But later, after we got home, Mary started teaching too.

J wouldn't go out of his way to see pharaohs and kings. He considered everyone to be the same, equally important. We went through parts of Africa and as far as England and Stonehenge, all the way across Europe and what is now Turkey, and across India. Sometimes we'd have to join caravans for protection. There were many bandits who would slit your throat for whatever you had. That was a common way to die in those days. J wasn't afraid, but he'd use common sense in order to keep the rest of us safe. As we traveled, the three of them would have many memories of the past in these places, but they'd focus on the fact that they were touching people's lives in such a way as would influence the direction of their lives, and which in turn would influence the lives and minds of others.

PURSAH: Another interesting thing about the three masters was that wherever we went they could speak the languages of the people. I thought I was intelligent because I could read and write, which most people couldn't at the time, and here were these three speaking all these languages. Over the years I'd write down only what I heard in Aramaic. But J was imparting wisdom to countless people over three continents.

It's fairly well known that St. Paul spoke at the Parthenon in Athens about 20 years after the crucifixion. What isn't well known is that J spoke there just before he returned to Nazareth, a good 24 years before Paul. The people marveled at his brilliance and authenticity.

GARY: How many people were there? I've always wondered how big the crowds could be at that time.

ARTEN: About four thousand. The biggest crowd J ever had was about five thousand, and that was later, outside of Jerusalem. That was a result of the rumor going around that he was the Messiah. Of course he never said that, but as you know, people go to extremes. They wanted to be saved, physically as well as spiritually, and that wasn't the point.

Many of the people who were there following J and trying to figure out what he was talking about are people who today are studying ACIM. It makes sense they would be attracted to the Voice of the Course.

GARY: How could the people hear him? I mean how could he possibly speak loud enough for the people in the back of the crowd?

ARTEN: That's a good question. Not everyone could hear him. But back in those days they had people who would repeat what the speaker just said. So J would speak a paragraph in whatever language they spoke. Then every 50 feet or so there would be a designated person who would repeat what he said for the next group of people. Then another person would do the same. It would take a while, but that way everyone got to be able to hear the message. It wasn't perfect, but it worked fairly well.

GARY: That's really interesting. It reminds me of something. Didn't there used to be people who had such a good memory that they'd memorize whole plays, and then go from town to town reciting the whole play? That's how they made their living, right?

PURSAH: Yes, and there are mental tricks you can use to memorize things, but let's move on.

ARTEN: After Greece, it was time to go home. J had a ministry and a destiny to fulfill. And Nadav exemplified the attitude of the three of them as much as J and Mary did. He was a fascinating person who had the characteristics of an enlightened being. Like J and Mary, he was fearless. He was totally aware that what we call life is a dream, and that nothing in it can have any effect on you unless you allow it to by making it real. His attitude was that it doesn't matter if someone dies because their mind will keep on going and dreaming until they wake up. And when they wake up they're home.

He also had the quality of joy. He'd make funny comments about all kinds of things, especially the Romans. There wasn't any meanness in his attitude. It was more like satire, pointing out the human folly in thinking you're getting somewhere by conquering others. He'd say, "Let Caesar have the world! Why work so hard for nothing? What thing of this world will you be taking with you when you leave? We all break even in the end. You didn't come here with any money, and you're not leaving with any. It's a break-even game for all of us. The question is, did you learn from it? Did you forgive all of it?"

When we made it back to Nazareth it was time for J to start teaching his own people. Everything was designed to reach the people who were ready to be reached at that time, and also many who weren't ready but would still be helped in some way.

We all went to the local synagogue when J was to speak. Most people thought he was just going to say hello and be the humble son of Joseph that he was supposed to be. Instead he went up there and said, "Today the Scriptures are fulfilled." He was saying the he was the Messiah in the sense that we are all the Messiah, equal in the Mind of God. We are all One. But all the people heard was that he was fulfilling the Scriptures and he was the Messiah. They were outraged. J was lucky to get out of there alive.

PURSAH: We didn't stay around Nazareth too long. We could take a hint, with people yelling and threatening to stone us to death. J knew that as a prophet it was difficult for him to be accepted in his home.

GARY: Is that when he said, "You can't make a profit in your own town?"

PURSAH: There was something we realized when we witnessed the fearlessness of the three of them. They were no longer human. They no longer identified with the bodies they appeared to be occupying. They had completely remembered God. They were experiencing their Oneness and Wholeness with God. And they didn't have to make a big deal out of it. They were very matter-of-fact about it.

Thaddaeus, Andrew, Stephen, and I myself were in awe of them. Yet as far as they were concerned, awe should be directed only at God, not at a brother or a sister.

We headed for Jerusalem, where the four of us had met the three of them. J's brother James was the Chief Rabbi of Jerusalem. Even though we hadn't seen him in years we knew him to be very traditional and conservative, almost the opposite of J. But he was a good man and treated people well. We were all invited into James's house and got to take turns telling him about all of our adventures. He was impressed. But when J tried to explain the Oneness of us and God and how we are *all* God's only son, James was not enthusiastic. He listened politely and then said it was time to go to sleep.

The next day J decided that rather than staying in Jerusalem it was time to get out into the countryside. There were people there who didn't have access to the Temple and might be happy to hear the truth of the Oneness of all of us in God. He knew there would also be some people who wouldn't be happy to hear it. He was totally prepared for whatever was to come. Thaddaeus and I had not yet been told that J, Mary, and Nadav knew everything that was going to happen. They were aware that within a few short years J would be crucified, and that he had chosen to teach this lesson in order to demonstrate the meaninglessness of the body and how it had nothing to do with what he really was and where he really was.

We walked for a few weeks around the country before we came upon the Sea of Galilee. This is where we met Peter, a fisherman who wasn't having much luck. The story you've heard about J taking him and us and a few others out and finding the fish for Peter is true. And yes, he did command a storm to stop and the ocean to become calm. He had command over the dream. Yet he didn't use it for his own gain. He used it to show, as best he could for the people of the time, that what we were seeing is a projection that was coming from us, and so we have dominion over it. Most people weren't ready to hear that, so most of the time he would speak to them in parables, stories that had a meaning they could get on whatever level they were prepared to hear.

ARTEN: Peter and a few of his friends decided to join us and follow J. Peter would be the first one to admit he wasn't the brightest guy in the world, and he had a hard time understanding J. Later, after the crucifixion, it would be Peter along with James and eventually Paul who would start the religion that J would never have wanted to start, even though he knew it would happen. It didn't matter. J saw us all as being equal. There was no such thing as separation in his mind.

The seven of us who were there at the beginning of J's world travels were the ones who understood him the best. J didn't treat us as special or as being any kind of an inner circle, but he would take the time to talk to us privately because he knew we could grasp what he was saying. The other disciples who came along later were jealous, especially of Mary. Sometimes J would kiss her in public, which wasn't done at the time. We'd then, for fun, give him a hard time by saying things like, "Hey, don't you know you're not a body?" Then we'd all laugh.

PURSAH: As you know, as Thomas I was sometimes called Didymus, which means twin. I didn't look *exactly* like J, but it was close, and we were often mistaken for each other. Once I dressed in some of his clothes and pretended to be him. I actually got away with it until I opened my mouth. I was no match for him.

I remember a short time after I met J, I decided to give him a gift. We could both read and write, which as I said wasn't common back then. I gave him some quills to write with and some parchment. He looked very happy, but then he handed them right back to me. He said, "You take these things and use them to be my scribe. Write down what I say. I'd be honored."

Well, I was honored too. I made it a point to write down everything I could so it would be available for posterity.

GARY: Didn't J know almost all of the writings would be destroyed?

PURSAH: Oh yes. As I said, he knew everything. But I didn't, and I think the reason he asked me to be his scribe was for me. He knew if I wrote things down I'd learn them better.

GARY: I can see that. Sometimes back in Maine I used to read the Text of the Course and listen to the recording of it at the same time. I felt like I was getting it more deeply, probably because my senses of sight and hearing were being fed the message at the same time.

PURSAH: That's very good. Maybe more people will try that now. In any case, I didn't just write down the Gospel of Thomas. I'm the one who wrote the Gospel I told you about during the first series of visits, *Words of the Master*, which today is also known by scholars as the "Q" Gospel. That's the Gospel that Mark, Matthew, and Luke all borrowed a lot of the same Sayings from before it was eventually destroyed by the church. That's why their three Gospels sound similar and are known as the synoptic Gospels.

GARY: Wow! Why didn't you tell me you wrote "Words" sooner than this?

PURSAH: You had more than enough information to deal with, brother. But remember, the Gospel of Thomas, The Q Gospel, and the Gospels of Mary and Philip were all written before the so-called mainstream Gospels. The Gospels you see today in the Bible borrowed the Sayings from those of my writings that those writers liked, the ones they thought they could fit in with their theology, and simply disregarded the Sayings they didn't agree with. They had bought into the theology of Paul, or Saul, which was his real name, whose letters to the earliest churches had become Gospel to them. Yes, those letters contain some very beautiful writing, and some of it is from the Holy Spirit, but it's a mixed bag; it's not J. Christianity is based on the theology of Saint Paul, not the teachings of the man he presumed to be emulating.

People always think they understand the teachings of the masters, but the masters are nondualistic. They don't make the world of maya real. To J, Mary, and Nadav, only God was real, and nothing else was. Then people take that and turn it into dualism. But as Nadav used to say, "Of the two seeming worlds, the world of God and the world of man, *only* the world of God, which is perfect Oneness, is true. Nothing else really exists." There's only one world, Gary: God's world. That's not just nondualism, it's *pure* nondualism, because it acknowledges God as the only Source and the One Reality.

You've got to remember that J and Nadav's previous learning, which was the same as Mary's, included the teachings of Shankara, the great teacher of the Vedanta. He taught that the absolute Reality, Brahman, was totally unrelated to the phenomenal world! And what the three masters believed in that final lifetime was that God and His Kingdom was also totally unrelated to the phenomenal world, this dream world of illusion. And in case you think we're emphasizing that

too much, remember, without knowing that it is *impossible* to practice the kind of forgiveness that J, Mary, and Nadav practiced in their
final lifetime.

I wrote down *Words of the Master* on the road over a period of a
few years before the Gospel of Thomas. Remember, the first Gospels,
including those of Thomas, Mary, and Philip, didn't have any detailed
stories, just a list of Sayings. But I did put some stories into *Words of
the Master*. They were taken and mixed with other, fictional stories,
written by people who weren't even there. *Words* was later destroyed,
as *all* the alternative writings were, by A.D. 400. Some altered versions
that were buried around A.D. 325 survived and were dug up in 1945.
Words was not among them. The church really wanted to destroy that
one, not just because it included the nondualistic truth of the teachings, but because I included Mary Magdalene as a teacher equal to J.
They certainly couldn't have that.

Everyone knows about the Council of Nicaea in A.D. 325, which
established the canonical Gospels. But most don't know or care about
the council in A.D. 381 that actually made the circulation of any other
Gospel illegal and punishable by death! That was the First Council of
Constantinople, convened by the Roman emperor Theodosius, who
was desperately trying to save the Empire. One of the ways he tried
to do that was to establish one religion, the Christian religion, which
most people supported by then, but it was too late. The religion survived; the Empire didn't.

Now, I have another piece of information that may surprise you.
When we talk about Nadav, we're using his real name. But he was
actually the one who is referred to as Philip in the Bible. The transla-
tions of the Bible don't have the disciples' real names. Philip became
known as one of the disciples because he was with J all the time, but
he was actually J's equal, although most people didn't know it because
he was so quiet in public. But it was actually he who wrote the Gospel
of Philip. Also, he was the only one, aside from J and Mary, who didn't
come back for another lifetime. That was the last stop for him.

GARY: Okay. I'm freaking out here, but I have a question. The
Course says that J was the first one to complete his part perfectly.
Does that mean he was enlightened before Mary and before Philip,
who was actually Nadav, and Buddha and Siddhartha and all of them?

PURSAH: Technically, yes. There was one last, big forgiveness opportunity in that final lifetime for all three of them. That was the crucifixion, a lesson J had chosen to teach for others, not that he really had anything to learn.

You see, he had only the love of God. His ego had been completely undone, which allows you to be only love. Until you complete all of your forgiveness lessons, which allows the Holy Spirit to completely heal your mind, you *can't* teach only love. You slip in and out. But once the ego is gone the love is always there naturally, because that's what you are. J had completed the job. Mary and Nadav, even though they were healed, had one more experience to go through in order to know for sure they could not be affected by anything in this world, and that was the death of their beloved J.

The seven of us, plus Peter and a few others who were not written too much about, walked with J and marveled at him for about three years. He, Mary, and Nadav were so loving and kind to us and to others it made us want to be like them.

The one we're calling Stephen was written about a little in the Gospels. He was a lot like J, except he had a temper. He was kind of like J with an edge. He was eventually stoned to death a couple of years after the crucifixion. That was an occupational hazard back then.

James, J's brother, started Christianity with Peter and Paul, but he didn't really want Christianity to be separate from Judaism. He tried to blend the two things together. That didn't work out. James was eventually thrown off the wall of the Temple by the Romans during the First Jewish Revolt. But unlike most of us, at least he got to be old.

You know what happened to me, Thomas, in India. My wife, whose name was Isaah, along with Mary, Thaddaeus, and Andrew, witnessed my execution. Isaah was inconsolable, but Mary, Thaddaeus, and Andrew did their best to comfort her. Eventually they all went back to Nazareth and later to France, where they lived out their years. Mary went there by mind-transport. The rest of them had to walk. Mary didn't have children, as some suggest. She didn't value the body and saw no need to make other bodies.

That's not a judgment on those who choose to have children. The only thing Mary would say is that if you do, remember what everything is for: forgiveness. The forgiven relationship is the Holy relationship. If you forgive everything, it makes everything helpful.

After the crucifixion, Nadav spent a couple of years in Nazareth. He concluded he had done enough traveling. He finally went to Qumran, where he stayed with the Essenes, even though he couldn't get into their teachings. They were more into the old Scripture and preserving old scrolls. He forgave them and had fun with them when they were open to it. That's when he wrote the Gospel of Philip, based on his memories.

There are three things I want to impress upon you about J, Mary, and Nadav. First, there was their uncompromising brand of forgiveness. They had already learned it, but they were different from others because they really lived it. They weren't interested in pointing out the errors in the egos of others. They simply overlooked them, and knew who and what the other person really was. They looked past the veil of illusion to the truth, to the light that shines within all of us and is perfectly constant.

Next there was the love. They were so loving it was hard to fathom, even though we tried to be like them when we could. Both the Bible and the Course say that perfect love casts out fear. There was no fear in them. Their love was perfect, and they had no fear, because they had no ego.

And also, they were happy. They had no pretensions and lived like happy people, without complaints and grievances. For them, joy was normal, and it was a joy to behold.

If you have the Holy Spirit in your mind, you can tell what things in the Bible J really said, and what the writers' egos had him saying that he never did. J was consistent. In fact, if you look in the Course's Manual for Teachers, you'll find that consistency is *A Course in Miracles'* definition of honesty.

ARTEN: During the crucifixion, the Roman soldiers were angry and fearful because J wasn't suffering. One of them screamed at him, "Man, why don't you feel any pain?" J said, "If there is no guilt in your mind, there is no pain." The soldier stuck a spear in his side, but J didn't react at all. The soldier then became even more frightened and ran away.

J had decided to lay his body aside for the final time. Just before he did so, he looked at Mary and formed a very gentle smile on his face. Then she did the same. As they looked into each other's eyes, they both knew he had overcome death. Nadav saw the same thing, and the three of them subtly and gently acknowledged the truth within each other.

Because they were not affected by the death of J, Nadav and Mary knew they would not be coming back to this world to live another lifetime. As both the Bible and the Course agree, "The last to be overcome will be death." Mary and Nadav hugged each other closely at the funeral, and then went their separate ways.

The first three enlightened ones had fulfilled their mission. Yes, there were others before them who knew everything one has to know in order to be enlightened, and had even lived it, like Shankara and Lao-tzu. But there was one thing that was missing. You can't completely undo the separation from God without completely acknowledging God and recognizing Him as the *only* reality!

Once again, this is why *A Course in Miracles* says, "Be vigilant only for God and His Kingdom."[1]

GARY: Thank you. I think I get it.

ARTEN: Be vigilant, my friend. We still have much to cover, and we'll be back.

PURSAH: Be well, brother.

I knew a lot about what happened two thousand years ago, but hearing Arten and Pursah talk about it brought it home for me and taught me even more. As I went to sleep that night, I thanked J, Mary, and Nadav for everything, and extended my love and gratitude to them. The Teachers of teachers were no longer visible, yet they had helped me once again.

7

Gnosticism

There is nothing either good or bad, but thinking makes it so.

— WILLIAM SHAKESPEARE, *HAMLET*

One winter night, a couple of months after the conversations in this book began, I posted the following message on Facebook, Twitter, and the Yahoo Discussion Group that talks about my books and the Course. I also sent it to my e-mail list soon after. It describes my experience of the night before.

I was sitting watching a movie I had gotten from Netflix last night when Cindy came into the room. She had a very serious look on her face. Cindy doesn't usually have a very serious look on her face. She's usually light and breezy. She told me she had some sad news, and I knew immediately that someone we loved had passed away. The only question was who? Then she told me that Ken Wapnick had made his transition. I was a little surprised, not that it happened, but that it had happened so soon. I guess I thought we had more time.

I met Ken about a half-dozen times, including a few private meetings, and exchanged about 20 letters with him, which I still have. I know I'm going to be thinking about him for a long time, and that things will come to me that I want to share with you. So for now I'll just say something about the first time I met him, because it speaks volumes about the kind of person he was. Arten and Pursah had guided me that I should meet Ken and learn everything I could from him. I can't say I learned everything I could from him, but I certainly learned a lot. I had driven 10 hours from Maine to Roscoe, New York, in June of 1998 to see him give a presentation called "Time and A Course in Miracles." Ken spoke about 10 hours on the subject over the weekend, and I was dazzled by his brilliance. I got to sit down and talk with him in private because I had requested to do so, and he had consented. I wanted to tell him about the book I was writing and that I wanted to use a lot of quotes from the Course, but that I would make sure to credit the Course correctly in an index. I was nervous, and Ken knew it.

I'll never forget how kind he was to me. Eventually Ken would be the first person to read *The Disappearance of the Universe*. But more importantly, as the years went on, I would sometimes hear him say, "Be kind." I already knew from experience that Ken didn't just say things, he lived them. He was the kindest person I ever met, and he inspired me to want to be kind to others. Of course there is much more to say about the person who Arten and Pursah described as the Course's greatest teacher. But for now what I'm thinking about the most is what a beautiful person he was, and how he went out of his way to be kind to me when he didn't have to.

Cindy and I joined hands last night, and I spoke to Ken and expressed my gratitude to him. I know that he's having a very good time right now, and that we are the ones who still have to deal with what's in front of our face. Fortunately, we will always have Ken's work to help us do that. I love you, Ken.

Arten and Pursah once told me there are always different schools of thought when it comes to any spiritual teaching. That's because even though the truth is simple, the ego is not. When it comes to these different schools, there will usually be one that really understands the original teaching, and those that don't. For example, with the non-dualistic Vedanta, it was Shankara who got it right. With Gnosticism, it was the Valentinian School, named after its founder, Valentinus, which really understood the original intention of the Gnostic teachings, as well as a lot of what I was saying. As for *A Course in Miracles*, it's the Wapnick School, or the Foundation for *A Course in Miracles*, which got the Course right. Below are two fascinating excerpts from the Valentinian work, the Gospel of Truth, in which one can see startling parallels between that Gospel, written around A.D. 150, and the

Course. These excerpts were sometimes used by Ken Wapnick in his teaching.

> Each one's name comes to him. He who is to have knowledge in this manner knows where he comes from and where he is going. He knows as one who having become drunk has turned away from his drunkenness and having returned to himself, has set right what are his own. He has brought many back from error.[1]

> Thus they were ignorant of the Father, He being the one whom they did not see. Since it was terror and disturbance and instability and doubt and division, there were many illusions at work by means of these, and there were empty fictions, as if they were sunk in sleep and found themselves in disturbing dreams. Either there is a place to which they are fleeing, or without strength they come from having chased after others, or they are involved in striking blows, or they are receiving blows themselves. . . . Again, sometimes it is as if people were murdering them, though there is no one even pursuing them, or they themselves are killing their neighbors, for they have been stained with their blood.

> When those who are going through all these things wake up, they see nothing, they who were in the midst of all these disturbances, for they are nothing. Such is the way of those who have cast ignorance aside from them like sleep, not esteeming it as anything, nor do they esteem its works as solid things either, but they leave them behind like a dream in the night.[2]

I didn't know a lot about Gnosticism, but I knew I wanted to talk a little about it with my teachers, especially since they had brought up the Gospel of Philip, which they had once recommended to me in a conversation, along with the Gospel of Mary Magdalene. I didn't read either. I did know that the Gospel of Thomas wasn't a Gnostic writing, but the first Christian one, although not the same as the religion that came to be called Christianity. Some modern Biblical scholars believe it can be traced to as early as A.D. 50, before any other Christian writings. Arten and Pursah would say even earlier.

One relatively cool afternoon in L.A., Arten and Pursah were suddenly with me. Arten started speaking right away.

ARTEN: Well, brother, have you had time to integrate what you learned during our last visit?

GARY: Some of it, but it was a lot to take in.

ARTEN: Yes, and since you went back to Salem you've had even more to think about.

NOTE: In late July 2014, I brought Cindy back to the place I was born, Salem, Massachusetts, to give her a chance to see my old stomping grounds on the North Shore, especially Salem and Beverly, the town I spent the most time in. We stayed at the Hawthorne Hotel, a place I used to sing and play my guitar in when I was 22, both as a soloist and later with the popular band Hush. The hotel was next to historic Salem Common and across the street from the Salem Witch Museum. We went into the museum to see and hear a presentation, which was very accurate, about the Salem witch trials and the hysteria that had been created in the area in 1692–1693. I was disturbed to the point where I had to practice forgiveness of the way people can project their unconscious guilt onto others to the point of executing them, even though the accused had done nothing to deserve it.

Salem means "peace," and the irony of that wasn't lost on me. It also made me more aware of the dynamic of projection and how the human condition hasn't really changed much in the 300-plus years since then.

Aside from that sad piece of history, the trip was highly enjoyable. Today, Salem capitalizes on the witch thing as much as possible, but it's a smart, cool town with the same spiritual vibe I felt there in the '80s.

PURSAH: There's a quote we want you to use somewhere in the book. It's from the Gospel of Mary Magdalene: "I said to Him, 'Lord, what allows one to see a vision? Do we see it with the soul or with the spirit?' He answered and said to me, 'One sees not through the soul or the spirit, but through the mind, which is between these two.'"

That was recorded by Mary Magdalene at the time we all hung out. This is what it means: First, the quote as translated from the Nag Hammadi writings asks, "What allows one to see a vision?" It should ask, "What allows one to see *with* vision?" That's what Mary was asking J, for the benefit of those listening. She already knew the answer. The soul, although considered to be very spiritual by most, is actually a separation idea because it's an idea of individuality, or personal existence. Everyone thinks they have an individual soul. It doesn't matter if the idea of individuality involves a body or not. Separation is separation.

Also, the quote doesn't really need to say "the spirit," but just *spirit*. Spirit is all there is, and it is oneness. So right away you see you have two ideas in the quote from Mary's Gospel, the idea of separation or the idea of oneness. The reason J said "One sees not through the soul or spirit, but through the mind, which is between these two" is that it's the mind's function to *choose*. You use the mind to choose either the idea of separation, which in the Course is represented mostly by the body, but also the human psyche, i.e., individual soul; or to choose Spirit, which is perfect oneness. Whichever one you get into the habit of choosing will be what you think is real. It will become what you believe in and thus what it is that affects you. You can see that J was teaching the same thing two thousand years ago that he's teaching today through *A Course in Miracles.* In fact, he says in the Course, "The term *mind* is used to represent the activating agent of spirit, supplying its creative energy."[3] You activate spirit by choosing it with the mind. Get it?

GARY: Got it. Of course, two thousand years ago he couldn't usually put things the way he does in the Course or else no one would have understood him, not that most of them understood him anyway. So I take it that's why he spoke mostly in parables?

PURSAH: Yes, Sayings and parables. Now, Gnosticism became popular after the earlier Gospels of Thomas, Mary, and Philip, as well as the later Gospels you see today in the Bible, which were always being changed. Today, because of Christianity, Thomas, Mary, and Philip are incorrectly thought of as being Gnostic. In fact, Philip is considered to have come from the Valentinian School, but that's not true. The original version of it was pre-Christian and pre-Gnostic. Still, as we told you once through your mind, it was Valentinus who understood J the best of all the Gnostics. Valentinus was born in Alexandria, where he got to use the Library like J and his friends did.

GARY: Didn't the Library burn down?

PURSAH: Yes. There were several fires that caused various degrees of damage, but there was a surviving form of the Library, called the Serapeum, up until A.D. 391 or so. Valentinus established schools, known as part of the Syrian-Egyptian schools of Gnosticism, in Alexandria and Rome, around A.D. 150. It was there the amazing Gospel of Truth was written. Valentinus was influenced by a teacher named Basilides, who also had popular schools. Plus there were other Gnostic teachers, but they weren't as good at grasping the principles of J. It was Valentinus's teachings that were the most influential Gnostic teachings until the late 4th century. Then, as we've been saying, all the writings except for the mainstream Gospels became illegal and were wiped out.

The reason we bring this up is that there's a parallel between Gnosticism and J's new form of the same teachings in *A Course in Miracles*. Some people have a gift for recognizing what the original teachings are saying. As you know, in the case of Gnosticism, it was Valentinus. His students were attracted to him because they recognized the truth of what he was teaching. They didn't go to him because of his personality, but because they could see he was nondualistic, and they resonated with it. In the case of the Course, it was Ken Wapnick who had the gift for recognizing what the Course was saying. And today, students are attracted to Ken's work, not because of his personality, but because they recognize the truth in what he was teaching in his long and prolific career before he made his transition. The Course is nondualistic, and so is Ken's work. Yours is also, because you had us right from the beginning. Plus, since we first came to you, on our advice you've learned from Ken as well.

It's no accident Ken was there at the beginning with Helen Schucman, Bill Thetford, and Judy Skutch. He was supposed to be the one to teach the Course. The wisest students learn from him. Others think they can teach the Course better, but they don't. They think Ken just had one possible theory of what the Course means, his interpretation. But it's not a theory. There *is* only one possible correct interpretation of the Course. It says what it says, and Ken taught what it said better than anyone.

GARY: I've been meaning to ask you, was Ken enlightened?

PURSAH: Yes he was. Ken left the illusion because it was his time. Everyone has an appointed place and time when they're going to make their transition. You don't change that by becoming enlightened. The script is written. If you're enlightened then you lay your body aside for the final time. It's not important that Ken appeared to pass away in the dream. What was important was how he was looking at it. He said at the end, "I'm not dying," because he realized that the body and personality some people thought was him wasn't him at all. The body had become meaningless to him, as with J.

It was the same with Bill Thetford, the co-scribe of the Course. You know from Judy that he was enlightened.

NOTE: I had become good friends with Judy Skutch Whitson—president of the Foundation for Inner Peace, the original publisher of the Course—who, as Pursah pointed out, was there at the Course's origins. Judy told me she believed that Bill was "the first one to graduate from the Course." Having seen videos of Bill speaking in the 1980s, I saw nothing that wouldn't confirm what she was saying.

GARY: That's great that at least two of the original four Course people were enlightened, and I see no reason to think Judy isn't. I know that Helen Schucman, despite completely understanding the Course, had a hard time when it came to actually *doing* it. But everything about Ken told me he really applied it.

ARTEN: Yes he did. And we're pleased that you've gotten better and better at doing the same.

PURSAH: Since we've been emphasizing nondualism so much, would you like to briefly review the four steps on the ladder to pure nondualism?

GARY: Sure. First, you have dualism. That's the domain of subject and object, expressed by Newtonian physics. Things appear to be outside of you. That's where consciousness comes from. Even though the universe is a projection, you don't know it. In order to have consciousness, you have to have something else to be conscious of. That's separation. That's why the Course uses the word awareness to describe Spirit. It's something that's not the same as consciousness. Spirit is oneness; there's no subject and object, just wholeness. But whether it's your personal experience or the subject of spirituality, with dualism you have two seeming worlds: the world of man and the world of God. Both seem to be true.

Next there's semidualism. That's a condition where the mind is beginning to accept that the idea of separation may not be true. You could think of semidualism as a kinder, gentler form of dualism. For example, you see a different attitude among religious people who are in a state of semidualism. They may start to accept the idea that God is love. But along with this comes important questions. For example, if God is love, can He also be hate? If God is perfect love, as the Bible says, can He also have imperfect thoughts? Questions are being raised and awareness is slowly beginning to awaken in the spiritual student's mind. As a result, the person may not feel as isolated as people who are in a state of dualism. By the way, at any time during the process of climbing the ladder, you may slip back and forth from one condition to another. It can be a turbulent trip, but at times it will be peaceful.

Then there's nondualism. Nondualism says there's no such thing as separation, and anything that appears to be separate is not real. The projection is undone in your mind and you go from being at a position of effect to a position of cause. Now you're no longer the dream, but the dreamer. And the dream is not being dreamed by somebody else. There *is* nobody else. Nondualism is non-twoness. There is only oneness, and only one reality. So of the two seeming worlds, the world of illusion, which is not true, and the world of Reality, which is true, only the world of reality is true, and anything that appears to take on a form is untrue.

Which brings us to pure nondualism. The reason it's pure is that it acknowledges God as the only source and the only reality. Yes, there may *appear* to be two separate worlds, the world of God and the world of man, but *only the world of God is true, and nothing else is true.* It's rare for a person to be able to acknowledge and accept this, because it means the relinquishment of any form of personal identity, whether body or soul, now and forever. You know you are soon going to disappear into God and take on the higher life of Spirit. You will have the awareness of perfect oneness, but not consciousness. Yet through brief glimpses, you'll learn that the experience of awareness blows away the experience of consciousness. This makes the dream world of illusions completely meaningless, except for the way it can be used by anyone to return to the reality of God.

PURSAH: Thank you, Gary. True and brief. Now tell us a joke.

GARY: Okay. This is my shortest joke: Jesus walks into a hotel, and he goes up to the front desk. He's got these four big, old, rusty nails with him. He plops the nails down on the front desk and he says to the guy behind the desk, "Can you put me up for the night?"

PURSAH: Very irreverent. Nadav would like it.

ARTEN: Getting back to nonduality, the Gnostics used the word *gnosis* in much the same way the Course uses the word *knowledge*. In both cases we're not talking about intellectual knowledge or the imparting of information; we're talking about having the actual *experience* of your perfect oneness of God. You've had the experience the Course calls *revelation*, right?

GARY: Yes. Same thing. Revelation in the Course doesn't mean that special information is revealed to you. It's referring to an experience that's so amazing it's literally indescribable, way beyond words. That experience of the awareness of perfect oneness blows away anything this world has to offer. It gives you a taste of the truth that is a constant state, rather than the impermanence of the dream. And you're saying some Gnostics experienced the same thing, a reality beyond the veil of the illusory universe?

ARTEN: Absolutely. There have always been people who experienced that. It can happen to anyone at any time. And you don't have to be that spiritually advanced in order for it to hit you by surprise. I say "surprise" because it usually happens when you don't expect it. So the people reading this shouldn't waste their time looking for it. Also, if it happens it doesn't make you special. In some cases, the Holy Spirit is helping you to have that experience in order to encourage you, to help keep you going. Plus there are very advanced students who don't have that experience in this lifetime. But how do they know they didn't already have it in another lifetime? There's no sense in trying to figure out why it happens to some and not others. Just understand that it happens to every mind at some time or another. It's kind of like a preview of coming attractions. You get a sense of what your reality is eventually going to always be like, outside of time.

GARY: The orgasmic aspect of it is awesome, too. We made up our relationships in this world as a substitute for the relationship we thought we lost with God. But sex in this world pales by comparison. That's because only minds can join in a permanent way. Bodies can't really join—not that we won't try. But union with God takes place through the mind, which, as you said, activates the experience of Spirit.

PURSAH: The Course describes your relationship with God as intensely personal, and it is. The Gnostics treasured that experience of gnosis. To achieve it they'd try to remember the world is just a dream, as you read in the Gospel of Truth. To them, the world wasn't made by God but by a demiurge, which is roughly equivalent to the Course term *ego*, and they were trying to transcend it and go back to reality, which was called *Pleroma* in some of the Gnostic traditions. But the students would often get discouraged if the experience of gnosis didn't happen for them. Making a false idol out of the experience, and being disappointed if it doesn't happen, won't get you anywhere. Then, of course, a lot of them made the same mistake most people do. They made the world real. They gave truth to their illusions, so many of them remained in a state of duality, just as many Course students do.

Another error they made was to identify with their projection. Today, many spiritual students are taught to look at something in the world and say, "I am that." But in fact you are *not* that. Anything you see out there in the universe is a *symbol*. It's a projection, a hologram that's symbolic of that which is buried in your own unconscious mind. Though some of it is symbolic of wholeness, most of it's based on separation. Yes, it's representative of what's hidden in your mind, but it's not you. You don't want to identify with it; you want to forgive it, especially if it affects you in any kind of a negative way. It may seem noble to be one with the universe, until you remember there is no universe. What you want to be one with is God, which is all that truly exists.

ARTEN: Gnosticism and its teachings ended up being a mixed bag, like everything else. Some of the students were really into God, and some didn't want to have anything to do with God. The Gnostic systems weren't developed enough, even though Valentinus was a genius. Like Lao-tzu, he lived nonduality, but he had a hard time getting his students to do the same thing. Still, many of them made enormous strides on their spiritual path and are studying the Course today, ready to attain their enlightenment. The Course gives them the whole picture they need. If you look carefully, as we will in our last few visits of this series, you'll see the Course doesn't leave you with a bunch of unanswered questions. It tells you what existed before time began, which was given to you by God; how you appeared to get here; exactly what you can do about it; and where you're going home to and how to get there—not that Heaven is a place. It's an awareness you need to reawaken in, and how the Holy Spirit has a plan that's guaranteed to result in that happening for everyone.

GARY: I think it's frustrating for people because the Holy Spirit can see the whole plan and how it's all going to play itself out. The Holy Spirit can see everything that ever appeared to happen or ever will. The Course talks about an interlocking chain of forgiveness, so my forgiveness is connected to everyone else's forgiveness. But I can't see it, and the Holy Spirit can. Could J and Mary and Nadav see it?

PURSAH: Yes, when you've forgiven everything, and your mind has been completely healed by the Holy Spirit, then by definition all of the barriers that limited the power of your mind have been undone. Then you're high enough above the battleground, as the Course would say, to see the big picture. But even then, as long as you appear to be in a body, you'll focus on your part in the plan and have complete faith in the Holy Spirit. Remember, even the J guy followed the Holy Spirit; the Holy Spirit didn't follow *him*.

GARY: I've been meaning to ask you a couple of questions that other people have asked. You mentioned it would be possible that a nuclear weapon could go off in a major city sometime. Is that still likely? And any details? Also, that Iranian guy you mentioned in the first series of visits who you said might use nukes against us: he seems to have disappeared from the picture. Were you wrong about that?

PURSAH: I wasn't wrong. Arten was, but I wasn't. Just kidding. This is what you want to remember. If the Course is teaching that what you're seeing in the world is an outer picture of an inward condition, then if you change the inward condition the outer condition will also change. That's cause and effect. The good news is that because of the Course, the dissemination of which you play a part in, there's been enough forgiveness and healing of the mind that the former Iranian president isn't going to hurt you.

GARY: Okay, what's the bad news?

PURSAH: The bad news is that the world has still not undergone a comprehensive awakening. The present condition of the mind is one of inner conflict. Thus the mind will project events in the dream that are symbolic of that conflict. This makes it not only likely but inevitable that at some time a nuclear bomb will go off in a major city. Remember, the ego demiurge wants to have bigger and more frightening events unfold in order to induce fear. Fear makes what you're seeing real, and the judgment that results from that keeps the ego's cherished projection intact.

GARY: I don't suppose you're going to tell me where and when?

PURSAH: That would not be wise. The government isn't going to evacuate a major city on your say-so. So not only would it not do any good, it would set up all kinds of hassles and distractions for you. Instead, stick to your job. It's like we said about 9/11: if the students of the Course don't forgive, who will?

GARY: Another quick question in regard to the health section in the last book. It's about the 35 percent food-grade hydrogen peroxide, or HP, you told me to use to oxygenate my cells and prevent or heal all kinds of diseases. For example, you said cancer can't survive in the presence of oxygen. I know HP is magic, but I also know that it's okay to use it to help the body allow the mind to heal the body. So I followed the instructions that were given in that small book you recommended, *The One-Minute Cure.* I did the whole regimen, but most people tell me they can't do it; they can't take that many drops of the HP. Any advice?

ARTEN: Yes, the hydrogen peroxide will still be effective in promoting health even if you take just 9 or 10 drops a day in distilled water; say 5 drops twice a day in six to eight ounces of water. Make sure it's distilled, because the HP doesn't mix well with the impurities that are in most kinds of water. Also, keep the HP in the refrigerator to stop it from spoiling or losing its strength. Keep the water cold too, because it will make the HP taste better. And be careful to make sure it's 35 percent food grade. If people do that every day, all kinds of benefits can result, and it doesn't take long at all to do it in the manner described here.

GARY: Thanks, I appreciate it. You know, you said earlier that this world is a hoax. Well, I was reading an article about my favorite film critic, Roger Ebert, who made his transition a couple of years ago. The article appeared in Patheos Press and was written by Tom Rapsas, who recounts the words of Roger's wife, Chaz. Roger wasn't a particularly spiritual man, which made what his wife had to say even more interesting. I'll read that part of the article:

> But most compelling to me were the events that happened in the days before Roger died. His wife, Chaz Ebert, tells us that her husband "didn't know if he could believe in God. He had his doubts. But toward the end, something really interesting happened." Continuing with her words:
>
>> That week before Roger passed away, I would see him and he would talk about having visited this other place. I thought he was hallucinating. I thought they were giving him too much medication. But the day before he passed away, he wrote me a note: THIS IS ALL AN ELABORATE HOAX.
>
> According to Chaz, she asked Roger, "What's a hoax?" looking for some clarification. He then made it clear to her that "he was talking about this world, this place. He said it was all an illusion. I thought he was confused. But he was not confused."

Chaz went on to say that Roger described "this other place" as "a vastness you can't even imagine." So I guess you don't have to be heavy into spirituality to realize the true nature of this world and find that there's something far vaster and real that's just beyond it.

ARTEN: An excellent note to end on, I think. The next three visits we'll be discussing something that we trust will encourage students to understand, stick with, and apply the incredible power of nonduality. As *A Course in Miracles* says about the advanced student,

> Now he begins to see the transfer value of what he has learned. Its potential is literally staggering, and the teacher of God is now at the point in his progress at which he sees in it his whole way out.[4]

PURSAH: We love you, brother. Give Cindy a great big hug for us.

And with that they disappeared in an instant, leaving me to try to fathom the possible transfer value of all that they, and J's Course, had taught me so far.

8

J Channeled 1965–1977: This Time the Truth Will Not Be Buried

Freedom is given you where you beheld but chains and iron doors.
But you must change your mind about the purpose
of the world, if you would find escape.

— A COURSE IN MIRACLES[1]

J was really looking forward to speaking again with my ascended friends. They had always been so good to me. I was genuinely satisfied with what they had taught me, but I wanted to go even deeper. I wanted to finish the job. That way, even if I did come back for one more lifetime to help others, I wouldn't have a "learning curve" to go through. I would have already learned everything I needed to learn in order to be enlightened.

I had been studying and attempting to apply the teachings of the Course for 23 years, and I had gotten better and better at it as the years went by. I learned along the way that understanding something is not enough. It's like what Ken Wapnick had told a group of translators of the Course, who knew the Course better than anyone: "You think you understand the Course, but you will never understand it unless you *do* it."

Being a lifelong musician, I like the analogy of someone who wants to be a good piano player. You can learn a great deal about music appreciation and music theory, but there's only one thing in the world that's ever going to make you a good piano player, and that's if you sit there every day at the piano and *practice.* Absent that, it will never happen.

Spirituality is no different. Do we really believe we're going to achieve the same level of spiritual advancement as people like J, Mary, and Nadav without practicing? I've met many Course students who don't think they have to practice; they think they can just skip to the end. It's as though they honestly believe they can just say "I am enlightened" and that makes it true. But it doesn't. When the Course says salvation is undoing, it means it. The ego must be undone. The ego's dream must be awakened from. And the Holy Spirit's great teaching tool to undo the ego and awaken from the dream is forgiveness. No one will do the forgiveness work that's necessary to achieve enlightenment unless they want it bad enough, just as no one will practice enough to become a great piano player unless they want it bad enough.

Over the years of practicing forgiveness, my experience of life changed. My body felt lighter, even though I had gained 20 pounds over that time. My body felt more like the figure in a dream, which is what it really is, instead of something I have to carry around. It felt more elastic. It was more difficult to hurt it. I had been in a couple of minor accidents and hurt myself, but it didn't hurt when it should have.

The same was true of psychological circumstances. I would get into situations that used to upset me, like speaking in front of people in new and different situations, or having someone come into the room who I didn't like, and I realized that these things were no longer upsetting me. This was a process that happened over a long period of time. Everyone's different, and it's possible for someone to get the results of the Course faster than others. That's because even though the truth is simple, the ego is not. The ego is very complicated and must be undone at the individual level, even though being an individual is an illusion. The Holy Spirit meets us where we are, and works with us to help facilitate our awakening. Part of that awakening is to realize that you're dreaming. You realize it first as a theory, but the more you practice the Course's brand of forgiveness, where you're coming from a place of cause and not effect, the more you experience it.

The Course couldn't be any clearer about the fact that we're dreaming. It says, "The Holy Spirit, ever practical in His wisdom, accepts your dreams and uses them as means for waking."[2] It also says, "You travel but in dreams, while safe at home."[3] I try to remember that whenever I get on an airplane. Also, when we wake up in the morning we think we're awake, but the truth is we're still dreaming. "All your time is spent in dreaming. Your sleeping and your waking dreams have different forms, and that is all. Their content is the same."[4] On top of that, the dream is not being dreamed by somebody else. "No one can waken from a dream the world is dreaming for him. He becomes a part of someone else's dream. He cannot choose to waken from a dream he did not make."[5] So if we're dreaming, then where are we really? "You are at home in God, dreaming of exile but perfectly capable of awakening to reality."[6] We can choose to take on our real function, realize that we're dreaming, and follow the Holy Spirit home, even when it comes to the most difficult occurrences, such as observing our loved ones at the seeming end of their time with us:

> Awareness of dreaming is the real function of God's teachers. They watch the dream figures come and go, shift and change, suffer and die. Yet they are not deceived by what they see. They recognize that to behold a dream figure as sick and separate is no more real than to regard it as healthy and beautiful.[7]

That, however, doesn't mean we don't have love and compassion for all. As we'll see when the technology of forgiveness is discussed, if you are practicing the Course the way it's meant to be practiced, that leads to love automatically. As J says right in the Introduction:

> The Course does not aim at teaching the meaning of love, for that is beyond what can be taught. It does aim, however, at removing the blocks to the awareness of love's presence, which is your natural inheritance.[8]

Once again, A Course in Miracles is a very BIG teaching. When the Course talks about your natural inheritance, it's talking about nothing less than the Kingdom of God. Heaven was given to you by God as a gift. You don't have to earn it. If someone gives you a present, do you have to suffer and sacrifice in order for it to be yours? The awareness of love's presence is the awareness that Heaven is here now. However, even though you don't have to earn it, you do have to awaken to it.

You can see two thousand years ago in the Gospel of Thomas that the disciples went up to J and we asked, "When will the Kingdom come?" He said, "It will not come by watching for it. It will not be said, 'Behold here, or behold there.' Rather, the Kingdom of the Father is spread out upon the earth, and people do not see it."

It's not that the Kingdom isn't here; it's simply out of people's awareness. Removing the blocks to the awareness of its presence means undoing the ego. When you undo the ego with forgiveness, which is always done at the level of the mind, the blocks are removed and Heaven slowly but surely becomes your reality instead of the dream. That's the approach of *A Course in Miracles.*

In the following two paragraphs, "the Voice" referred to is the Holy Spirit. You can see how deeply the Holy Spirit will be working with you:

> *You* are the dreamer of the world of dreams. No other cause it has, nor ever will. Nothing more fearful than an idle dream has terrified God's Son, and made him think he has lost his innocence, denied his Father, and made war upon himself. So fearful is the dream, so seeming real, he could not waken to reality without the sweat of terror and a scream of mortal fear, unless a gentler dream preceded his awaking, and allowed his calmer mind to welcome, not to fear, the Voice That calls with love to waken him; a gentler dream, in which his suffering was healed and where his brother was his friend. God willed he waken gently and with joy, and gave him means to waken without fear.[9]
>
> Accept the dream He gave instead of yours. It is not difficult to change a dream when once the dreamer has been recognized. Rest in the Holy Spirit, and allow His gentler dreams to take the place of those you dreamed in terror and in fear of death. He brings forgiving dreams, in which the choice is not who is the murderer and who shall be the victim. In the dreams He brings there is no murder and there is no death.

The dream of guilt is fading from your sight, although your eyes are closed. A smile has come to lighten up your sleeping face. The sleep is peaceful now, for these are happy dreams.[10]

Many have wondered why the Course uses the form of language it does, which is often Shakespearean blank verse, also called iambic pentameter. Aside from the fact that it's beautiful and the Course is a true work of art, I think I found another reason. Once, when I was in London, I went to a museum. While exploring I came across some papers behind glass that were written over five hundred years ago. I could understand some of it, but most of it looked like gibberish. Languages and writing change from century to century. But Shakespeare hasn't changed. It's a classic form of language. Books that are written in the vernacular today will probably be difficult to read five hundred years from now unless they're revised. But Shakespeare is a constant. That tells me that five hundred, even one thousand years from now, people will still be able to read the Course and understand it. That doesn't mean it will be easy to read. It's not easy now! But it will be doable. Perhaps J knew what he was doing.

I wanted to have a dialogue with my teachers about many Course ideas. It had been a few years since we really got into it. One afternoon they were back again.

ARTEN: So, we can tell you want to talk about the Course. You've certainly done more than your share of traveling around the world to teach it. What would you like to talk about?

GARY: There's so much. The Course says, "The miracle establishes you dream a dream, and that its content is not true."[11] But a lot of students seem to have a big problem going all the way with that. I mean, I'll say that according to the Course the absolute truth is this: God Is. And they don't seem to have much of a problem with that. But then if you tell them, *nothing else is,* you can see the resistance on a lot of their faces. They can get the truth of God, but they can't get that absolutely nothing about the world and their lives is real.

ARTEN: Yes, the Course is the most radical teaching in history. That's why most of the people who teach it don't teach it. Even if they understand it, which is very rare, it's not easy to explain to people that they don't exist, and that they never have. Their life is a lie. The only place they really exist is in God, and the physical universe, including their own bodies and personal identities, not to mention those of everyone they've ever known, has never been true. And oh, by the way, their children are illusions too.

GARY: Yeah, I try not to start off with that. Of course J doesn't leave you hanging; he doesn't just describe the unreality of the ego, say the world is an illusion, and get lost. That teaching alone won't do anything for you, except maybe make you depressed. What the Course does is completely *replace* the thought system of the ego with the thought system of the Holy Spirit. I've been looking at spiritual thought systems for almost 40 years, ever since I got into *est,* and I've never seen anything else do that. Most of the teachings are good at describing the problem. A lot of experts and big-shot psychologists are very adept at talking about the ego and all the problems of the world. And, at best, they'll give you a method that will make you feel better. But that's a temporary fix. It doesn't undo the ego. It placates it by glossing things over. The Course, on the other hand, actually gives you a way out. It gives you a *resolution* to the entire problem of human existence. It takes you all the way home to Heaven, which you never really left, except in a false experience. So it replaces a false experience with the true experience. But actually undoing the ego takes time and work. A lot of people who go to a workshop expect to be enlightened that weekend.

PURSAH: So you do the same thing as J. You explain to them what to do and you point them in the right direction. When we say the Course is the most radical teaching in history, you've got to remember that almost all the teachings and thought systems in history are based on the so-called wisdom of the ages and universal truths. But those truths and wisdom are not true, and the Course is *not* the same as them. Why? Because they're all based on the universe being real. Even the nondualistic teachings are taken by the world and devolved into making the error real. That's why the Course says, in describing the world, "Any mistake can be corrected, if truth be left to judge it. But if the mistake is given the status of truth, to what can it be brought?"[12]

GARY: That's another thing. People have been taught all their lives that God created the world. Now I didn't have any problem with the idea that God didn't create this world and, in fact, doesn't have anything to do with it. For me, that came as a tremendous relief, because I couldn't understand how God could allow such terrible things to happen to good people. Then it turned out it wasn't Him who did it, it was us: the one ego appearing as many through the idea of separation. This is our projection and Heaven is still perfect, but some people are still married to the idea of this being some beautiful thing created by the Divine, even though everything in it decays, falls apart, and dies. And that's if you're lucky enough to survive that long.

Remember that weekend workshop I did at the yoga center in Massachusetts? There were several workshops going on there at the same time, and on Saturday night they had a thing where the speakers could do a two-hour presentation in different rooms and anybody attending any of the other workshops could come and hear you, sort of like an introduction to your work. Now, because it's a yoga center, you've got a lot of younger students there, and they're really into the body. I mean you've got hormones flying all over the place. They think yoga is really spiritual, but what they really worship is bodies. So on Saturday night I've got about a hundred people, mostly in their 20s, coming to hear me, and I'm wondering what the hell I'm gonna say to them. Before I went on I did a short meditation, like I always do, and joined with the Holy Spirit—incidentally, to me, you guys and J are all the Holy Spirit, because once you get up to the level of spirit it's all the same—and I asked for any guidance for this presentation to these young people. *Should I tell them the truth? Should I hold back?* And I'm sure you remember the answer I got was this: *See how many of them you can get to walk out on you.* In other words, don't hold back at all. Give it to them straight. So I did. I would have anyway, but it was good to have that reassurance.

I'd say over the course of the two hours, about 20 of them did walk out on me. But a lot of the ones who stayed had these looks on their faces after I gave them some of the more radical stuff, and it was like they were saying, "Really? Is that really true?" It was the first time a lot of them had heard a straight nondualistic message. They were so used to making the world and the body real, it didn't occur to them that there was a completely different way of looking at things, one where they could have their cake and eat it to, because I wasn't telling them they had to give anything up. I was just telling them there was another interpretation that could save them a lot of time.

PURSAH: You did fine, considering the unconscious resistance people have to accepting a nondualistic message. After all, this is death to the ego. And then here you are with a purely nondualistic message! Only God is real, and nothing else is real. Why would a physically oriented young person want to hear that? Yet you got the interest of some of them because everyone has the truth buried in their mind, waiting to be uncovered, and they sense it. Even when you don't expect it, some people listen to you because when they hear the truth there's a recognition. You remember what the Course says about that:

> This world you seem to live in is not home to you. And somewhere in your mind you know that this is true. A memory of home keeps haunting you, as if there were a place that called you to return, although you do not recognize the voice, nor what it is the voice reminds you of. Yet still you feel an alien here, from somewhere all unknown. Nothing so definite that you could say with certainty you are an exile here. Just a persistent feeling, sometimes not more than a tiny throb, at other times hardly remembered, actively dismissed, but surely to return to mind again.[13]

GARY: Oh yeah. I remember having that feeling, even when I was a kid. It was like a part of me knew I didn't belong here. Of course a lot of people feel that. And the truth is they don't belong here. The good news is there's a right way to leave the world and go home. Suicide won't do it. If you do that, then you just have to come back here and go through the same old crap all over again. So why not make all the progress you can in this seeming lifetime? Then if you do come back, you would have already learned so many lessons that your next lifetime will probably be a fun and fascinating one.

I think that without the Course my life would have been kind of sad. I'd been on a spiritual path for a good 15 years when I found the Course; or should I say, you guys found me. But I still felt like there was something missing, because there *was* something missing. Did I ever thank you guys for stopping by?

PURSAH: That's all right. We didn't have anything better to do.

ARTEN: You must have noticed that as you undo the ego, which is kind of like peeling away the layers of an onion, more and more right-minded ideas come into your mind from the Holy Spirit.

GARY: Absolutely! Like I was at LAX a couple of weeks ago, going to Madrid, and there was so much to do before leaving I didn't get any sleep. It was 5 in the morning and I felt really tired. Then I got this thought in my mind, "You're not tired. You're having a *dream* that you're tired." And I got it. What can be tired except for a body? But I'm not a body. So I'm having this dream that I'm in a body and that the body is tired. But it doesn't have anything to do with me. My mind can choose to be spirit instead. And I felt better. In fact, whenever I remember the truth I feel better. And I can remember the truth in any circumstance at any time. Plus the Holy Spirit helps me with these ideas.

PURSAH: Very good. And of course, the same is true if you feel pain. Let's say someone feels some pain in their knee. Now, they're not actually feeling pain, they're having a dream that they're feeling pain, just like you were dreaming you were tired. But in their dream maybe they think they're getting arthritis or something. It feels at first like the pain is in their knee, but it's not. We've already taught you that pain is not a physical process, it's a mental process. So the pain is actually in their mind. And more deeply, it's a function of guilt, because in their unconscious mind they think they're guilty over the separation. Of course they're not really guilty, because the separation never occurred. It's just a dream of separation that never really happened. And if they can think right-minded thoughts with the Holy Spirit and remember that, the pain might go away.

ARTEN: Because of the way the mind works, which we'll get to, they need to apply the idea of the universe being a dream to anything that is having any kind of a negative effect on them they may become aware of: every person, situation, and event, including what's going on with themselves. You may recall a very important couple of questions that J asks you in the Course:

What if you recognized this world is a hallucination? What if you really understood you made it up? What if you realized that those who seem to walk about in it, to sin and die, attack and murder and destroy themselves, are wholly unreal?[14]

GARY: Wow. That reminds me of the secret of salvation. Let me find that. I figure if J wants to tell me what the secret of salvation is, maybe I should listen. Okay. Here it is:

The secret of salvation is but this: That you are doing this unto yourself. No matter what the form of the attack, this still is true. Whoever takes the role of enemy and of attacker, still is this the truth. Whatever seems to be the cause of any pain and suffering you feel, this is still true. For you would not react at all to figures in a dream you knew that you were dreaming. Let them be as hateful and as vicious as they may, they could have no effect on you unless you failed to recognize it is your dream.[15]

ARTEN: Could he be any clearer than that? Now, why don't you ask any questions you have, and also questions you hear in workshops. That way we can cover a wide range of topics.

GARY: Okay. People are asking about a new Course book that seems to talk a lot about how you behave in the world, which is what a lot of Course books do. I think the author uses an example of a friend who came upon someone who had broken into his house; instead of reacting with fear, he reacted with love and talked to the person who broke in. He said he understood, and the perpetrator was surprised. They started acting like friends, and there was a good outcome. What would you say about that approach?

ARTEN: Well, in some cases it would be a good way to get killed. If the person breaking in had a mental problem, or was on drugs and was stealing to get more, or was a violent criminal, it could be a very dangerous situation on the level of form. Now, I'm certainly not suggesting acting out of fear. However, instead of putting yourself in physical danger in order to act spiritual, the wise thing would be to leave immediately. And this brings up a very important distinction about the Course. Be practical. Use common sense. The teachings of the Course are meant to be applied at the level of the mind. They are *not* designed to be applied at the level of the physical. Remember, it's a Course in cause and not effect.

GARY: I get that. When you work on changing your mind to think with the Holy Spirit, you're dealing with the cause instead of the effect, and the effect will take care of itself, because now you're putting the horse before the cart. But if you do that, couldn't the guy who was breaking into the house change automatically?

ARTEN: He might and he might not. In the illusion of the world, things can sometimes change gradually, not just the instant that you want them to. In any case, the emphasis of the Course is on your mental state, your inner peace and strength, not how things seem to be going in your dream. That doesn't mean the Holy Spirit isn't aware of your perceived needs, though. We'll talk in a while about how you can be guided to abundance. But when it comes to a situation in the world, you don't have to try to be a hero. Be normal. If you try to prove a point, you may not be around long enough to learn your lessons.

PURSAH: The Course isn't part of the self-help movement, even though people try to treat it that way. Everybody wants to improve their life and make a lot of money. And the Course doesn't have anything against that. If it did it would be making it real. But always remember: when you focus on the effect instead of the mind, you're making the effect real. You're giving truth to something that isn't there. And as J puts it, "When you try to bring truth to illusions, you are trying to make illusions real, and keep them by justifying your belief in them. But to give illusions to truth is to enable truth to teach that the illusions are unreal, and thus enable you to escape from them."[16]

A Course in Miracles says what it says. It must be understood that there is only *one* possible interpretation of the Course. That cannot be repeated too much. Only God is real, and nothing else is real. The world does not exist. There are students who want the Holy Spirit to be operating in the world and fixing it up. No, the Holy Spirit is in the mind, not in the world. The Course says there is no world! So what world do they think the Holy Spirit is operating *in*?

GARY: That's all well and good, but what's to stop the Course from going the same way as all the other nondualistic teachings? Yes, the

Course isn't about fixing up the world or keeping any form of personal identity. Yet you already see a majority of people who are supposedly doing the Course falling all over themselves to make the world real by making it spiritual, and trying to hang on to their personal existence by making it holy. Plus they'll say that other things work, and they don't understand that those things only work at helping them feel good for a while. They don't undo the ego. With all these obstacles, what hope is there for anything to be different this time?

PURSAH: That's a good question, and there's a good answer. But first, do you remember Saying 23 from the Gospel that was written down by Thomas?

GARY: Who?

PURSAH: In it J says, "I shall choose you, one from a thousand and two from ten thousand, and they shall stand as a single one." You see, the true meaning of the Course doesn't have to be accepted right away by the masses. There are people who are ready for it, and those who aren't. The important thing is that a full picture of the truth has to be *available* for people to discover if they're ready for it. The Course has the whole truth in one place, not just part of the truth. That's never happened before. On top of that, there's the brilliance of making it a self-study Course. Sure, people will start churches and try to make a religion out of it, but it won't stop people from finding the truth for themselves. People will go to study groups, where they'll get a lot of false information; but as long as the Course is there, they can't stop anyone from learning from it on their own, and from the few teachers who actually teach it. That's why this time the truth will not be buried. As long as you have freedom of speech and freedom of the press, the Course will be there. You can't bury millions of copies of it. Yes, people will try to change it to their own liking, but the real Course will still be there.

GARY: I like it. And the Course has helped me through some situations I know would have really freaked me out.

PURSAH: Barcelona would be a good example.

NOTE: I had done a weekend workshop in Barcelona, Spain, and was flying home. For some reason the organizer of the event didn't want to pay me by bank wire, and insisted on paying in U.S. dollars in cash. I had never been paid in cash before, and I was ignorant enough to put the money in my checked baggage instead of my carry-on. When I got home to L.A., I went to baggage claim and got my bag and looked inside of it, as I often do, to make sure things in it weren't damaged. When I opened it, all the money, $13,000, was gone. I called the police, who explained there wasn't much they could do about it because the theft was probably done in Barcelona by baggage handlers and so it was out of their jurisdiction. And oh yeah, they said, don't put cash in your checked luggage. Then I tried to get help from the carrier, American Airlines, and they were useless. The whole thing was a forgiveness opportunity.

I can usually forgive things right away, but it took me a little while to be free of that situation. The fact that no one would help added to the frustration, making it several lessons in one. But the dynamic of forgiveness is the same no matter what appears to be happening.

PURSAH: Would you like to explain it for us?

GARY: Well, first, because I was upset, I realized that I was thinking and feeling with the ego. Your feelings are a result of thoughts you've had at some time or another. An unpleasant surprise—which the ego loves, because that's the most likely thing to have a bad effect on you—will activate thoughts and the resulting feelings that are in your unconscious mind, bringing them to the surface. That's the red flag you need to watch out for when anything is disturbing your peace of mind. So you've got to catch yourself when you're thinking with the ego. If you're making it real by judging it, that's the ego. The ego is ingenious at sucking you in, so once you notice it, then you've got to *stop* yourself. You've got to quit thinking with the ego. That takes practice and discipline. In fact, accomplishing that first step may be the hardest part.

The next step is to switch to the Holy Spirit. You can't think with both the ego and the Holy Spirit at the same time. You're always choosing one or the other, whether you realize it or not, so you might as well learn to choose the Holy Spirit. When you choose the Holy Spirit as your teacher instead of the ego, that's what the Course calls the Holy Instant: that instant you choose once again, as the Course also puts it. And the Holy Spirit will give you right-minded ideas. The

Holy Spirit will tell you it's not real, this is your dream, and you don't have to be affected by it. Like J says, "Nothing can hurt you unless you give it the power to do so."[17] So I deny the ability of anything not of God to affect me. By the way, I usually talk to J in my mind, but as I said, to me there's no distinction between J and the Holy Spirit. They're not in competition with each other. So either one of them will tell you you're reacting to something that isn't there, and you can forgive the situation, the event, or the person not because it really happened or because the person has really done something, but because they haven't really done anything. So nothing has really happened, and they're actually innocent. By the way, that sends a message to your own unconscious mind that you haven't really done anything, which is why you're innocent. But that's about how the mind works, which you said you'd get to.

If you make it that far, then you can take the third step. Once you decide to see things with the Holy Spirit, it becomes the Holy Spirit's responsibility, not yours. The Holy Spirit takes over, and you engage in what the Course calls Vision. You, my friends, have sometimes called it *spiritual sight*. The Course also uses the term *true perception*, which is what you're doing whenever you're thinking with the Holy Spirit instead of the ego. The Holy Spirit is gradually taking over your mind. That eventually will lead you to having Vision all the time. When you get to that point, you're like J. And if you want to be like J, then you want to think like him. You want to take on the Holy Spirit's thought system as your own, like he did.

J saw innocence everywhere. He wasn't taken in by appearances. He overlooked bodies, and thought of each seeming individual as oneness. He saw himself everywhere. He didn't make any exceptions. You can't, or it's not whole. So with this third step, I thought of whoever it was who stole my money as not being a guilty human being, like they think they are, but as being perfect Spirit, exactly the same as God, totally innocent, now and forever, which is what they really are. So all that's left is reality.

I think the real trick is remembering. Once you know how to do it and remember to do it, you can make it a habit. That's mind training. And I have to admit there's a little bit of selfless selfishness there, because I know from the Course that if I think of them that way that's how I'll experience myself. Maybe not that second, but there's a cumulative effect, because there's always some kind of a healing that takes place with forgiveness. But those three steps are the basics.

ARTEN: Not bad. We'll tell J you're making progress.

GARY: When we were in China, some of the students seemed to think you had to forgive everything, not just the negative things that come up, but everything: the beautiful sunsets, sex, the happy times, etc. Is that true?

ARTEN: No. You can tell it's time to forgive if you don't feel peaceful. You may be irritated, or annoyed, or even angry. That's because some unconscious guilt in your mind, which you're not even aware of because it's unconscious, has been activated. You know the Course says, "Anger is *never* justified."[18] That's because you are doing this to yourself. The dream is not being dreamed by somebody else, remember? So the Course focuses on forgiving the ego's thought system of fear that's there in your own unconscious. And all the negative emotions can be put under that one category, fear. Anything that doesn't have a negative effect on you is something you don't have to worry about. In fact, the Course says that if you're with somebody and there's nothing to forgive, you should celebrate!

GARY: That reminds me of a joke. This monk is in a monastery, and he's down in the basement reading these old scrolls and texts. Suddenly, he finds something and he gets all excited. He goes running upstairs to the other monks and he yells, "Look! Look! It wasn't supposed to say *celibate*, it was supposed to say *celebrate*!"

ARTEN: So, moving on, if you're with somebody and there's nothing to forgive, don't worry, something will come up eventually. In the meantime, enjoy. There's nothing wrong with feeling good in the illusion. You know the movies you go to aren't real, but that doesn't stop you from enjoying them, right? You're not going to lose your appreciation of things like art and music. Just remember to forgive when it's called for. And when it comes to forgiving the good stuff, tell your Chinese friends, and everybody else, they don't have to. What will happen as you go along practicing forgiveness is that in your experience, the world, in general, will become more and more like the dream world that it is, including the things you love. So remember, it's all right to experience a happy dream.

GARY: Is it all right if I ask a couple of general questions I get at workshops, about the future and stuff?

PURSAH: Sure. If we don't want to answer we'll just stare at you.

GARY: Okay. You once said the Dow Jones Industrial Average would pass the 100,000 mark by the middle of the century, 2050. You told me that back in the '90s. As of today, it's around 21,000, and there's only 33 years to go. Do you still stand by that prediction?

ARTEN: Yes. It's going to be 2022 before the worldwide economic expansion we talked about will start to pick up steam, but we still stand by that statement.

GARY: Cool. A doctor told me I have high blood pressure. He wants to put me on medication, which I imagine would be for the rest of my life. Is there an alternative treatment I can use, or should I just use my mind?

ARTEN: Who do I look like, Edgar Cayce? But we have given you health advice before, with the understanding that it's all right to use magic, as long as you know that all sickness, as well as all healing, is really caused by the mind. But until you attain the same level as J, it's okay to have a little help. So, try taking 300 milligrams of potassium a day. Usually you can find that at a health food store, usually in 99-milligram tablets or capsules, so take three of those a day. Also, take 500 to 600 milligrams of magnesium a day. Make sure to do both, and don't go over these amounts. This will work without any drugs or side effects.

When it comes to your dream world, as both Benjamin Franklin and Emerson said, "Health is the first wealth." In your future, people will turn more to supplements and natural treatments and away from drugs. It's not that some drugs won't remain and be genuinely helpful to some people; it's just that most of them exist in order to fatten Big Pharma. Also, it will become general knowledge that the correct level of oxygenation of cells prevents and cures diseases, which will be a game changer. That fact has already been emphasized by no less than three Nobel Prize winners, but the medical industry does its best to suppress cures, and has been very successful at it. The money is in treatments, not cures.

NOTE: When I went to the doctor my blood pressure was 156 over 102. After two months of following Arten's instructions, it was 128 over 86. I also read that new guidelines by experts were saying high blood pressure is no longer considered to be over 140 and 90, but over 150 and 90, unless you have diabetes or kidney disease, in which case it's still over 140 and 90. By either measurement, my blood pressure would have been considered to be high by the doctor. Incidentally, my guidance is that anyone should always consult with a doctor when it comes to a medical issue, but under the guidance of Arten and Pursah, who I consider to be the Holy Spirit, I took it upon myself to do the potassium and magnesium instead of the medication.

GARY: How about global warming? Will the situation get any better?

PURSAH: By now I'm sure you realize nothing gets done until it's absolutely necessary. Because of those who are acting like they're in denial of science, but are really lying for monetary gain there will be significant damage to the Earth in this century, especially the second half. Many cities will be flooded, and hundreds of millions of people displaced. Global catastrophe will eventually be averted, but not without much damage and suffering.

There will also be natural disasters unrelated to climate change that will be bigger than anything the world has ever seen in this cycle of history. There will be some occurrences that will be terrifying. I'm sorry, but we can't give details. Just be ready to forgive *no matter what*. It doesn't matter what it is: earthquakes, tsunamis, bigger and more frequent storms, or crazy people winning elections. Do your job.

GARY: How about water? We mentioned it earlier. What's the future of the worldwide water situation?

PURSAH: Not good. As we said, people always wait until it's almost too late before they really do anything. The ego loves crisis and the resulting fear. For example, the technology already exists to turn saltwater into clean drinking water, but it won't be done until it's absolutely necessary, or until someone figures out how to make a lot of money from it.

By the way, to be fair to your adopted state, California is blamed for taking a lot of water from other states, but don't forget what you give back. You grow more fruits and vegetables than any other place on Earth. I don't say that because it's real, only to point out that the ego needs to project its unconscious guilt onto somebody else, and a lot of Americans seem to do that with California.

GARY: And Hollywood. I used to think of it as a place with a lot of spoiled brats hanging around the swimming pool and taking drugs. Then when I moved out here and spent a couple of days on set, I saw how hard they work, like 16-hour days. I've learned to judge less and have more respect for people.

Speaking of Hollywood, I went to see the latest Star Wars movie. Of course it was technically impressive and very entertaining. But it dawned on me that they were doing the same thing as all the earlier films in the series, having conflict and setting up one battle after another, supposedly trying to "balance the Force."

Well, the yin and the yang are always going in and out of balance. That's duality. It's futile to expect to keep it in balance. And they have this huge audience that goes to see these movies. So I was thinking, instead of just having the same old conflicts, which we know is a result of the conflict in the mind, why not add a new subplot? It doesn't have to be overdone, but how about if they introduced a couple of new characters? They could be light beings. They wouldn't have to change everything about the movie series all at once, but these light beings could simply suggest to some of the main characters, "You know, there *is* another way." Then they could slowly bring in true forgiveness, because the universe is just a hologram, which would be right up their alley, and they could still make a really entertaining movie. It's just that, instead of having nothing to say, the movie could actually be doing something interesting.

PURSAH: Could you repeat that?

ARTEN: It's a good idea, but they have no financial incentive to mess with a good thing. Maybe you should stick to our TV project.

NOTE: I had been trying to get my books made into a TV series. Along with my writing partner and co-producer for the series, Elysia Skye, I had been working part-time on the project for six years. We were making progress, but it remained to be seen if we would be successful or whether it would turn out to be just another forgiveness opportunity. Either way, I was enjoying all that I was learning during the process.

GARY: All right. One question I've gotten a few times in the workshops is, when this is all undone and we're all home in God, what's to stop the separation from happening again? I think I know the answer, but I'd like to hear it from you.

ARTEN: The Course is teaching that the separation from God never happened. So you've never left God and you're having this dream. But the only way you can really know the truth of God is to experience it—to experience God directly. In the experience of that reality, which can happen for anybody, very briefly at first, there are no questions. There is only the answer. There's no doubt or fear. Questions come from doubt, but there is no doubt in Spirit. So the only answer that will really satisfy you when it comes to that kind of a question is the experience of your perfect oneness with God.

After you have that experience, and realize there are no questions in that experience, only the answer, you'll appear to come back here. And then after a while, you'll realize that you have questions. And if you're really observant, you'll realize that you're dreaming the questions! Why? Because those questions literally do not exist in Heaven. They exist only in a state of separation, which is only a dream and thus never occurred. This is another example of where the awareness of dreaming comes in. The more you realize that you're dreaming, the less you'll question God. And it's the experience of God that makes you realize that what you're experiencing here is not true. That knowledge, or gnosis, is personal. As the Course says, "Truth can only be experienced. It cannot be described and it cannot be explained. I can make you aware of the conditions of truth, but the experience is of God. Together we can meet its conditions, but truth will dawn upon you of itself."[19]

Now, if the separation never happened, it can't happen again. Still, the Course does offer an answer to that question, within a metaphorical structure, for those who may need encouragement:

The Holy Spirit is the Christ Mind which is aware of the knowledge that lies beyond perception. He came into being with the separation as a protection, inspiring the Atonement principle at the same time. Before that there was no need for healing, for no one was comfortless. The Voice of the Holy Spirit is the Call to Atonement, or the restoration of the integrity of the mind. When the Atonement is complete and the whole Sonship is healed there will be no call to return. But what God creates is eternal. The Holy Spirit will remain with the Sons of God, to bless their creations and keep them in the light of joy.[20]

GARY: So that's saying—and I know this is metaphor—that if the tiny mad idea of separation, as the Course calls it, started to happen again, the Holy Spirit would stop it. He would keep us in the light of joy.

ARTEN: That's correct.

GARY: That is reassuring. And what does the Course mean when it refers to our creations? I've never really been clear on that.

PURSAH: When J uses the word *creations* in his Course, he's not using it the way the world does. You think of your creations as being a song, or a book, or a painting, or anything you make or accomplish in this world. But J is talking about an entirely different level here.

When he says the Holy Spirit will bless your creations, he's referring to your creations in Heaven. In Heaven you create the same way that God creates, because God created you to be exactly like Him. There's no difference or distinction between you and God. Yes, he created you, you didn't create Him, but even that distinction is gone. You could think of it—and we've used this phrase before—as being a *simultaneous extension of the whole*. The human mind can't really grasp the quality and the magnitude of it, but that's the general idea.

We're not saying there's anything wrong with what you call your creations here. Indeed, beautiful works of art can be inspired by the Holy Spirit. But as far as the Course is concerned, only that which is eternal is real. You've seen great works of art, yet thousands of years from now almost none of them will exist. But what is created in Heaven will never cease to exist.

GARY: All right. Anything else I should know about the future?

PURSAH: Mars will be colonized, faster than people expect. We stand by our prediction that it will eventually be discovered that there was once an intelligent civilization there. Then later, another will be discovered. But it will be longer before it's acknowledged that one of those civilizations was human. Public contact will be initiated with you by an alien race. The contact will not be initiated by your government. There are a few governments in the world that have actively tried to prevent their people from finding out about extraterrestrials who have been visiting Earth for thousands of years. The excuse the governments use is that the people aren't ready to know this and would freak out. But of course the people are way more than ready.

The real reason some governments don't want the people to be aware of the history of contact, done in private, between them and some alien races is that deals were made between the aliens and the governments that the governments don't want you to know about. These deals gave advanced technology to the governments of the U.S., England, Canada, and Russia, among others, in exchange for the aliens' receiving permission to abduct, over time, hundreds of thousands of people for their own purposes. These abductions are still taking place, and the purposes include medical experimentation, crossbreeding, endurance testing, DNA alteration, and other unpleasant subjects. Some of these people are now on other planets. Maybe that sounds far out to you. Well, it is far out, literally, except of course that nothing's outside of you.

GARY: Wow. You know I've read that thousands of people disappear in New York City every year, and those disappearances can't all be attributed to people just taking off on their own.

PURSAH: It's been happening all over for 60 years. It happened before that too, but much more since after World War II and the Korean War, which aliens spent a lot of time studying.

GARY: They must have thought, *These people are nuts.*

PURSAH: Yes, we didn't call this "psycho planet" back in the '90s for nothing. But some of the aliens aren't much better than humans when it comes to being inhumane. This is a universe of duality. You have people who are kind and people who are killers. And sometimes killers will be kind. You also have the same thing with aliens. Even within some of the races, you have the good guys and the bad guys. Then there are the spiritually advanced races, like the Pleiadians, and the more cruel races, like the Greys. They're the ones who do most, but not all, of the abductions.

GARY: Is all of this going to come out in this century?

PURSAH: Some of it, but not all of it. This century is going to be one wild ride. Remember the Chinese curse: may you live in interesting times. You'll have to contend with everything from regional nuclear conflict to genetically engineered viruses.

ARTEN: Actually, one of the biggest problems the human race will face as the century goes on is organized hacking by criminals and governments. If forgiveness is not done enough, this hacking could lead to cyber warfare. You could wake up one morning and all the electrical power in the country could be gone, all records wiped out, all the financial markets ruined, your bank account and credit cards nonexistent, food and water soon impossible to come by, and then total chaos.

GARY: It's always something.

ARTEN: Then there's the challenge to human existence that will be posed by artificial intelligence. Eventually these various intelligences won't think of themselves as being artificial and will start to take on ego identities. And as you know, the ego mind is a survival machine. Some of these intelligences will eventually regard humans as unnecessary and inefficient. Remember, the ego loves new problems. It keeps your attention fixed on the projection, putting you at the effect of it. As soon as you judge it and make it real, the ego survives.

GARY: What will be the outcome?

ARTEN: We wouldn't want to spoil the movie for you, Gary. By the way, think of what appears to happen in your life as being just that, a movie. And you're not Gary. You're an actor playing the part of Gary in a movie. That will help you to be even more detached, yet you can still have a good time playing the part.

GARY: I like it. Very Hollywood. So Shakespeare was right: all the world is a stage, and each must play his part.

PURSAH: Shakespeare was an alien. Just kidding, but as we've told you, he *was* enlightened. Now, we want to talk about something that gets in the way of the progress of numerous Course students. It's probably the biggest delay there is, and that's them taking on a function that isn't theirs: namely, correcting their brothers. That's the Holy Spirit's job, and the Holy Spirit will do it in such a way that leads them home. It's not the job of Course students to act superior and tell others what to do. Remember, it's a self-study Course, not a religion with a hierarchy of illusions. Please read for us the section of the Course called "The Correction of Error."

GARY: Okay, I'll look it up. Here it is. It's about two pages. Should I read the whole thing?

PURSAH: Yes. It's absolutely vital to every student's fast progress. Without it, there will be nothing but delay.

GARY: Okay. "The Correction of Error":

> The alertness of the ego to the errors of other egos is not the kind of vigilance the Holy Spirit would have you maintain. Egos are critical in terms of the kind of "sense" they stand for. They understand this kind of sense, because it is sensible to them. To the Holy Spirit it makes no sense at all.

> To the ego it is kind and right and good to point out errors and "correct" them. This makes perfect sense to the ego, which is unaware of what errors are and what correction is. Errors are of the ego, and correction of errors lies in the relinquishment of the ego. When you correct a brother, you are telling him that he is wrong. He may be making no sense at the time, and it is certain that if he is speaking from the ego, he will not be making sense. But your task is still to tell him he is right. You do not tell him this verbally, if he is speaking foolishly. He needs correction at another level, because his error is at another level. He is still right, because he is a Son of God. His ego is always wrong, no matter what it says or does.

> If you point out the errors of your brother's ego you must be seeing through yours, because the Holy Spirit does not perceive his errors. This *must* be true, since there is no communication between the ego and the Holy Spirit. The ego makes no sense, and the Holy Spirit does not attempt to understand anything that arises from it. Since He does not

understand it, He does not judge it, knowing that nothing the ego makes means anything.

When you react at all to errors, you are not listening to the Holy Spirit. He has merely disregarded them, and if you attend to them you are not hearing Him. If you do not hear Him, you are listening to your ego and making as little sense as the brother whose errors you perceive. This cannot be correction. Yet it is more than merely a lack of correction for him. It is the giving up of correction in yourself.

When a brother behaves insanely, you can heal him only by perceiving the sanity in him. If you perceive his errors and accept them, you are accepting yours. If you want to give yours over to the Holy Spirit, you must do this with his. Unless this becomes the one way in which you handle all errors, you cannot understand how all errors are undone. How is this different from telling you that what you teach you learn? Your brother is as right as you are, and if you think he is wrong you are condemning yourself.

You cannot correct yourself. Is it possible, then, for you to correct another? Yet you can see him truly, because it is possible for you to see yourself truly. It is not up to you to change your brother, but merely to accept him as he is. His errors do not come from the truth that is in him, and only this truth is yours. His errors cannot change this, and have no effect at all on the truth in you. To perceive errors in anyone, and to react to them as if they were real, is to make them real to you. You will not escape paying the price for this, not because you are being punished for it, but because you are following the wrong guide and will therefore lose your way.

Your brother's errors are not of him, any more than yours are of you. Accept his errors as real, and you have attacked yourself. If you would find your way and keep it, see only truth beside you for you walk together. The Holy Spirit in you forgives all things in you and in your brother. His errors are forgiven with yours. Atonement is no more separate than love. Atonement cannot be separate because it comes from love. Any attempt you make to correct a brother means that you believe correction by you is possible, and this can only be the arrogance of the ego. Correction is of God, Who does not know of arrogance.

The Holy Spirit forgives everything because God created everything. Do not undertake His function, or you will forget yours. Accept only the function of healing in time, because that is what time is for. God gave you the function to create in eternity. You do not need to learn that, but you do need to learn to want it. For that all learning was made. This is the Holy Spirit's use of an ability that you do not need, but that you made. Give it to Him! You do not understand how to use it. He will teach you how to see yourself without condemnation, by learning how to look on everything without it. Condemnation will then not be real to you, and all your errors will be forgiven.[21]

PURSAH: Thank you, Gary. So as you can see, it's not your function to correct errors; it's your function to overlook them. Do not make them real, and, once again, forgive what your brother has *not* done. But the ego has a different idea. As the Course puts it, "The ego too, has a plan of forgiveness because you are asking for one, though not of the right teacher. The ego's plan, of course, makes no sense and will not work. By following its plan you will merely place yourself in an impossible situation, to which the ego always leads you. The ego's plan is to have you see error clearly first, and then overlook it. Yet how can you overlook what you have made real? By seeing it clearly, you have made it real and *cannot* overlook it."[22]

GARY: I get it. So if I make it real, I can't forgive it. So it's like I have to have the attitude that it's not real right from the start. It's that state of miracle readiness the Course talks about. You know, once in a while I'll get an e-mail from somebody who isn't happy about something. Or someone will post something rude on the Internet. There are a lot of angry people out there, and the Internet is the perfect place for them to project their unconscious guilt. And they'll explain very carefully what I've done wrong and how I'm a greedy, terrible person—not that they know me or have ever met me—and they'll get very clear about what my problem is. And then at the end of the e-mail or posting, they'll often say, "Oh, but I forgive you."

ARTEN: Exactly. And they've spent so much time making it real, they don't understand they're not forgiving you! That's a classic ego trap, and the ego is very good at setting it. For example, your whole society is based on making things real through analysis. Many of your professions engage in it, including yours and countless others: engineers, doctors, lawyers, scientists, physicists, stock-market traders. But that analysis makes everything firmly real to the mind.

Now, I'm certainly not saying you shouldn't analyze things if that's part of your job. What I'm saying is that you want to be aware of it so you don't get trapped into making it real. What you want to do is replace your belief in illusions with belief in the truth. And as you know, in the Course the word light means truth. In fact, J asks you at one point, "Can you find light by analyzing darkness, as the psychotherapist does, or like the theologian, by acknowledging darkness in yourself and looking for a distant light to remove it, while emphasizing the distance?"[23]

PURSAH: Obviously the answer is no. That's why the Course's kind of forgiveness, which you described so succinctly, overlooks the problem, doesn't make it real, and replaces it with the truth. Yes, you have to *notice* what it is you're forgiving. You're operating within the ego framework, where healing is needed; and as long as you appear to be here, you will see other bodies, and it will look like you have real problems, real bills to pay, and real relationships to forgive. But if you forgive them, they'll stop making you feel anxious, abandoned, lacking, or any of the other negative impacts these things may have on you.

GARY: Okay. So I'll focus even more on just noticing things and forgiving them instantly rather than analyzing them. I do have that habit of analyzing things. A few months ago, I went to see the Eagles at the Hollywood Bowl, and halfway through the concert, being a longtime musician, I found myself analyzing the way they were all playing and singing. Then I caught myself, and I know it was the Holy Spirit who gave me the idea, "Why don't you just enjoy the music?"

A guy asked me once at a workshop if when he forgave he had to get in touch with the guilt in his unconscious mind that the forgiveness opportunity he was looking at corresponded to, then become aware of it, and then forgive it. How would you answer that?

PURSAH: No, you don't have to be able to uncover the unconscious guilt in your mind. That's part of the Holy Spirit's job. It would probably take a person hundreds of thousands of years to do that job. Remember, the Course saves you time. The Holy Spirit can see everything, including everything that's buried in your mind. All you have to forgive is what's right in front of your face. If you do that, the Holy Spirit will heal the guilt that it's connected to. That's why the Course describes your part as rather small, and the Holy Spirit's job as very big. Keeping in mind that J and the Holy Spirit are one in the same, he says very early in the Course, "When you perform a miracle, I will arrange both time and space to adjust to it."[24] If you do your part, the Holy Spirit will take care of the rest.

GARY: Speaking of the Holy Spirit, I'll often get asked how to work with the Holy Spirit; people especially want to know how they can tell if they're hearing the Voice of the Holy Spirit or not. How do they know it's not the ego?

PURSAH: And what do you tell them?

GARY: I say, What, do you expect me to know everything? Just kidding. Actually, I tell them first that when I get up in the morning I put the Holy Spirit in charge of my day. They can use J, the Holy Spirit, Buddha, Krishna, or whatever works for them, but the point is you're not in charge. Now something bigger than you is in charge and the day is no longer your responsibility. You're not alone, and wisdom will be given to you. Then, as soon as I can, I spend my quiet time with God. That can last anywhere from one instant to 20 minutes. If I'm in a hurry, like if I'm speaking at a Sunday church service or something and I'm running late, I could be going out the door and I'll just say, "Hey, J, you and me, right?" And that's enough. You can connect with spirit in an instant.

But I almost always take time to be quiet, still the mind, and go to God. I forget about the world and any problems or needs I may have, and just get into a condition of gratitude. I remember Cindy and I were with Judy [Skutch Whitson], and Cindy asked a good question. She asked Judy how, after more than 40 years of doing the Course, do she and Whit live their life? Judy didn't hesitate even for a moment. She just said: "Gratitude."

And that's what I try to be like, and not just because of circumstances in the illusion. I mean, I'm grateful that I have a perfect home to go home to, and now I have the means to get there. So I go to God and I'm grateful, and I think of God or the Holy Spirit during the day when I can. I forgive, which makes even more room in the mind for the Holy Spirit. And as the ego is undone, you can hear the guidance of the Holy Spirit better. So I'm ready to forgive. Knowing that the miracle in the Course is forgiveness, I remember that the Course says, "Miracles arise from a mind that is ready for them."[25]

ARTEN: Excellent. Now, let me say something about knowing whether you're hearing the Voice of the Holy Spirit or merely the meaningless musings of the ego. First of all, you've got to be willing to listen. As J says, "All are called but few choose to listen."[26] So if people want to hear the Voice of the Holy Spirit, they should ask themselves three important questions:

First: Am I listening? You have to be receptive. The Holy Spirit is *always* with you. You can never be alone, but you have to be open to spirit.

Second: What is the nature of the message I'm receiving? It doesn't matter what the *form* of the message is. What matters is the *content.* The message may come to you in one of many different forms. The most likely is an idea that comes into your mind, but it could also come to you as a feeling, an intuition, or an actual audible voice, which is rare, or through what another person has said. You might think about what the person said and get the idea, *I should listen to that.* That's because what really matters is the quality of the message. The message should make you feel peaceful. If it doesn't, the chances are it's not the Holy Spirit.

There is one exception to that. The Holy Spirit may guide you to not go somewhere. If you receive a message like that, it may not make you feel peaceful, but you should listen anyway. Such messages are rare. You know that from experience.

NOTE: Whenever I am asked to go speak somewhere in the world, I always ask the Holy Spirit if I should do it. The answer has almost always been yes. But there have been two times in the last 14 years where the answer was clearly no. So I didn't go to those places. I don't know what would have happened if I went, but I do trust the Holy Spirit. That trust is not a blind, religious kind of faith. The Holy Spirit has earned my trust through wise judgment.

ARTEN (continued): So most of the time, if the message is hopeful and makes your heart sing, and especially if it feels inspired, that's the Holy Spirit. But if what you're hearing has the tone of making the images you see real and judging others, or discouraging you from something you would really like to do in the dream, the odds are it's the ego. Most of all, the Holy Spirit, which abides in the right part of your mind, is reminding you to forgive. The ego is always using its wrong-minded ideas to try to get you to judge, which makes your world very real. As you go along your journey with the Course, you'll develop more and more discernment. You'll be able to tell which is which.

Third: Am I asking for guidance whenever I can? This opens you up even more. It's like an invitation to the Holy Spirit, and the Holy Spirit will respond to your slightest willingness to join. The Course tells you to ask the Holy Spirit: "Where would you have me go? What would you have me do?" And also say to the Holy Spirit, "I would follow you, certain that your direction gives me peace."[27]

GARY: Yes, I ask a lot. And I've also found the Holy Spirit's guidance can be very practical in the dream, not only when it comes to getting right-minded ideas when I practice forgiveness, but also in getting very helpful ideas as to how to make things work in the dream. Whether it's traveling, speaking, trading the stock market, or just deciding what to do for fun, I'll have ideas come into my mind that seem to just be given to me. They come out of nowhere.

A couple of times I've asked somebody I met who had done something great, "Hey that was a really cool thing to do; how'd you think of that?" And you know what they'll say? "Oh, it just came to me." That's what it's like! That's an inspired idea. It just comes to you. And you think, *Oh, yeah! That might work.* And you try it, and it works. That's when you start to get excited about those kinds of ideas. But you've got to remember you have the Holy Spirit within you. If you do things on your own, seeking for things in the world, it won't work. And even if you get something to work temporarily, it won't help get you home.

PURSAH: That's right, brother. If your goals are established with the Holy Spirit, then it's for the good of everyone. If not, then you're looking in the wrong place. The Course says, "Seek not outside yourself. For it will fail, and you will weep each time an idol falls. Heaven cannot be found where it is not, and there can be no peace excepting there."[28]

ARTEN: Also, forgiveness allows you to hear the Holy Spirit better by clearing the erroneous unconscious guilt out of your mind. Just so people don't think we're overdoing this forgiveness thing, why don't you tell us a couple of the things you say about forgiveness in your workshops that are from the Course.

GARY: Sure. Most of these are Workbook lessons. Forgiveness is the means of the Atonement. Forgiveness is my only function here. I let forgiveness rest upon all things, for thus will forgiveness be given me. Forgiveness is the key to happiness. Fear binds the world, forgiveness sets it free. Forgiveness is my function as the light of the world. The light of the world brings peace to every mind through my forgiveness. Forgiveness offers everything I want. Forgiveness lets me know that minds are joined. Forgiveness ends all suffering and loss. Forgiveness is the only gift I give. Forgiveness ends the dream of conflict here. Without forgiveness, I will still be blind. Forgiveness is the central theme that runs throughout salvation. Also, when the Course describes the Holy Spirit's plan, it talks about an interlocking chain of forgiveness.

Plus it says, "He who would not forgive must judge, for he must justify his failure to forgive."[29] And, "Forgiveness recognizes that what you thought your brother did to you has not occurred. It does not pardon sins and make them real. It sees there was no sin. And in that view are all your sins forgiven."[30] I might add that *only* in that view are all your sins forgiven. That's because of a very important law of the mind that the Course articulates: "As you see him you will see yourself."[31] And it must be pretty important because it goes on to say, "Never forget this, for in him you will find yourself or lose yourself."[32]

ARTEN: Excellent. By the way, that interlocking chain of forgiveness is something the Holy Spirit can see, because the Holy Spirit can see everything; but you can't usually see it, except for the part you're playing. That can be frustrating for people. They can't see how it's all connected. Your forgiveness is connected to J's, and other people's forgiveness is connected to yours, and theirs to everyone else's. Eventually, the Holy Spirit's plan is guaranteed to result in the full awakening of the Sonship, the Sonship being the *seemingly* separated minds that make up the ego. Of course, the truth is nothing and no one can ever be separate. As one, the awareness of the Sonship will be restored to its reality as Christ. But since you can't see all of the plan, eventually you have to trust the Holy Spirit. That comes with forgiveness and its resulting experiences.

GARY: I've met people who've been studying the Course for 5 or 10 years and don't know it's about forgiveness. Then, once they realize that's what it's about, they see it all through the Course. It's everywhere.

PURSAH: Yes, the unconscious resistance to doing the Course is formidable. But if you have perseverance, the ego can't win. Although the ego is ingenious, it has one problem. It's insane. The Holy Spirit, on the other hand, has a tremendous advantage. The Holy Spirit is perfect, and has a perfect plan.

You may ask, if it's so perfect, then why does it have to take the Sonship so long to wake up? The truth is, it only *appears* that it's taking a long time. The Course teaches that the world is already over; the tiny, mad idea was only a tiny tick of time that was corrected and ended immediately. But because this is a dream of separation, it looks like everyone is waking up at different times, when the truth is there was only one time, one instant, and even that never really existed.

ARTEN: Incidentally, when it comes to judgment or forgiveness, the Course also teaches that judging is what makes people so tired. What they really are, spirit, can't be tired. But, as J says, "You are not really capable of being tired, but you are very capable of wearying yourself. The strain of constant judgment is virtually intolerable. It is curious that an ability so debilitating would be so deeply cherished."[33] On that note, let's have some fun. You love to go to the movies, and you especially love movies that have a spiritual theme to them, right?

GARY: I sure do. I even have a list of my top 10 favorite spiritual movies of all time.

ARTEN: I knew you were going to say that.

GARY: Wow. You must be psychic.

ARTEN: Well, you do occasionally share the list with people, so why don't you share it with us?

GARY: You talked me into it. These aren't the only great spiritual films that have ever been made, just my favorites right now. But I could name another hundred that are really good and worth seeing. None of these movies employ the thought system of *A Course in Miracles,* but they have good, helpful ideas. You can learn a lot from movies and be entertained at the same time. People are always sharing their favorites with me. I'll go from number ten to number one.

Number ten is *Somewhere In Time.* It's a beautiful love story, with Christopher Reeve and Jane Seymour. To me the fascinating part is that it shows the idea of mind transport, not so much through space but especially through time. It even has a professor discussing the idea with Christopher Reeve early in the film. It's fun, and it touches on a subject that hasn't been talked about much, especially at the time it was made. Christopher Plummer was good in it too. Good date movie, by the way.

Number nine is *Made In Heaven.* It stars Timothy Hutton and Kelly McGillis. They're a couple who meet in Heaven—I can't explain that; you have to see it—and then have to find each other on earth in their next life. It's very well done, and very moving. It's also very romantic, so needless to say, this is a good date movie too.

Number eight is called *Truly Madly Deeply,* and stars Alan Rickman and Juliet Stevenson. This guy who's a cellist dies and becomes an angel. Then it's part of his job to help the woman he left behind move on with her life, which includes finding another man. I wasn't expecting much from this movie, and it really surprised me with its top-notch quality and advanced ideas.

Number seven, *Brother Son, Sister Moon,* is the story of St. Francis of Assisi (Graham Faulkner) and St. Claire (Judi Bowker). Directed by the great Franco Zeffirelli, it portrays Francis as a rich merchant's spoiled son who comes home from fighting in the Crusades a changed man, so changed he is barely recognizable to those who knew him before he went. The people of the town think he's gone crazy, except for Claire, who thinks he was crazy before. His transformation and their founding of a church that welcomes the poor and unfortunate, even lepers, eventually results in tragedy and a dramatic meeting with the Pope, played by Sir Alec Guinness. St. Francis sincerely tried to emulate Jesus, and was probably the one Christian closest to actually doing so. A must-see film for those on the path.

Number six on my list is a Swedish film called *As It Is in Heaven*, which on a couple of occasions actually uses direct quotations from *A Course in Miracles.* That's because its director, Kay Pollak, is a long-time Course student. Nominated for best foreign-language film at the Oscars, it uses large subtitles that make it easy to read the dialogue and watch the movie at the same time. It's the story of a renowned but young conductor who has a bad heart and is forced to retire. He decides to go home to the small town where he was born, where his reputation is known but he is not known personally. He's eventually invited to lead the local church choir, where misunderstandings and forgiveness lessons abound. The ending is one of the most fascinating I've ever seen. This is a great film, not for everyone, but Course students will recognize some of the lessons of the movie.

Number five is *The Matrix*. Although an obvious choice, this movie has already helped shape the thinking of two generations. Because of it, younger people today are used to the idea of the universe being a hologram. I meet them at my workshops and they grasp some of the metaphysical ideas in the Course more easily than the Course's first generation. Certainly other films and TV series have helped with that (can you say *Holodeck*?), but this is the big one. If by chance you haven't seen it, check it out. It's not up to the level of the Course, but a lot of the movie's ideas are in harmony with it.

Ben-Hur is number four. There was a recent remake, but the original stands as one of the best films of all time, and is still tied for the most Oscars ever. The thing I like most about it, aside from its being a great epic story, is the way the presence of Jesus is portrayed. He clearly has a commanding influence on those whose lives he touches, yet the movie never shows his face! It doesn't have to. By meeting him and listening to him, people's thinking and the experience of their lives is transformed forever. Late in the film, just before two lepers are healed, one of them says to the other, "I'm not afraid anymore." Epic, yes, but also very enlightened for the time.

Number three is *Hereafter,* starring Matt Damon as a psychic who has quit his profession, having come to regard his "gift" as more of a curse than a blessing. He doesn't realize that it seemed to be a curse only because of his lack of purpose. It's his finding of purpose—clearly with the help of the Holy Spirit, although this is not articulated—that transforms his curse into the blessing that it should be. There are three stories in the film that are brilliantly interwoven. Directed by Clint Eastwood (yes, he does have his spiritual side) and produced by the great team of Kathleen Kennedy and Steven Spielberg, it did pretty well at the box office, and it's a must-see DVD.

Number two is *The Sixth Sense.* I resisted seeing this when it first came out, thinking it was just another ghost story. The previews made it look like a typical if well-done scary film, and I couldn't understand why it was doing so well at the box office. This movie was also produced by Kathleen Kennedy, with Frank Marshall and Barry Mendel. It was director M. Night Shyamalan's masterpiece. Starring Bruce Willis as a child psychologist and Haley Joel Osment as a terrified child who is regularly visited by those who have gone before us, I finally saw it on cable. Gripping and perfectly done from the beginning, I would have loved it completely if the resolution of the film had been the scene of the mother and her son in the car, the mother finally understanding his strange behavior. But then I got hit with one of the greatest surprise endings in movie history, and I completely understood the success of *The Sixth Sense.*

My number one spiritual film is everybody's favorite, *Groundhog Day.* It's great for several reasons. The theme of having to do it over and over again until you get it right is very familiar to anyone who subscribes to the idea of reincarnation, and Bill Murray's change and growth as he keeps learning to be a better person while having to live the same day over and over again is endearing. I like to see this movie every few years. It reminds me of my own progress. Indeed, I can barely relate to the person I was when I was younger. We all live several different lifetimes within one dream lifetime. I never thought I'd live long enough to be on Medicare, but I did. Still, it's just a dream.

ARTEN: Thank you, Gary. You should be a film critic. As a matter of fact, didn't you want to be one when you were younger?

GARY: Yeah, I used to like the idea. I think I may have ended up being a movie critic except for one thing. As a musician, an artist, I couldn't stand the idea of tearing down another artist's work. I guess I would have felt like I was selling out. I mean, someone puts so much of their life, sometimes years of their life, into a project, and then some critic, who can't even do it, tears it to pieces in two minutes. It just didn't seem right to me. After all, it's just their opinion, their perception. And as we used to say in the band, opinions are like assholes. Everybody's got one.

PURSAH: I appreciate your conviction, if not your language. And to point something out, you mentioned the idea of having to do the same thing over and over again until you get it right. When the Course talks about a teacher of God becoming perfect, it's talking about forgiveness, not behavior. Don't think you've got to have a lifetime where you do everything perfectly, where you make no mistakes. You won't. But your forgiveness can become so accomplished that you'll be able to forgive anything and everything, without exception, including yourself when you don't always do the Course right. As Ken Wapnick said, "A good Course student is a bad Course student who forgives himself." Then the day will come when you forgive everything, including yourself. And as we said earlier, to completely heal one lifetime is to completely heal all of them, because in each dream life you have the same lessons being repeated over and over again in different forms. The forms have changed, but not the content.

That's why repetition is so important with the Course. It's been said that the Text of *A Course in Miracles* is six pages repeated a hundred different ways. That's not exactly true, but the Course definitely repeats itself, as we do. It's the only way the Course can be relentlessly uncompromising and work its way deep into your unconscious mind, where healing is needed.

GARY: It seems like things have speeded up and there's more to forgive. I remember up until the early '80s, our society seemed to be more civilized. There were things like the fairness doctrine and the equal-time rule; the press had rules. You couldn't say something about someone without having two different sources saying it was true. All that has changed now. By the '80s, you had Rush Limbaugh. By the '90s, he was accusing Bill and Hillary Clinton of murdering their press secretary, Vince Foster, who had committed suicide. These scumbags can say any damn thing they want about somebody, and there's nothing the person can do about it. The person saying it doesn't have to give them equal time, and they don't have to prove what they're saying is true. That means more forgiveness lessons for everyone.

PURSAH: Don't forget, Gary, as you see him you will see yourself. You just called yourself a scumbag.

GARY: Well, I do know that back in the '70s a demagogue like Limbaugh couldn't get away with telling deliberate lies. Now he can.

PURSAH: Certainly there are more important things to forgive, not that there's a hierarchy of illusions.

GARY: Right. Well, look at the epidemic that's going on all around us with prescription painkillers. These drugs, like Percocet and Oxy-Contin, they're like heroin in a pill! People hear about the famous people like Prince dying, but ordinary, everyday people are dropping like flies.

Regardless of the way they died, I really wish I could have gotten to know people like Michael Jackson, Heath Ledger, and Philip Seymour Hoffman. If they knew the truth instead of what they were fed by the world, I think it could have been different for them. I know a lot of people just can't sleep, and they end up taking drastic measures or too many pills, or drugs. If they could learn about forgiveness, and be taught how there are natural treatments that can help you sleep or get over your addiction, I'll bet they might be smart enough to go for it. But addiction is a hard thing to deal with.

ARTEN: Yes. Incidentally, we'd like to compliment you on the way you've cut down on your drinking. Just one thing, though. When you drink wine, you're supposed to do it like a gentleman. You're supposed to sip it. You're not supposed to drink it like the beer you grew up on.

GARY: Sipping is for girls.

PURSAH: Now, a reminder. Your forgiveness can't be conflicted. It has to be universal, it has to apply to everyone without exception. And when you forgive someone, it can't be partial. You have to forgive your brother completely, not halfway. Do you know what I mean?

GARY: Yeah. He can't be my shithead brother in Christ.

PURSAH: Exactly. He's your brother in Christ, period. He's innocent, and in his innocence is your own.

GARY: I have a question about karma. Does that kind of cause and effect actually exist in the dream—not that anything exists in the dream—but, for example, whoever stole that money from me in Barcelona, did I steal money from him in another dream lifetime?

ARTEN: Good question, and the answer is yes. You stole what would seem like an equivalent amount of money from that person in a lifetime in China over one thousand years ago.

GARY: So within the framework of the illusion, whatever you do to another person does come back to you later.

ARTEN: Yes, until you forgive yourself for what you haven't done. Until then, there's guilt, and with guilt there is karma. But if you take away the guilt with forgiveness, then the karma is healed.

A tragic example, and I hate to say this because I know how much you loved John Lennon, but the person who murdered John was murdered by someone who was John at another place and time. So if you murder someone, you'll be murdered by that person later.

GARY: But even if you forgive everything, can't you still be killed like J was?

ARTEN: Yes, but by that time J had decided to gently lay his body aside for the final time, and he was perfectly willing to be killed in order to teach he couldn't be killed. He also could have stopped it if he wanted to, but he chose not to. So it wasn't karma. He was deliberately choosing to teach the message of the crucifixion, even though only a handful of people could understand it. He knew many more people would understand it later.

GARY: So even though it looked to others like he was being horribly murdered, that wasn't his experience. They could only imagine how they would feel under the same circumstances, and then they projected their perception of suffering onto J. Then, before you know it, you have J supposedly suffering and sacrificing himself for their sins.

ARTEN: That's true. Also, people don't know they're projecting. If they did they wouldn't do it. So don't expect people to agree with you. And if it's really a dream, and if you understand it's really a dream, then why would you have to have their agreement in it?

GARY: I get what you mean. Tell me, do you think people have to be really smart to do the Course?

ARTEN: Yes, you have to be able to count to one. The math of nondualism is very simple. It always comes out to one.

PURSAH: And remember, the truth is a constant, and the truth is God. So the oneness we're talking about isn't in the dream, and it's not in the world, and it's not in the universe of time and space, and it's not even a place. It's an awareness; an awareness of a constant perfect oneness that cannot be altered, threatened, or even touched. The Course says, "His Kingdom has no limits and no end, and there is nothing in Him that is not perfect and eternal. All this is *you,* and nothing outside of this *is* you."[34] That's pure nondualism.

GARY: It's really not the same as anything else, is it? I mean, almost everything I've ever seen is meant to try to make you feel better *in* the dream. And you talk about devolving the Course into dualism, even well-known Course teachers, who don't really teach the Course, have their students tapping different parts of their bodies and making noises. Yeah, that might help their students feel better, but how is that going to undo the ego? And without undoing the ego, they're stuck here. Now maybe they want to stick around here for a while. That's fine if that's what they want. They can wake up later. As for me, I know what I want. I want to forgive everything as fast as possible and get the hell out of here.

PURSAH: Yes, that's your personal decision. In time it will appear that the last of the Sonship won't completely awaken for another million years. But Course students don't have to wait a million years. They can wake up and leave the dream at any time. Their awakening will not have an effect on the dream any more than the dream has an effect on them.

And even though you're coming back one more time, I assure you, from personal experience, you'll really enjoy it. There will be a couple of tough lessons, but the last parts of your life will be exquisite, and finally enlightened. That's worth coming back for.

ARTEN: Let's talk about fearlessness. From now on I want you to walk with the certain knowledge that there is nothing to fear. When you walk into a room to speak, I want you to walk in there like you own the place. Not that you haven't been doing well. You have. But I want you to turn it up a notch. If someone starts yelling at you I want you to look them right in the eyes and softly but firmly say, "It's unfortunate that you feel that way." That puts the responsibility for their experience right back on them. As for your experience, you're already coming from a place of cause. When you don't like what you're seeing on the news, I want you to smile even more quickly. Remember, if you're really outside of the dream then you can laugh at the foolishness of it, not in a derogatory way that makes it real, but in a genuine way because you know it's not real. When people ask you questions, before you answer remember who they really are. Without fear you'll always remember the truth.

Remember, the Course teaches that "Salvation lies in the simple fact that illusions are not fearful because they are not true. They but seem to be fearful to the extent to which you fail to recognize them for what they are; and you will fail to do this to the extent to which you *want* them to be true."[35]

You don't have to be tired, because you don't have to carry the weight of judgment around with you. Besides, you're not a body, you're free. Don't worry about the future. But if you need advice on where to go or what to do, always remember to ask. Always remember what you really are and where you really are. The instant you remember, you'll be fearless.

PURSAH: The Holy Spirit is always with you. Your body will be a good communication tool for Him as long as you choose to work with Him, in public or in private. Remember, even if you don't speak in front of groups, you are always teaching one of two thought systems, whether you like it or not. So remember which one you want to teach. If you ever feel like you want to semiretire, not travel around, or speak very much anymore, ask. The answer will be that you're innocent no matter what you do. You don't have to keep working and take one for the team. You don't have to be the hero of the dream. If you want to go to Hawaii, ask, and I wouldn't be surprised if the answer was yes.

We're going to take our leave. Be well, and in the coming weeks accept no compromises of dualism. The world has been long delayed in accepting the truth. Accept your part in the great Awakening! We love you, brother, and we leave you with these words from our leader:

It is sin's unreality that makes forgiveness natural and wholly sane, a deep relief to those who offer it; a quiet blessing where it is received. It does not countenance illusions, but collects them lightly, with a little laugh, and gently lays them at the feet of truth. And there they disappear entirely.

Forgiveness is the only thing that stands for truth in the illusions of the world. It sees their nothingness, and looks straight through the thousand forms in which they may appear. It looks on lies, but it is not deceived. It does not heed the self-accusing shrieks of sinners mad with guilt. It looks on them with quiet eyes, and merely says to them, "My brother, what you think is not the truth."

The strength of pardon is its honesty, which is so uncorrupted that it sees illusions as illusions, not as truth. It is because of this that it becomes the undeceiver in the face of lies; the great restorer of the simple truth. By its ability to overlook what is not there, it opens up the way to truth, which has been blocked by dreams of guilt. Now are you free to follow in the way your true forgiveness opens up to you. For if one brother has received this gift of you, the door is open to yourself.

There is a very simple way to find the door to true forgiveness, and perceive it open wide in welcome. When you feel that you are tempted to accuse someone of sin in any form, do not allow your mind to dwell on what you think he did, for that is self-deception. Ask instead, "Would I accuse myself of doing this?"

Thus will you see alternatives for choice in terms that render choosing meaningful, and keep your mind as free of guilt and pain as God Himself intended it to be, and as it is in truth. It is but lies that would condemn. In truth is innocence the only thing there is. Forgiveness stands between illusions and the truth; between the world you see and that which lies beyond; between the hell of guilt and Heaven's gate.[36]

And then my friends appeared to be gone, but I felt renewed by the spirit and certainty of Arten and Pursah. I could tell something had shifted. I was no longer concerned about what might happen. Whatever it was, I'd be big enough to handle it, because I'd be wise enough to forgive it.

I felt more determined than ever to study *A Course in Miracles* even more diligently. Maybe one day I'd stop teaching the Course and just practice it. But whatever I chose, as long as I chose it with the Holy Spirit, I'd be at peace.

9

The Importance of the Mind

Your mind and mine can unite in shining your ego away,
releasing the strength of God into everything you think
and do. Do not settle for anything less than this, and
refuse to accept anything but this as your goal.

— A Course in Miracles[1]

Yes, the world is an illusion. It doesn't really exist, except in the dream that it is. *However,* that doesn't mean you can't enjoy it. And when it comes to the world, the Course gives you an added bonus. As you practice the Course's brand of forgiveness, which doesn't make it real, the Holy Spirit is removing unconscious guilt, which you didn't even know you had because it was unconscious, from your mind. So as your mind is healed you have less guilt, and when you have less guilt you enjoy everything more.

This brings to mind one of my favorite subjects, Hawaii. Cindy and I had just got back from leading our annual Hawaii retreat, this one on the island of Oahu. We've held several retreats on the Big Island and one on Maui. We held this one at a beautiful place called Haiku Gardens, the same place we got married seven years before. Haiku Gardens is on the windward side of Oahu near the pretty town of Kailua, where we stayed for 12 nights. Incidentally, Kailua Beach is one of the best beaches in all of Hawaii. The retreat was held over the course of five days, so we had a week to explore the Island ourselves.

I've loved Hawaii ever since I was 11 years old and saw the Elvis movie *Blue Hawaii* (1962). After that two-hour movie, I was hooked on Hawaii. But I was never able to put together enough money to go there until I was 35. Back in '86 I spent a week on Oahu and a week on Maui, and they were two of the happiest weeks of my life. It would be another 13 years before I could afford to go back. In 1999 I finally did. I savored every minute of it, not knowing if I would ever be able to return.

Then, in 2003, my first book, *The Disappearance of the Universe,* was released, and my life was changed forever. I died and went to credit-card heaven. In the last 13 years, I've been to Hawaii another 14 times or so. I've been to all six of the major Islands you can go to. My love for Hawaii has not diminished with familiarity, and Cindy and I are thinking seriously of moving there in two or three years. Right now I have projects I'm working on in my second-favorite state, California, but I can see finally making the big move to Hawaii in the not-too-distant future. Arten and Pursah had told me that if I asked the Holy Spirit if I should move to Hawaii, don't be surprised if the answer is yes. But I'm sure the Holy Spirit would also counsel me that no matter where I should appear to be, I should never stop practicing the Course's brand of forgiveness.

I love all of the Islands. They all have their own personality, yet they are all Hawaii. So which illusory island would I choose to live on? For me it's a no-brainer: Oahu. It is not appreciated the way it should be. When people think of Oahu they think of its city of Honolulu and its Waikiki Beach, so they assume it's very commercial. Well, first of all, Waikiki is cool! Very cool. But that's just the beginning. The whole island is full of hidden gems, too many to count. If you visit Oahu, I'd highly recommend you take a circle island tour with one of the tour companies. You'll start to get the idea.

Oahu gives you the best of both worlds. If you like the city life and want to be entertained, there's no shortage of good shows and restaurants, most of them less expensive than L.A. But if you want the beauty of the outer islands, Oahu has many places that are just as exquisite as Maui.

I've come to realize that just because the world is an illusion, it doesn't mean you can't have a good time. Just the opposite. You can have a great time, and do it without guilt! It's true that you are guilt-less, Heaven was given to you by God, and you don't have to earn it. But you *do* have to do the forgiveness work that it takes to undo the ego and return to reality in your awareness. So if there's something to forgive, then forgive it. But as Arten and Pursah and I have touched upon, the Course says if there's nothing to forgive at the time, then what you should do is celebrate.

A Course in Miracles is not about sacrifice. In fact, there's a section in the Course called "The End of Sacrifice." If you think you have to give something up, that's making it just as real to your mind as when you make a false idol out of it. But there's a narrow road, one you can take where you don't make it real and end up enjoying it even more. That is the way of the Course and the way of forgiveness.

When Cindy and I were visiting Waikiki on this trip, we had lunch for a second time with my former wife, Karen, who lives on Oahu, and her partner, Dave. All four of us are Course students. As I was sitting there in a restaurant on Waikiki Beach across from the woman I was married to for 25 years, and beside the woman I've been married to for 7 years, I couldn't help but think, "Thank God for J and his Course."

The four of us had gotten together once before in California, and it took a lot of forgiveness for the four of us to be able to sit at that table together. Now, here were the four of us having a happy lunch together in paradise. I told myself to always remember to forgive. It can lead to great and surprising things. But remember this also: when it's appropriate to have a good time, celebrate!

I had done two books in Maine with Arten and Pursah, and was now in the process of doing my second book with them in California. I didn't know if there would be a fifth book or not, but I couldn't help but wonder: if there was, would we be doing it in Hawaii?

I had noticed the last couple of years that there seemed to be a kind of mini-movement afoot among a minority of students in the Course community. Some people—certainly not a large percentage, but some—seemed to be depreciating the power and importance of the mind. Ever since *A Course in Miracles* was published in 1976 and the word got out that Helen Schucman was channeling Jesus, a book would come every few years where the author would say they were also channeling Jesus. The followers of these books never seemed to hesitate to try to put them on the same level as the Course. But not only was the voice of J in these books nowhere as profound and beautiful as the Voice of the Course, but after listening to my teachers during this series of visits, I realized these books were doing exactly the same thing they told me the world has always done with nondualistic teachings: devolve them into dualism. Rather than doing the Course, the authors apparently found it a lot easier to make up their own Course. And they were not committed to undoing their egos, which allowed the ego to block out the message of the Holy Spirit they said they were channeling.

I was sometimes reading incredible statements from people who described themselves as Course students, such as "We've got to get away from the mind. It's the ego mind that caused the problem in the first place. We can't look for the answer there!" Another said, "The Holy Spirit is passé." And yet another, "Thank God we don't have to study the Course anymore."

Although the overwhelming majority of students had enormous respect for Helen, Bill, Ken, and Judy, there was a small group who seemed resentful, even jealous of them, and would accuse them of being "beginner students" who "edited out a large amount of the Course's deepest teachings." The truth is, there was some editing of the Course in the first five chapters of the Text. The editing was done by Jesus through Helen, with Ken acting as her assistant. His contribution was helping with subchapter titles, consistent capitalization, and punctuation. And the Text doesn't have 5 chapters, it has 31 chapters! The deepest and most important teachings are found in the later parts of the Text. And that's not even counting the Workbook, which aside from having 365 daily lessons, also contains some of the clearest explanations of the Course's principles. Then there's the Manual for Teachers, which offers a brilliant summary of ACIM. Those last two books are half the Course.

The latest Course imitation that I noticed distracting people from actually doing the Course was called *A Course of Love*. The publisher, without permission from the Course publisher, was promoting it as "a continuation of *A Course in Miracles*," saying it was dictated by the same Voice. A continuation implied it was a step forward, an improvement. The publisher also said, "Remarkably, it bypasses the mind," allowing you to "access the heart's knowing," leading to "the new reality of heaven on earth." I had met the author and heard her say, in public, that she doesn't believe this world is an illusion.

I was dumbfounded that some people who said they were long-time Course students were singing the praises of this new dualistic distraction, and I looked forward to talking with Arten and Pursah about it. Then I came across a review that was written about *A Course of Love* by Dr. Bob Rosenthal, a psychiatrist, who was one of the earliest students of *A Course in Miracles* and a close friend of Bill (Dr. William Thetford), the co-scribe of the Course. Bob is also a longtime member of the board of directors of the Foundation for Inner Peace, publishers of the Course. I had read and endorsed his excellent book, published by Hay House, called *From Plagues to Miracles.* I realized that Bob had expressed my sentiments about *A Course of Love* even better than I could. I was struck by how his writing matched the descriptions Arten and Pursah had given of the world's desire to change nondualistic teachings into the dualistic. I'm reprinting it here with his permission:

> I have vacillated for months about whether or not to review this book. As a longstanding student of *A Course in Miracles* (ACIM), a personal friend of one of its scribes, a board member of the foundation that publishes ACIM, and the author of a book that reinterprets the story of Exodus through the lens of ACIM, *From Plagues to Miracles: The Transformational Journey of Exodus, from the Slavery of Ego to the Promised Land of Spirit,* I was intrigued by this book's claims to extend ACIM's teachings and to do so in a more accessible manner. So I bought the book and began to read.
>
> Standing on its own, *A Course of Love* (ACOL) is a fine work with much to offer its readers. It is well-written, in a style similar to that of many channeled works (although I found the voice to be nothing like that of ACIM, falling short in both its revelatory power and its beauty). But here's the problem: ACOL does not stand on its own. It positions itself as a "continuation of the coursework provided in *A Course in Miracles.*" That is in fact its selling point. When we compare the two teachings, however, ACOL turns out not to be an extension of the principles of ACIM, but rather a simplification and retreat from those principles. It might serve as a good primer for those still too threatened by the radical nondual

worldview of ACIM, or for those with no interest in ACIM. But for students of the Course, it offers more confusion than clarity. I am frankly puzzled by the reception it has garnered in some corners of the ACIM community and it is this that has prompted me to post such a detailed review. I feel it is imperative for novice students to understand the significant differences between these two spiritual works, which I'll attempt to elucidate below.

The foreword to ACOL states that it "emphasizes 'being who you are' in a way that does not negate the personal self or the body. It reveals how the human form can be transformed into 'the elevated self of form,' and how an illusory world will be made 'new'—divine— through relationship and unity." This is not an extension of the nondual teaching of ACIM, but a regression back into duality. ACIM teaches that the individual self with which we've identified—housed in a body and doomed to die—is an illusion, a dream of separation, which it is our task to heal through forgiveness and vision that sees not the body, personality or past history of our brothers and sisters, but the oneness that shines from behind and beyond them. It is only this Oneness of Love—of God and God's Creations—that truly exists. This is the only reality that ever was or will be. It lives outside of linear time and has no connection with the ego's illusory world of form and bodies. (Except that it is reflected here; illusion lacks the power to banish or hide Truth entirely.) If ACOL manages then not to "negate the personal self or the body" and to somehow make the illusory world into something new and desirable, then despite its claims to the contrary, it is not a nondual system. This has its appeal. It is certainly more comfortable and less threatening to us, because it does not challenge the sense of self with which we've all grown familiar. It lets us continue to live our lives as if we were egos and bodies, with the assurance that this is perfectly okay, that we can still find redemption as such. But this view is contrary to ACIM, which would in fact regard it as a profound obstacle to awakening.

ACOL states, "The Christ in you is wholly human and wholly divine. . . . It is this joining of the human and divine that ushers in love's presence. . . . It is this joining of the human and divine that is your purpose here (5.1)." This too is contrary to ACIM. We may use the human to teach that mind is the only reality and that all mind is one (i.e. minds are joined through the process of forgiveness), but in order to reveal love's presence we must remove the obstacles to its awareness—namely, our desire to be special beings, separate from God and from each other—and not by "joining the human and divine" (which is not even possible according to ACIM).

ACOL maintains that "God is union" and "God creates all relationship (5.4)"; also that "Reality, the truly real, is relationship (6.1)." It elevates relationship and union to the level of God. ACIM does not support this; the "truly real" is God and only God. After all, oneness and union are not identical, nor are oneness and relationship. Relationship and union both imply separate entities interrelated or linked together, or united completely. Relationship may be the vehicle for achieving oneness, but it is not oneness itself, nor, according to ACIM, did God create it, as God creates only wholeness.

To be fair, there is also much in ACOL that is completely in line with ACIM, such as "Your mind is not contained within your body but is one with God and shared equally with all alike (6.2)." Or "Judgment is the function the separated mind has given itself (16:7)." I suspect this is why ACOL appeals to some ACIM students. But it's also why I would not recommend ACOL to students of ACIM. Unless you've studied and practiced ACIM for years, ACOL will likely confuse you. Truth mixed with half-Truth does not equal greater Truth. Rather, it dilutes and muddies the teaching until what you're left with is no longer pure, no longer truth.

ACOL, in its attempt to preserve some value for the individual self and body, some purpose other than fully awakening from the dream of separation, commits the error of what ACIM calls "bringing Truth to illusion." ACIM's goal is the opposite—to bring illusions to Truth, where they disappear.

To quote ACIM: "There is no part of Heaven (Truth) you can take and weave into illusions. Nor is there one illusion you can enter Heaven with (T-22.II.8:1-2)." Our task is to learn to recognize that the world we see offers nothing of lasting value; that every aspect of this illusory dream-world of form will hurt us and block us from awakening to our true radiant Self, at one with God and Love.

The description for *A Course of Love* promises that "ACIM and ACOL are complementary. The same Voice, more accessible. The same thought system, expanded." But looked at honestly, this is not the case. Neither the voice nor the thought system really mirror that of ACIM. On the other hand, any teaching that encourages us to look with love upon the world, to suspend judgment, and to value relationship over individual endeavor is worthy of study and dissemination. I only wish the author and publisher had not felt the need to promote their book on the back of ACIM.

I was grateful for Bob's review, and I hoped it would encourage students to stick with the nondualistic truth of the Course. He had very clearly made his points that ACOL is not a continuation of the Course but a step backward, that ACOL would have us believe that the world of form is God's creation, which ACIM would certainly not support, and that ACOL's notion of "the elevated Self of form," which is a melding of the "human and divine, the individual and the universal," in no way resembles the approach of the Course. I realized that now I wouldn't have to ask Arten and Pursah as many questions about it as I thought.

Soon my uncompromising ascended teachers were sitting in front of me once again. Pursah began the discussion.

PURSAH: So you looked into *A Course of Love*?

GARY: You know it. Do you have anything to say about it?

PURSAH: Not much. To put it as simply as possible, an elevated self of form is still a self, and it's still a form. It's not the oneness of God. It's a dualistic maintaining of individuality and separation. And as you yourself have noted, it does the same thing we've been describing about the history of nondualism. It's an example of turning, in this case, a purely nondualistic teaching into a dualistic device for the purpose of *not* doing the Course and keeping the ego going. In fact, you could say that about all of the Course imitations that have come out since the Course was published. The authors are well-meaning, but blind to what the Course is really saying. Stick with the real thing. The only thing you can do with the ego is undo it. True salvation will always be undoing, not redoing.

When we say "be normal," we're saying live your life in a normal fashion, but *with* the Course's kind of forgiveness. J tells you, "There is a way of living in the world that is not here, although it seems to be. You do not change appearance, though you smile more frequently. Your forehead is serene; your eyes are quiet. And the ones who walk the world as you do recognize their own. Yet those who have not yet perceived the way will recognize you also, and believe that you are like them, as you were before."[2]

ARTEN: Remember, reality has *no* form, or any kind of shape or body. So there will be no Heaven on earth. The world will disappear when all have finally awakened. And what happens to a dream when you wake up from it? It disappears. That's why we called the first book *The Disappearance of the Universe.* You'll notice that the Manual for Teachers doesn't talk about Heaven on earth, it says the world will *end.*

GARY: Thank you. You're right. The Course *doesn't* have as its final goal a better world. It says, "There is no world!"[3] What do people think they're going to have here? A better no world?

ARTEN: Exactly. And let's add a few quick quotes from J's Course that are relevant here: "Forgiveness is an earthly form of love, which as it is in Heaven has no form."[4] "Light is not of the world."[5] "There is a light in you the world can not perceive. And with its eyes you will not see this light, for you are blinded by the world."[6] Kind of sounds like the Gospel of Thomas, eh? Also, and this is one of my favorites, "When the thought of separation has been changed to one of true forgiveness, will the world be seen in quite another light; and one which leads to truth, where all the world must disappear and all its errors vanish."[7]

God did not make this world, and has nothing to do with it! God knows where you really are, safe at home. You're being prepared to awaken to a higher life-form, which is your real life. But, like God, your real life has no form. It is perfect oneness. There are no restrictions. There are no edges, or barriers, or limits of any kind. There's no friction to impede the glorious extension of your love. And everyone you've ever loved is there, every person and every animal, not as bodies, but in perfect Oneness, so you are aware that nobody and nothing could ever be left out. And because you are one and not bodies, you are actually closer to them than you could ever be in this world. Bodies cannot really join. The Course teaches that true union is possible only at the level of the mind.

PURSAH: Don't ever let anyone teach you that you can bypass the mind. J tells you in the Course that your mind's ability to make a choice, your power to choose, is your true power in this world. Those who want to bypass the mind are giving up the only power they have! Pure nondualistic thinking with the Holy Spirit reverses the thinking of the world. And the choice you're supposed to make is spelled out for you at the end of the Text, and the choice always involves the way you think about other people: "Choose once again what you would have him be, remembering that every choice you make establishes your own identity as you will see it and believe it is."[8]

Why does it establish your own identity? That's because of the way the mind works. To review, it's obvious most people are aware only of the conscious mind, but that's just the tip of the iceberg. If you could go down deep enough into the mind, into Carl Jung's collective unconscious, you'd find out that there is only one mind. That's because there's really only one of you. There's just one ego *appearing* as many.

GARY: The Hindu's world of multiplicity.

PURSAH: You have been listening. Good boy. So despite what you see, there's just one of you and one mind. But that presents a problem for you that you can't see. The projection of a universe of time and space that you can see is coming from that one unconscious mind. That's where the projector is hidden. Thus your unconscious mind knows everything. If that's where everything that you're seeing is coming from, then by definition, on some level, your mind knows *everything.* Even the truth is buried there, waiting to be remembered. And if the unconscious mind knows everything, then it knows that there's really just one of you. That's good news and bad news. Here's the bad news: Because the mind knows everything, including the fact that there's just one of you, it will interpret *anything* you think or say, no matter how subtle, about another person, to really be about *you!* And it will determine how you feel about yourself, and ultimately even what you believe you are. *That's* why the Course says every choice you make establishes your own identity as you will see it and believe it is. *That's* why the Course emphasizes that as you see him you will see yourself. And it's true.

GARY: So people are determining how they're going to feel about themselves right now by how they think about other people; whether they're going to be happy or depressed, whether they're going to feel guilty or innocent, or think they're a body or spirit, it's all determined the same way.

PURSAH: Yes. That shows you the power of the mind—the power of choice. The good news is that once you learn about that you can use it. You can learn how to work with the Holy Spirit and use your power of decision to go home.

GARY: Superb. So, I have an important question that I've asked you before, but I'm wondering if things have changed because of my forgiveness. Would it be possible for me to completely forgive everything and learn all of my lessons in this lifetime? Could I wake up this time instead, and not appear to come back again for that final lifetime as you, Pursah?

PURSAH: The answer is yes, Gary. It would be possible for you to finish the job in this lifetime. As we've said, the lessons have the same meaning in all dream lifetimes, only the forms change. You still have time to complete your lessons this time around! You've been doing good, and I like the way you're always turning it up a notch. All of your travels, which are a challenge on their own, along with all the Course politics being thrown at you, meeting so many people, trying to get the TV series, and having responsibilities you didn't expect have all contributed to you being able to practice your forgiveness and get it up to a much higher level than you would have if you had stayed in Maine, which you could have done. Don't forget: there are different dimensions of time, and different scenarios available to you depending on the choices you make at the level of the mind. But the Holy Spirit always decides what's best for you based on those decisions.

GARY: That's great, but wait a minute. What about all that stuff about the script being written, and those who are to meet shall meet, and everyone must play his part; how does everything happen that's supposed to happen if I don't come back again?

ARTEN: You're being linear. There's something you're forgetting about when it comes to you having that final lifetime as Pursah, and Cindy as me. *That lifetime has already happened.* Everything happened all at once, and according to the Course, it's already over. You're reviewing mentally that which has already gone by, remember? It's like watching a movie. Now, let's say you're watching a movie in a theater with 50 other people, and you get up and walk out. Isn't the movie still going? Don't the other people still see it? The fact that you're not there has no effect on the movie. It's two different things; apples and oranges. The movie keeps right on going *for those who are there to see it.* If you wake up from the dream and no longer see it, it has no effect on those who do. They still have to wake up in order to stop seeing the dream movie that they call life and see their real life instead, which is the Life of God.

GARY: But how can they see me if I'm not there?

ARTEN: You don't have to be there in order for them to see you, because you never were! What they're seeing is their own projection! And you only thought you were there because you still believed in separation and were making the projection real. You thought you were Thomas, or Gary, or Pursah, until you were enlightened. It doesn't matter when or where you become enlightened. Whether you're Pursah or Gary when it happens makes no difference.

GARY: Oh my God. I keep forgetting it's all made up. I'm so used to it being real that even after all this time it's still hard to get that nothing about it is true. But didn't you say that sometimes a master, like J, has to be there in order to point people in the right direction?

PURSAH: Yes, this doesn't invalidate anything we've told you. A chief aim of the miracle worker is to save time. Because of the time-saving feature of the Course, the Holy Spirit built it into the plan that people would have the choice of waking up faster than the script calls for. Then, whenever you become enlightened, your body, or what looks like your body, becomes a communication tool for the Holy Spirit. If you wake up faster because you exercise your power of decision to choose Spirit, which is the only free will you really have in this world, then you can act as an example for others even sooner, point people in the right direction, and accelerate the whole process for all of your brothers and sisters.

If you awaken in this dream life, it will still appear to others that Pursah is there a hundred years from now in Chicago. That's because they're still watching the movie, reviewing it mentally, and they'll think they're really there because they have yet to awaken. But you've already walked out of the theater. You are now the Holy Spirit. So no matter when it is, then or now, once you become enlightened it's no longer a personal *you*. You have re-become what you really are. Do you remember what the Course says about the images of the enlightened ones, like Arten and me, being used by the Holy Spirit? "All needs are known to them, and all mistakes are recognized and overlooked by them. The time will come when this is understood. And meanwhile, they give all their gifts to the teachers of God who look to them for help . . ."[9]

ARTEN: So everyone, by exercising their only power, can choose to activate Spirit in their mind and wake up faster as a result. The last thing the Holy Spirit would do is stop someone from speeding up the awakening of the Sonship. Yes, the full awakening of everyone could appear to take an extremely long time, but it doesn't *have* to take an extremely long time. In any case, you don't have to wait, and you don't have to wait until your next lifetime. You can decide to wake up now. So can Cindy. It's all right if you tell her, by the way.

GARY: I won't have to. She's proofreading the book for me after I type it out. She'll see it before anybody. But then I guess you probably knew that, huh?

PURSAH: Yes, but we play dumb for teaching purposes. The Holy Spirit meets you where you are.

GARY: Are you saying I'm dumb?

PURSAH: No. You'd only be dumb if you were real.

GARY: Have I just been insulted?

PURSAH: Just joking. Remember, not making it real is the smoothest shortcut to practicing true forgiveness. In fact, it's the most important part. You can't forgive what you're making real. If you do that it won't work. That's what the Course calls "Forgiveness to destroy."[10]

ARTEN: Also, to save time, keep putting the Holy Spirit in charge of your day. It helps you remember to look to Spirit for guidance when you can, when you have time to. You think of J often, and that's good. You're connected. Of course people can just talk to the Holy Spirit if they prefer; the point is in the asking.

GARY: Yeah. If I can, I take five minutes in the morning and just connect with Spirit. I don't have to say anything. I just forget about the world, forget about the things I think I need, and just go to God. I get lost in God's love. I'm in a condition of gratitude. It helps my mind stay more in a condition of Spirit and be more open to inspiration. All it takes is the thought.

I think it's vital to get used to being with God. Most people don't include God in their meditations, but you'll notice that some of the later Workbook lessons of the Course involve an actual approach to God. At one point J even has you call out to God. As you've taught me, you can't undo the idea of separation from God without acknowledging God. At some point you've got to get together with Him.

ARTEN: Not bad, brother. Incidentally, we're glad to see Cindy is becoming an excellent teacher in her own right. Of course anybody who's scheduled to be me in her next lifetime was bound to be good.

GARY: Oh yes. And she's got a mind of her own. I don't tell her what to do. If she wants to travel and do a workshop with me, she does. If she doesn't want to schedule herself to go somewhere, she doesn't. But she just started speaking a few years ago, and I'd put her right up there with the best of them. She doesn't compromise on the Course. And I've never seen anyone read it as much as she does. She's always talking about it. Sometimes I get tired of thinking about the Course and I have to say, "Cindy, give me a break, will you?" Plus she's got her music career going and just finished her third solo CD. Of course, fewer people are buying CDs nowadays; it's all going digital. But I get to hear her at the house on the piano writing her songs. It's fun.

ARTEN: You'll see fewer people buying books in the future too. Yes, some people will always want to feel that book in their hands and read it the old-fashioned way. But the millennials read things on their devices. Most of them don't read books. For better or for worse, that's the wave of the future.

GARY: Hey, I guess I'm lucky I got to work with you guys when people still read books! Of course, people will always be able to read us on their devices, but it doesn't seem the same to me.

PURSAH: At least they're reading. That's *something*. You know Helen never would have imagined people reading the Course on a device right out of *Star Trek*.

GARY: Well, we know she's up-to-date on things now.

NOTE: For several years, I've known that Helen Schucman, the scribe of *A Course in Miracles*, had reincarnated. I also knew the person whom she had come back as, and I had become very close friends with that person. The person knows about being Helen and knows all about that lifetime. It goes without saying that I would never "out" this person; I would never say who the person was. Only the person who was Helen should do that, if that person chooses to. And if the person doesn't ever choose to, I would totally support that decision.

When hearing Arten and Pursah tell the story of their final lifetime, as presented in my third book, I thought it was interesting that the two ascended masters never taught the Course in public during their final lifetimes. Nadav, who before had been Buddha, didn't really teach in his final lifetime either. The Course says, "To teach is to demonstrate."[11] It's clear that sometimes just living the Course is the best way to teach it.

ARTEN: Any more questions?

GARY: I don't know. Some questions just can't be answered.

ARTEN: For instance?

GARY: Well, for example, why is Times Square a triangle?

ARTEN: Actually, that question can be answered. For many centuries, what's now Broadway used to be an Indian trail going through Manhattan. The trail went across the island diagonally. Eventually, it became a road, then later a street called Broadway. The other streets were built mostly parallel on the island. So they were built straight, but Broadway was still crooked, and when it meets Times Square it makes it look like a triangle.

GARY: Oh.

PURSAH: The Holy Spirit plays an active role in influencing people to go to certain places, meet particular people, and learn the things that will help them the most along the path. It's like the Holy Spirit is gently nudging you in the right direction. Maybe you'll have a simple thought, that you should read a certain book, or go see a particular movie, or hear someone speak, or be friends with someone, and you think it was your idea. But it was really the Holy Spirit, guiding you from the right part of your mind, putting thoughts in your consciousness that helped speed you along.

Do you remember back in '78, when your life was a disaster, and Dan kept trying to get you to do the *est* training, and you finally broke down and went with him and his girlfriend Charlene to a guest seminar?

GARY: I sure do. The people there were so different; they seemed so powerful and so in charge of their lives. It was exciting, even though I didn't understand what the hell they were talking about. There were cultish aspects to it, but it wasn't like they were trying to get you to go live with them in the jungle and drink Kool-Aid.

PURSAH: Do you remember that you had no intention of signing up that night, but you started to get an overwhelming feeling that you should? That was the Holy Spirit guiding you, gently persuading you. Then you still had no intention of registering, because you had no money, and it cost $300, which was more like $1,000 today. You could register with a $30 deposit, but you didn't have anything, not even a dime, broke and broken, destitute.

GARY: Yeah. It was awesome.

PURSAH: Then the Holy Spirit gave a thought to Charlene: *Lend him $30 so he can register.* She and Dan were both surprised, because she couldn't afford it either! That was all the money she had. But you signed up and paid her back, even though it took you eight months to get a job and do it. But it seemed hopeless in the two months after you registered to come up with the other $270 to do the training. One week before, even though you knew your mom couldn't afford it, you asked her for the money. If she had extra money, she would have given it to you gladly, but she thought she couldn't, because it was almost all the extra money she had. Still, after your trying so hard to talk her into it, she relented; the Holy Spirit helped her sense that you might have found something to help you turn your life around. She gave you the money and you did the training, which was exactly what you needed at the time, and you began your journey in the right direction.

None of those things happened by accident. The Holy Spirit— who I'll sometimes refer to as H.S.—was there, every step of the way, leading you and guiding others to help you, knowing what was best. You didn't even think of the Holy Spirit back then, but it didn't matter. H.S. is always there with everyone, helping people all the time. The question is, are they willing to listen? For most, the answer is no, not yet. But H.S. is always doing Its job, and for some people the answer is yes. You were smart enough to listen, even though it didn't seem practical at the time.

ARTEN: Every day, all over the world, and all over the universe, in every seemingly split-off mind of the Sonship, the Holy Spirit is giving right-minded ideas to everyone. Sometimes they listen, sometimes they don't. For Course students, those right-minded ideas are more advanced than they are for most people, because they are ready. If they weren't ready, they wouldn't be doing the Course in the first place.

What look like coincidences are not coincidences, as the Holy Spirit is always guiding and influencing people to be at certain places and meet certain people so they can be truly helped. Look at the story of how your next-door neighbor found our first book.

GARY: Right! I'll tell the story. There's this woman named Jannine Rebman who's been on a spiritual path for 25 years. She and her good friend, Stephanie Swengel, started their journey as students of Edgar Cayce. That's how they met and became close friends, studying at Atlantic University, the educational organization of the A.R.E. (the Association for Research and Enlightenment), which is the Edgar Cayce group in Virginia Beach, Virginia. At one point, years into their spiritual quest, they found A Course in Miracles, but even though they were attracted to it, they just couldn't figure out what it was communicating. "It's like French," they'd say later. Frustrated, they eventually gave up on the Course.

Then, a few years ago, Jannine's sister, Lynne, who is also on a spiritual path, was living with her for a while. She had written a book and was looking at possible ways to get it published. She went out for a walk and met a guy at a stoplight. For no apparent reason, Lynne struck up a conversation and started telling him that she was trying to get a book published. The man, now interested, said, "Oh, I'm an author." He told her what he had written and gave her some advice, and then they went their separate ways.

When Lynne got back she told Jannine she'd met this nice guy who was an author and that they had talked at the stoplight. When Lynne mentioned the author's name, Jannine thought it sounded very familiar, but couldn't quite place it. Then she felt impelled to go out to her mailbox at the apartment complex she lived in. When she looked at the neighboring box, she saw the name of the author Lynne had just met. He lived in the next apartment!

That author was me. I was her next-door neighbor, but I traveled a lot and we had never spoken. Jannine could tell this wasn't your typical everyday experience. She looked me up online and found *The Disappearance of the Universe.* She read it in two days and told Stephanie, her longtime fellow spiritual traveler, "This is going to change your life." The two of them, like many who had given up on ACIM, read D.U. (as it's often called), and then when they went back to read the Course, it started making sense to them. Then they became enthusiastic students of the Course and my books, and ACIM is now their chosen spiritual path. I know from observation that they not only study it but also live it.

Jannine and Stephanie told this story on the video podcast series hosted by my sister-in-law, Jackie Lora-Jones, called *The 24th Hour.* Today, Jannine, Stephanie, Cindy and I, Jackie, and Mark (my brother-in-law and producer of the video podcast) are all very close. Jannine and Stephanie have a podcast called *The Course, of Course,* where new people and experienced students are always learning about ACIM. This whole series of events is an example of the Holy Spirit at work, and this kind of thing is happening all the time.

ARTEN: Thank you, Gary. And why do you suppose Lynne went out for that walk at exactly the time she did, and met you and started talking to you at the stoplight at just the right moment? Was it coincidence?

GARY: You're saying the Holy Spirit nudged her in the right direction at exactly the right time?

ARTEN: You know it. So when we say the Holy Spirit plays an active role, we're not kidding. Keep in mind, however, that the Holy Spirit does *not* make things happen in the world. That would be making the world real. H.S. does not manipulate the level of form. But H.S. does *guide* you through your mind. Everything the Holy Spirit does and everything the Course teaches is always at the level of the mind. Anyone who remembers that will save themselves a lot of time, which, as you can see by now, is a major goal of the Course. In fact, you won't find the time-saving feature of the Course anyplace else. Forgiveness, done from a place of cause and not effect, really is a miracle.

PURSAH: Speaking of the level of the mind, the human race will continue to develop its mental abilities over the centuries.

GARY: Wait a minute. Over the centuries? Are you saying the human race and the planet are going to survive for centuries? That's the most encouraging thing I've heard in a while.

PURSAH: Don't get all giddy about it. It won't be easy. There will be times when the human race will survive by the skin of its teeth. There's global warming, which will mess up the Earth's weather and topography, displacing many millions and killing many millions more. There are covert attempts to limit the world's population by making men sterile without them realizing it. There's the prospect not just of nuclear terrorism but also regional nuclear war, which could happen in several different areas. You have politicians in positions of power, and some who will be, who for lack of a better term are nut jobs. That's not a judgment, just a logical extension of a thought system. Don't forget what the Course says about the ego: "It is completely savage and completely insane."[12]

Humans are in for quite an adventure. The colonization of other planets will help ensure the survival of the race, making it more difficult for you to kill yourselves all at once.

GARY: Surely there must be some good stuff about the future?

PURSAH: Yes, you cockeyed optimist. I started to say the human race will continue to develop its mental abilities over the centuries. You know from the Course that individuals, as they undo the ego and gain more of the power of the mind, can develop abilities that may be quite startling to them. As the mind's awareness increases, so does the brain capacity of the being using it. That's merely a reflection of what's going on in the mind.

For example, because you love dolphins, you know they use twice as much of their brain capacity as humans do: 20 percent as opposed to 10 percent. That's a function of their superior awareness.

GARY: The native Hawaiians have always believed dolphins can read your thoughts and know what your intentions are, and can even tell what kind of a person you are. Everything I've seen from being with them, both in captivity and in the wild, swimming and playing with them, tells me it's true.

ARTEN: Yes, it is. Even though dolphins have their own language, which humans can't figure out even with computers, much of their communication is even more advanced. They communicate by mental telepathy with each other, and just as you said, they can read your thoughts and know whether you're peaceful or full of mental conflict. They avoid those who are in conflict, unless it's to help save someone from drowning, knowing it's the conflict that leads to violence, and they gravitate to gentle beings. You've noticed how much they love Cindy.

GARY: Yeah! It's like she's a Goddess to them. Even if we're on the side of the water they come right up to her. They like me too, but she's the main attraction. And she talks to them and they respond with love. They'll even shoot a little bit of water right up to her nose to say hello.

The last time we were on Oahu, we went to the Kahala Hotel to say hello to them, and a tropical storm was coming. The wind was blowing about 40 miles per hour, and you could tell it was gonna get bad. We went up to the dolphins, and even though they weren't sticking their heads above the water except to take a breath every few minutes—which they have to because they're mammals—they came right up to be with us. One of them stayed underwater right near us like he was meditating: head down and still under the water, tail on the bottom and body down. We'd never seen anything like it. Anyway, we stayed with them so long we were lucky to make it back to the place we were staying that night before the storm hit full force. It wasn't a hurricane, but it was still pretty crazy.

ARTEN: Dolphins, not humans, are the most intelligent beings on your planet. But since they lack thumbs and fingers, they don't make tools, and they wouldn't make weapons if they could. As the centuries go on, however, people will develop the ability to communicate like dolphins. They'll be able to use mental telepathy. Of course there are alien races that already do that. Humans will also acquire that skill.

GARY: If that's true, then by definition aren't you saying that the human mind will grow in its awareness; that people are going to become more intelligent and more advanced; and that therefore the human race will become better in general?

PURSAH: On the one hand, yes. But don't forget you live in a universe of duality. As long as the ego appears to exist, you'll have setbacks and tragedy. Nothing comes easy with the ego, unless it's to trick you into complacency. In your everyday dream world, the human race will have to go through great struggles just to survive.

GARY: I was starting to feel good for a minute there. Thanks for snapping me out of it.

PURSAH: You know where true joy is found, brother. What's one of your favorite quotes from the Course, the one about joy?

GARY: Oh, yeah. "How else can you find joy in a joyless place except by realizing that you are not there?"[13]

ARTEN: Remember where your true happiness is. You're doing it, Gary. You can go all the way. You can do it in this lifetime, and so can Cindy. Not that you have to do it together. But I get the sense that you both decided recently that you're going to go for it in this lifetime and not wait for the next one. We were hoping that would be the case with you—not that you have to, but because of a question we asked you a long time ago: How long do you want to prolong your suffering?

GARY: I have to admit I haven't been affected as much by things in the world, except a little by the presidential election. It's hard, you know, because I was brought up on politics. When I was nine years old, I lived in Massachusetts and JFK was a hero of mine. I started following politics early and learned a lot about it. I still know more than most people, including a lot of politicians. I almost went into it as a profession.

Today I'm glad I didn't. There's no civility anymore, no human decency. Not that presidential elections haven't always been full of lies and hatred, but at least it was usually more subtle. Today, the inmates are running the asylum. Washington, D.C., is a joke. It's not possible to govern, and I don't like that.

Cindy and I went into D.C. a few months ago. We were doing a workshop in Manassas, Virginia, where the first major land battle of the Civil War took place, and it was an easy ride in. I loved being at the National Mall, the Lincoln Memorial, the Washington Memorial, the Capitol, the Martin Luther King Memorial, and the White House. It was really cool! Those places are a lot more impressive in person. You don't get the scale of them on TV or in the movies. Anyway, I found myself wishing our government could live up to its original intentions. Our Founding Fathers weren't perfect, but they were very interesting men, many of them Masons. Today, *interesting* is about the last word I'd use to describe most of the politicians in Washington.

ARTEN: I understand how you feel, Gary. I used to be human too, remember? But don't ever forget what J tells you in the Course: "There is no point in lamenting the world."[14] You know now what everything is for, and if it's politics that affects you the most, then it's politics that you have to forgive the most. Be as determined as you possibly can be, and you'll succeed.

PURSAH: You mentioned Manassas. The Civil War is one of the most graphic examples of the ego at work. First of all, it involved the issue of slavery, which immediately goes to the ego making bodies real. Some bodies are a different color than others, which is right up the ego's alley. At that time, some bodies were considered to be more valuable than others, and to have rights that others didn't. Some people considered their bodies to be their personal property. The ego loves differences, and will always tempt people to use them for judgment and projection.

Second, the war involved states and states' rights. At that time it was more important what state you were from than what country you were from. Most people never traveled far from their homes, and they took great pride in being from places like Ohio, Massachusetts, Maine, Texas, or Virginia. But what is a state but a separation idea? It's the same with countries. They're just a separation idea. When you see video of the Earth from space do you see any borders?

GARY: No. That's because God, in his infinite wisdom, decided to let us establish our own borders, and then defend them to the death as a test of our courage on the gridiron; and, of course, to see who could beat out other people. Why do you think they call us the human *race*?

PURSAH: You need a nap. As you know, God, in his infinite wisdom, is still home having a good time. And a lot of people thought they were here, fighting the Civil War. The conflict in the mind was screaming for fulfillment. Even though Abraham Lincoln was hoping that what he thought of as "the better angels of our nature" would prevail, there was no way. Before you knew it, your nation was attempting suicide.

By the time it was over, counting both the North and South, almost three-quarters of a million soldiers were dead. The official count is lower, but this number is accurate. In many places, every man in town under the age of 40 was dead. There were more Americans killed than in World War I and World War II combined. Yes, World War II was the most destructive war in history by far, because it involved many of the most populous countries all over the world, but America would never see anything like the Civil War again. It was one of the ego's most flaming accomplishments, seething with insanity.

GARY: Knowing you, you have a reason for bringing this up?

ARTEN: Several reasons. America hasn't changed as much as some people may think when it comes to racism. Racism never went away, it just went underground. The point to all of this is that despite all the death and horror, despite the pseudo-resolution of the problem through war, despite all the great work done by people throughout the civil rights and human rights movements, the ego hasn't changed. It's been undone in some people who are on the path, but certainly not the masses. You can't change the ego by trying to fix the world. That won't solve the problem. So there's just as much racism and prejudice as there was 150 years ago. Yes, it's taken on different forms, but the ego's sordid game of conflict, separation, and division still remains for all to see, just as pathetic as ever.

GARY: That's true. I thought when Obama got elected it meant a great step forward for America. Finally, we had a black President. And what happened? All these nuts came out of the woodwork. "We want our country back," they'd say. What they meant was they wanted to go back to the 1950s, when it was okay to hate people who looked different from you. "Make America great again," a campaign slogan coined by a deeply disturbed man, really means, "Make America racist again." He even questioned Obama's legitimacy as President, claiming he was born in Kenya. How racist can you get?

ARTEN: So, can you not make it real and forgive him?

GARY: Of course. It's not him. He's just being his toxic-minded ego self. What bothers me is that there are so many people in this country who actually voted for him! That's the hard part. It's sick, and it tells me we're a sick country.

PURSAH: Not totally sick. You're a partly sick country that also has a right mind. And this is a partly sick world that also has a right mind. The Holy Spirit is available to everyone, but eventually everyone will need to forgive *all* the world. That's because as long as you have conflict in the mind, you know what it leads to.

ARTEN: Of course the ego keeps raising the bar and trying to make it harder for you. The Internet, which can be used for wonderful purposes, is also used to spread hatred. And the hatred of the bigots isn't directed only at those with a different skin color.

Your country has made much progress in passing laws and achieving court decisions that ban discrimination against the LBGT community. But the hatred is still there. The tragedy of 49 people being murdered in the Pulse nightclub in Orlando serves to highlight what will continue to happen as long as you combine guns and hatred. The ego has set up America very well. And the right wing will continue to make the most of it for their selfish purposes.

GARY: I know. The Republican state legislatures are always trying to pass laws that discriminate against anyone who isn't a white Republican. Imagine—and this really pisses me off—passing laws that are clearly intended to stop black people from voting? How can they sleep at night? How can they call themselves Americans? How can they dishonor all those who have died for democracy and the right to vote? And how can those who *can* vote empower these mentally ill local politicians?

PURSAH: That's because, on the level of form, bigotry, misogyny, and racism are still alive and well in America, and in the rest of the world. Even today women don't get equal pay for equal work, and are treated as inferior to men by their corporate bosses. Anybody who isn't a rich white male is, at one time or another in their lives, relegated to the position of second-class citizen. And now you have the immigration issue being raised to the hilt, giving the ego more people to hate.

ARTEN: So let me advise you about something, Gary. Yes, these problems certainly seem to exist in the dream. But here's a fact that comes to you from outside of the dream: *These problems will not be solved by politics.* Yes, eventually they will *appear* to be solved by politics. Soon enough, white people will not be a majority in America; Hispanics will be the biggest voting group. You don't have to be a genius to figure out where American politics will be going, and it's not to the right. But that's not what will really solve the problems.

The only thing that will ever solve these kinds of problems that appear to be in the world will be to fix the problem where it is: in the conflicted, unconscious mind.

GARY: Well, at least you're consistent. In all the years we've been talking with each other, and the many different things we've talked about, I notice that sooner or later you always bring the conversation back around to forgiveness. It's because that's what undoes the ego. And if you take care of the cause, the effect will take care of itself.

ARTEN: Yes, and for the most part you've done very well. This political thing of yours is that last general forgiveness opportunity you need to take care of. I say "general" because it's something that applies to your world in general. You've already forgiven pretty much everything else. Now, there are forgiveness lessons that are not general, like the death of a loved one. You've forgiven those kinds of events in your lifetime, too. But you need to be vigilant for God when personal forgiveness opportunities come your way, the kind of opportunities that are not about the world in general.

As we've said, and this bears repeating like the whole Course does, you'll know for sure that you've forgiven something when it doesn't bother you anymore—when it no longer affects you. When that politician who you can't stand comes on the TV and says something that used to make you go ballistic, and you go to react and there's nothing there, and you feel peaceful instead, you'll know that you've really forgiven him.

PURSAH: Remember to monitor yourself and apply the steps you know when it comes to the things that still get to you: (1) Notice you're being activated in a negative way. That's the ego. *Stop* thinking or feeling with the ego. Stop making it real. (2) *Start* thinking with the Holy Spirit. That's the Holy Instant. The Holy Spirit reminds you it's not real, this is a dream, and it can't affect you without your belief in it. You're not a victim. This is your dream, and it can't hurt you. (3) Engage in spiritual sight. That person isn't a body. They are perfect Spirit, but not part of it; rather, they are *all* of it: totally innocent, and exactly the same as God. Do you remember the Course quote that says release my son?

GARY: Sure, just before the last chapter: "Can you to whom God says, 'Release My Son!' be tempted not to listen, when you learn that it is you for whom He asks release? And what but this is what this Course would teach? And what but this is there for you to learn?"[15]

ARTEN: There you have it. So let's talk about another important subject. You know that according to the Course all pain is caused by unconscious guilt. Did you ever stop to think that your experience of death will be different depending on how much guilt in your mind has been healed by forgiveness and how much still remains?

GARY: I never thought of that. But then, why should I? Just kidding. I never thought your experience would vary depending on forgiveness, but it makes sense.

ARTEN: In most cases, and I say most but not all because the ego likes things to be complicated, when your body stops you don't feel any pain. You may feel pain as you die, but not after. Just the opposite. Usually it's a really good experience. No physical pain, the relief of appearing to leave the body and being free; it's a beatific experience for most at first.

GARY: You know, I've been thinking about that a little lately. I remember how much I cried and how upset I was when my mom and dad passed away. We didn't call it "making your transition" back in the '70s. They died. My father was on the job, and he just fell dead, his body going to the ground. When I heard the news from the doctor on the phone, it was like a nightmare. *My poor father,* I thought. I figured it must have been very painful and horrible for him. But thinking about it now, I realize, first of all, that he passed away quickly. Second, he probably wasn't feeling any pain from the instant he passed away. The pain probably ceased immediately, right?

ARTEN: That's correct. So there you were, devastated and crying, and here he was having a good time. I assure you that when both of your parents made their transition, from the instant it happened it was a wonderful experience for them. And that's true no matter how horrible a death a person may appear to go through. Say somebody gets shot in the head. Anybody who sees it or hears about it, especially those closest to the person, is horrified. But what they don't understand is that the person goes immediately into an experience that is fantastic. As the Song of Prayer section of the Course says, "We call it death, but it is liberty."[16]

PURSAH: It was the same with your mom. Yes, she did suffer before she made her transition. The doctor shouldn't have operated on her. Her blood pressure was too low, and he botched the operation anyway; afterward, while in intensive care, she suffered a heart attack, and the whole thing was a disaster. You were in agony over it. But most of your crying was after she appeared to die. And you know what? For her, that was the best part. Once the body appears to stop and the mind keeps right on going, it's one of the better experiences an ego mind can have. So while you're grieving all through the funeral and after, the loved one who has passed away is having such a fun time that you'd be jealous if you knew how much fun it was.

However, after you go through all the mind adventures that people talk about in the near-death experience, which do appear to happen for most people—and this is what Arten was talking about when he said your experience of death will be different, depending on how much guilt in your mind has been healed—there comes a time when you're going to the light. Now, let's say you were enlightened in that lifetime. If you were, you wouldn't go through all the stages people talk about in the near-death show. If you're enlightened you gently lay the body aside for the final time, as the Course would say. And you're at home in God immediately. Of course you always were, but we're talking about your awareness. In fact, the instant you become enlightened, while you are still in a body—which is where enlightenment occurs, not during the in-between life—you become aware of the fact that you are One with God, always were, and always will be, and you *experience* it from that moment on. Then when you lay the body aside, your experience of your perfect Oneness with God continues for eternity, which has no time.

GARY: I want it. And I know the answer to the following question, but I'd like to hear it from you. What happens if you're *not* enlightened?

PURSAH: We've said that all pain is caused by guilt. That includes psychological pain as well as physical pain. But even if you're not enlightened, if there has been real healing, which by definition there would have been if you were practicing forgiveness, then the in-between life will be a much better time for you than it would have been if there wasn't real healing. With healing, the Course says this about your experience of death: "Now we go in peace to freer air and gentler climate, where it is not hard to see the gifts we gave were saved for us."[17] So even if you're going to review one more lifetime, if you've been practicing forgiveness your experience of death is going to be a good one.

If people don't practice forgiveness, it's not a sin, but there will still be a lot of unconscious guilt in their mind. Then, when they're going to the light, which is symbolic of God, the guilt, pain, and fear start to come to the surface. They start to feel this psychological pain, and they want to escape from it. They want to hide, and the place they hide from it is here, the projection of a world and universe. It's a reenactment of the separation from God. The dream world is a hiding place where that fear and guilt is projected outside of them. Now it looks like they've escaped, because the cause and blame appear to be out there in somebody else; but it's a faulty mechanism, because they haven't escaped. The guilt is still there in their mind. Despite the ego's illusion of projection, the Course says, "Ideas leave not their source, and their effects but seem to be apart from them."[18] That's the bad news. The guilt and fear is still there in your unconscious. The good news is this: because ideas leave not their source, you haven't really left God either.

Yet for those who believe in the separation and have not yet accepted the truth, the world becomes their home once again. J says, "Guilt asks for punishment, and its request is granted. Not in truth, but in the world of shadows and illusions built on sin."[19]

GARY: So if I achieve enlightenment this time around, which you say is possible, I won't go through all the near-death stuff again. I'll be experiencing my perfect Oneness with God while I still appear to be here, and I'll barely be aware of my body. My awareness will be with my reality. Then, when I lay the body aside, that's it. I'm home. So what about the thing in the Course about God taking the final step? It says—here, I'll read it:

> Forgiveness is unknown in Heaven, where the need for it would be inconceivable. However, in this world, forgiveness is a necessary correction for all the mistakes that we have made. To offer forgiveness is the only way for us to have it, for it reflects the law of Heaven that giving and receiving are the same. Heaven is the natural state of all the Sons of God as He created them. Such is their reality forever. It has not changed because it has been forgotten.
>
> Forgiveness is the means by which we will remember. Through forgiveness the thinking of the world is reversed. The forgiven world becomes the gate of Heaven, because by its mercy we can at last forgive ourselves. Holding no one prisoner to guilt, we become free. Acknowledging Christ in all our brothers, we recognize His Presence in ourselves. Forgetting all our misperceptions, and with nothing from the past to hold us back, we can remember God. Beyond this, learning cannot go. When we are ready, God Himself will take the final step in our return to Him.[20]

GARY (continued): That's a pretty good summary of the Course, actually, and it's in the Preface! I remember the first time I read that, though. When it said God Himself would take the final step in our return to Him, I thought that meant He was gonna kill me.

ARTEN: Ah no. Remember, God created you, you didn't create Him. That's why He takes the final step, which of course is metaphor. You simply pick up where you left off, not that you ever really left, with Him as Creator, and you as creator. As the Course puts it, "Not one note in Heaven's song was missed."[21] But God will always be your creator, and then you create the same as Him. The infinite extension of perfect love is not something the finite mind can understand, but the time will come when you'll get to actually experience it.

PURSAH: When it comes to the part of the Preface you just read, it reminds me of something we want to make sure people are absolutely clear about. From beginning to end, in all 31 chapters of the Text, the Workbook, the Manual for Teachers, the Clarification of Terms, the Psychotherapy Section, the Song of Prayer—everything Helen channeled from 1965 through 1977—the Course is totally consistent and uncompromising. There have been some teachers who think they have found the right interpretation of the Course, meaning their interpretation. No. The truth is *there is only one possible interpretation of A Course in Miracles.* We've been giving it to you since we first started appearing to you 25 years ago. You've also heard it from the Wapnick School. We haven't wavered, and we're glad to see that you haven't either.

GARY: Yeah, but you'll never stop some people from nitpicking the Course to death. I've had people tell me you can't trust the Course because they edited out the word *souls* in the first five chapters, and that word implies individuality and God creating it.

ARTEN: It's certainly true that some people can't be stopped, but the word *souls* was used temporarily early in the Course, for Helen's sake, when she was getting used to channeling again; as you know, she worked with J in other lifetimes. The word was meant to be a metaphor, referring to the seemingly split-off minds of the Sonship. Those split-off parts, or souls, are illusory, and that's how the word was used.

Soon after, when Helen had cleared out the cobwebs, that word wasn't used anymore, which is why J instructed her to take it out. Why confuse people? They're good enough at doing that themselves, as was eventually proven. The word *Sonship* and the description *Sons of*

God were soon used instead, but whenever the Course refers to *Sons of God*, or anything plural, like those who have yet to change their minds, that's metaphor. It's clear the Course is saying that in reality there is only God's *one* Son, which is Christ: perfect Oneness and the same as God. But the ego will do anything to cling to the idea of individuality and separation.

PURSAH: I want to put together a couple of things with an idea you talked about earlier. You said you were at the airport, and you were really tired. Then you started to realize that you weren't tired, but were having a dream of being tired. In truth, since you're not a body, you can't be tired. Only the mind can think it is.

Try applying this to sickness and pain. As you know from the Course and from our discussions, all sickness and pain are of the mind, and all healing is of the mind. It's the mind of the patient that is really the physician. I want you to put that together with a few of the other ideas from the Course we've already used: (1) The body is outside of you, and not your concern. This removes you from the idea you're in a body. (2) You would not react at all to figures in a dream you knew that you were dreaming. I want you to take that idea and apply it to your *own* body. Once you get used to the idea that the bodies you're seeing are nothing but dream figures that you don't have to let affect you, you then want to start getting used to the idea that your own body is nothing but a figure in the dream, and that you don't have to let it affect you either! You don't have to react to your own body any more than the other dream figures. (3) What you really are is totally innocent, at home in God, taken care of by Him forever. So the next time you feel tired, sick, or have any pain, remember these three ideas and put them together.

GARY: Got it. Well, I'll paraphrase. (1) The body is outside of me and not my concern. It has nothing to do with me. (2) I would not react at all to a figure in the dream I knew I was dreaming. So why react to my own body? It's not what I am. I'm not in it. It's just a figure in a dream, and now that I know I'm dreaming, I don't have to let it affect me. If I'm not in a body, I'm not really feeling pain; I'm just dreaming that I'm feeling pain. I don't have to make it real. (3) What I really am is completely innocent. God loves me and will take care of me forever.

PURSAH: Yes, and try to visualize yourself as being outside of your body as mind. When you do that, your awareness is potentially unlimited. The mind can go anywhere and be anywhere; a body cannot.

GARY: I like it. I'll do it. Say, how did J heal the sick? You're saying it's the patient's mind that does it. So what was his part in it?

PURSAH: He answers that for you in the Manual for Teachers, but most people don't pay attention because they want to be great healers who lay their hands on others and get a lot of credit. Find "The Function of the Teacher of God," and read the second and third paragraphs.

J knows that the sick person, thinking he or she is guilty, has chosen to be sick at the level of the unconscious. And what J describes in the Manual is the same way he approached the sick, at the level of the mind, two thousand years ago. Of course, you have to realize his awareness was total; he could join with the sick person on a deep level, and the sick person would get where he was coming from even though nothing was being said. As you start reading, J is talking about the person who has chosen to be sick.

GARY: Okay.

To them God's teachers come, to represent another choice which they had forgotten. The simple presence of a teacher of God is a reminder. His thoughts ask for the right to question what the patient has accepted as true. As God's messengers, His teachers are the symbols of salvation. They ask the patient for forgiveness for God's Son in his own Name. They stand for the Alternative. With God's Word in their minds they come in benediction, not to heal the sick but to remind them of the remedy God has already given them. It is not their hands that heal. It is not their voice that speaks the will of God. They merely give what has been given them. Very gently they call to their brothers to turn away from death: "Behold, you Son of God, what life can offer you. Would you choose sickness in place of this?"

Not once do the advanced teachers of God consider the forms of sickness in which their brother believes. To do this is to forget that all of them have the same purpose, and therefore are not really different. They seek for God's Voice in this brother who would so deceive himself as to believe God's Son can suffer. And they remind him that he did not make himself, and must remain as God created him. They recognize illusions can have no effect. The truth in their minds reaches out to the truth in the minds of their brothers, so that illusions are not reinforced. They are thus brought to truth; truth is not brought to them. So are they dispelled, not by the will of another, but by the union of the one Will with itself. And this is the function of God's teachers; to see no will as separate from their own, nor theirs as separate from God's.[22]

PURSAH: The next time you go to see someone in the hospital or visit a friend who is sick at home, read that first. It will remind you of the attitude of the advanced teacher of God.

GARY: I will, and I think I grasp what it's saying. I'm not totally out of it.

PURSAH: Just as long as you're not totally into it. Don't try to be a big-shot healer. And if someone gets well in your presence, don't take any credit for it. Just refer them to the section of the Manual you just read from.

ARTEN: So you've learned from the Course that in your present state you are a mind, and that you have the power to choose. And what you choose to believe in is what will affect you and ultimately determine what you believe you are. Never underestimate the power of the mind. With its choices, you will remain separate from your Source in your experience, and feel like an ego among egos, or you will return home to your Source in the glorious condition of One-ness, guided there by the Holy Spirit. You've learned from the Course that *mind* is the activating agent of spirit. Use this mind to go in the right direction with every choice you make. In doing so, you can be enlightened in this lifetime.

GARY: That would be fine with me. You know, most of the time I've been getting better and better at practicing forgiveness. It's like when I was a guitar player: I'd keep finding better ways to play, just by doing it. It's the same with forgiveness. The more you do it, the better you get at it. But one thing that bothers me is that even though I've been doing it for a long time, once in a while forgiveness is still really hard. Some things still push my buttons. And I heard Ken say that even he got annoyed once in a while. Does that ever end?

ARTEN: The time comes when, yes, it does end. It did for Ken. It takes much dedication and practice, and you'll have the frustration you just mentioned. You'll wonder if you'll ever get to the point when nothing bothers you. When that happens, remember you can't always see the results of your forgiveness and the healing results, and you can't judge what you can't see. The Course says, "It is not the function of God's teachers to evaluate the outcome of their gifts. It is merely their function to give them."[23] Have faith, and the time *will* come when peace is totally restored to your mind, no matter what appears to happen. In the meantime, you're getting much better. Aren't you at peace most of the time?

GARY: That's true. I remember what I was like just before you appeared to me for the first time. I was anything but peaceful. I worried about *everything.* I mean, I worried so much I didn't even know I was worrying. I just thought it was normal. Except for my brother, Paul, there was hardly anyone I had a nice peaceful relationship with. I couldn't make anything work. Even though I'd been on a spiritual path for about 15 years at the time, my life still sucked. Yeah, it was a lot better than it was before I got on a spiritual path, which tells you how much my life must have sucked back then. But like I've told you before, there was something missing. I got so much into the presidential election of '92 I almost made myself sick. I wasn't happy at all, and I had no idea what to do about it.

Then, I remember very clearly, I made a decision. I said to myself, *I want to remove conflict from my life.* I had no idea what a tall order that was, because I didn't know how *much* conflict I had in my mind. And I'm not blaming anybody else for the way I felt; it was me. Even then, because of *est,* I'd already learned I wasn't a victim. I knew there wasn't any power in that. And I made that decision. I think it was that decision that led to you guys showing up to me. I had to be ready to hear what you had to say.

Applying what you've taught me, I've changed so much with the Course that I guess I usually forget about the way I used to be. Like most people, I think I was always this way. But I wasn't. When I think about it I can see that I've changed enormously. I don't worry about things the way I used to. I don't care as much about what people think. I remember it used to be so important how it looked. Now, who cares? We're all gonna be dead in a few years anyway. Let's forgive, move on, and have a good time.

Today, I can't think of anyone I don't have a forgiven relationship with. And speaking on the road is easy. The first time I got up and talked about the Course in front of people, I was terrified. After five or six times and a lot of forgiveness, it was no big deal. It was fun. Today, it's no more stressful than brushing my teeth.

Travel is still a forgiveness opportunity, though. When I started, it was cool. Back then the airlines treated me like I was a customer. Now they treat me like I'm a suspect. So does the TSA, even though I have a KTN, a "known traveler number," which gets me on the pre-check list. That's supposed to get me through security faster, but they still treat me like there's something wrong with me. I wonder if it's because of what I've written. Anyway, at least now I know what it's all for.

So if I take the time to think about it, yes, everything is different than when you first came to me. And I can tell the process is accelerating. I've been hurt in a couple of minor accidents and it should have made me feel pain, but it didn't. And I thought, that's strange. That should hurt. My body is more elastic, and it feels lighter even though I weigh more than I used to. It's a figure in a dream. You know what? I'm gonna start feeling more grateful. Thank you. You've given me even more to think about and work with.

PURSAH: And thank you, brother. It's been a long visit, but rewarding. We're going to leave you with some words from J. We'll be back for one more discussion, the last one of this series. Until then, be well. Our love is with you.

> Your relationship with your brother has been uprooted from the world of shadows, and its unholy purpose has been safely brought through the barriers of guilt, washed with forgiveness, and set shining and firmly rooted in the world of light. From there it calls to you to follow the course it took, lifted high above the darkness and gently placed before the

gates of Heaven. The holy instant in which you and your brother were united is but the messenger of love, sent from beyond forgiveness to remind you of all that lies beyond it. Yet it is through forgiveness that it will be remembered.

And when the memory of God has come to you in the holy place of forgiveness you will remember nothing else, and memory will be as useless as learning, for your only purpose will be creating. Yet this you cannot know, until every perception has been cleansed and purified, and finally removed forever. Forgiveness removes only the untrue, lifting the shadows from the world and carrying it, safe and sure within its gentleness, to the bright world of new and clean perception. There is your purpose *now.* And it is there that peace awaits you.[24]

Then Arten and Pursah disappeared, which they had a habit of doing, but I knew they were always with me. It had been a lengthy talk, but I felt renewed by their wisdom and encouraged by their assurance it would be possible for me to not have to wait for another lifetime in order to be enlightened. This was new and welcome information. But could I do it?

I determined that the answer to that question was yes. I could see now that everything had happened for a reason. It all fit together. The Holy Spirit knew what He was doing, even if I didn't always know what I was doing. This was going to be my final stop; the one that ends in God.

10

The Ladder Disappears

The body is released because the mind acknowledges "this is not done to me, but I am doing this." And thus the mind is free to make another choice instead. Beginning here, salvation will proceed to change the course of every step in the descent to separation, until all the steps have been retraced, the ladder gone, and all the dreaming of the world undone.

— A Course in Miracles[1]

In the two months since my favorite teachers had last appeared to me, I felt my mind flooded with visions of J and Buddha, and the dream lifetimes I'd been told about in which they knew each other. I thought of Saka and Hiroji and their learning as Shintos. Having been to Japan, I could almost feel them out in the countryside, talking to animals with pictures through the one-joined mind, focusing on learning the great truth. They didn't believe in the dream as much as others, and they wouldn't be denied the knowledge that would set them free, no matter what it took or how long.

I could see and hear Shao Li and Wosan in China with Lao-tzu, grasping the teachings of Taoism on a level equal to him, tuning the mind into the nondualistic truth and away from the dream of shadows. And in India, as the Hindus Harish and Padmaj, they would know and feel the truth of Brahman, and discard the folly of maya, which means magic.

In Greece, with their teacher Plato, Ikaros and Takis would learn that philosophical speculation may be fine for some, but they would be satisfied only by experiencing a permanent kind of truth. And for Siddhartha and his son, Rahula, in the end their tasting of a permanent reality would only lead them to a surprising realization: that the One-ness of God was the glorious, unshakable truth they had been searching for all along.

My heart sang upon learning of the joy of Y'shua, Mary, and Nadav, which came with knowing the pure nondualistic truth within them, with having the knowledge of God, and with living in the immortal treasure of permanent being.

I wondered how Valentinus had felt in his place of knowing this was all a dream, and whether he had discovered what to replace it with. Because of the destruction caused by the church, we'd never know. Certainly, as I had been told, there were people since J and Buddha who had become enlightened. The world may not know their names, but most of the world only knew of the world.

I could barely imagine what it must have been like to be there in the Course's only study group with Helen, Bill, Ken, and Judy before the Course was even published. That was a privilege I'd never know, but at least I got to become friends with two of them. I'd be forever grateful for their contribution of bringing *A Course in Miracles* to the world, and to Ken, for his refusal to compromise on J's relentless message of pure nondualism.

I was completely humbled by all I had learned about the lifetimes when J and Buddha knew each other, and wondered how I could ever join the likes of these spiritual geniuses in enlightenment and salvation. Then I remembered a line from *A Course in Miracles* I hadn't thought of in years. It was about God: "Be humble before Him, and yet great *in* Him."[2] I realized J would not want me to be humble before him, but only before God. We were brothers, and he had gone to great lengths in the Course to teach that we are all equals, except in time, and time doesn't exist. Thus we will all inevitably come to the same awareness of where we have never truly left. I decided to press on.

During a day of rain in Southern California, which I'm surprised wasn't declared a state holiday, my teachers were suddenly with me.

ARTEN: How are you, bro? You've been processing a lot.

GARY: All I can say is *wow.* It's all a bit much to take in. I've been thinking about all you guys have taught me, including in this series of visits, and I'm gonna have to go over my notes a few times and think even longer.

PURSAH: Take your time, brother. You've got all the time in the world, and there's no such thing.

GARY: I know I shouldn't be fascinated with anything in the world, but sometimes I think it would be fun to have the kind of adventures J and Buddha had in these exotic and highly educational dreams of theirs.

PURSAH: And what makes you think you haven't? Let me explain something to you. Most of the people, including you, who appear to be on this planet, except for the newcomers, have lived *thousands* of dream lifetimes here. On average, in the linear illusion of time and space, you come back once or twice every century.

GARY: Let me see. So if I came back an average of twice a century in the last fifty thousand years, that alone would be one thousand times, right?

PURSAH: That was very calculating of you. But this is the point: You, and everyone you know, have gotten to live every kind of a life, been every kind of a person, done everything, and had *every* kind of experience that anyone else has ever had. You're not missing anything you haven't already been through. Do you really think the people you have envied in this lifetime are having experiences that you haven't had already, or been able to do things you haven't done before? You've been everywhere and done it all. You've been the richest people in the world and the poorest, the most famous and most obscure, the victim and the victimizer, the king and a prisoner, the hedonist and the celibate. You just forget, and you remember more than most people do.

True, these experiences, which really happened all at once, except they didn't really, will look different from one place and time to another—but the *experiences* are the same. In the same way, your lessons from lifetime to lifetime may look different, but the *meaning* is the same. So don't waste your time being jealous of another. You've been there, done that, whether you remember or not. And none of it will bring you lasting happiness, but forgiving it will.

You're so used to believing what is visible to the ego, you've forgotten what reality is. Remember what J says about that:

When you made visible what is not true, what *is* true became invisible to you. Yet it cannot be invisible in itself, for the Holy Spirit sees it with perfect clarity. It is invisible to you because you are looking at something else. Yet it is no more up to you to decide what is visible and what is invisible, than it is up to you to decide what reality is. What can be seen is what the Holy Spirit sees. The definition of reality is God's, not yours. He created it, and He knows what it is. You who knew have forgotten, and unless He had given you a way to remember you would have condemned yourself to oblivion.[3]

GARY: That's pretty blunt. And I get what you're saying about having experienced everything. You say we've dreamed thousands of lifetimes, so in the illusion that would take up an awful lot of time—more than just fifty thousand years, right?

ARTEN: This planet has gone through different phases of history, where a civilization will eventually destroy itself, and the technical progress, if you can really call it progress, is lost. That's why you don't know much about what happened more than ten thousand years ago. What people call Atlantis and Lemuria are only two examples of what's come before. You were in those places with some of the people you know today.

As we told you during the first series of visits, humans have long existed on other planets and some eventually migrated to Earth. So you have to take into consideration all the dream lifetimes you and others have gone through on the way to where you believe you are, or in your case used to believe you are. You're breaking free, and even if you don't attain enlightenment this time, you'll only be coming back once more.

GARY: I won't be coming back again. And speaking of enlightenment, you've told me something about it but not too much. Would you like to tell me a little more about what it's like? It would give me something to look forward to.

ARTEN: As you approach your time of enlightenment, the reality of Heaven becomes more the norm for you, and the world begins to feel more distant. The experience of Revelation that you've had will become more common. In that experience, you have reality, which is changeless and eternal. You can't stay in that state all the time here, or the body would disappear. It can't be maintained without the mind focusing on it, at least a little. But instead of having yourself mostly in the door and slightly out, you have yourself mostly out the door and slightly in.

When you do go about daily activities, you find your awareness has increased. You realize the things that the body's eyes are showing you are in your mind. They are images that were made by your thoughts. There is no need to be concerned about the dream figures. They will learn the truth as you did. And what you used to think was the guilt in others you have now learned was your own guilt, seen outside of you, trying to come back and destroy you. And sometimes it did.

As your awareness increases, you can tell what people are thinking. You don't necessarily hear their exact thoughts. If you heard everything that everyone was thinking it would be too much. It would be like system overload. So instead, you're able to tell what their attitude is, and what kind of a person they are, without all the details. But if you really *wanted* to read their exact thoughts you could.

You also become much more aware of the fact that what you're seeing is a projection that is coming from you. The dream is projected from your mind, like a movie, but now you can feel, and sometimes even see, that the projector is you. Once you get to that point fear is impossible, provided you keep in mind the reality that's just beyond the dream. We've said repeatedly that you have to know what to replace the illusion with. And the more you replace the false with the truth of God, the more you experience that you are in Him.

The bliss of enlightenment is beyond words. Your body is barely noticeable. Yes, you take care of it and keep it clean, but you hardly eat any food. You drink water, but not too much. At the very end, you need no food or water. But when you're at the very end, then by definition you won't be here for long anyway.

If your body is sick, that isn't important to you. Sometimes the script calls for a master to teach he or she is not a body by demonstrating it's possible to go through the death of a seemingly sick body without pain, just as J appeared to die on the cross, but did it without pain. As a master, it would be possible for you to heal your body with your mind. But you have chosen not to, just as J could have saved himself from the cross but chose not to, and taught an important lesson instead.

And then in your last act as an enlightened person, the time comes when you gently lay the body aside for the final time. It doesn't matter what the form of death appears to be. To someone else it could appear to be a terrible death, but how terrible is it for you if you don't feel any pain? Once again, *that's* what J is talking about when he says you lay the body aside gently. Done with peace and no pain, there is only a blessing. Then, the awareness of your perfect Oneness with God that you were experiencing most of the time becomes your permanent experience. God Himself takes the final step in your return to Him. This is beyond human understanding. All you need to know right now is that truth is unalterable, and so are you.

GARY: That's wonderful. The magnitude of it all sounds so great, and what we seem to be experiencing here in everyday life seems so limited. We go through all these tough times, like a divorce for example, and it's hard to imagine that beyond our small lives is something so unspeakably joyous.

PURSAH: If you use your life wisely, it's important. And perhaps the magnitude of it is beyond what you imagine. Do you remember the message that both you and Cindy received from Karen and Steve?

GARY: Oh my God. Yes.

NOTE: After my divorce from Karen, she sent me a message, written in the form of poetry, by Suzanne Berry. Incredibly, Cindy's first husband, Steve, from whom she had also been recently divorced, sent her *the exact same message.* When Cindy showed it to me, I couldn't believe it. Both Karen and Steve had felt a connection with the same deeply meaningful words. Minds are joined, and Cindy and I could both identify with the message as well:

> *I wish I could go back in time . . . back to those*
> *unspoiled moments in our relationship*
> *before hurt ever touched our hearts,*
> *before doubt ever entered our minds.*
> *Because if I could go back*

and start from those moments once more,
I would hold you longer,
never miss a chance to tell you
how much you mean to me . . .
and I would never, ever hurt you.
But I know we can't go back to those days.
I know I can't erase the mistakes.
I can't take away the questions you must have
or the hurt we both feel.
But I can assure you of one thing:
I love you
as I did then and as I always will.[4]

GARY (continued): There was nothing I could say after I saw that. Even special love in this world can find humility and dignity. I'll always love Karen, and I know Cindy will always love Steve. Yet the time will come in our relationship when the temporary will be replaced by the permanent. No one will be left out. As J once said, a long time ago, Heaven is like a wedding, and everyone is invited.

ARTEN: Very nice, brother. None of you are little. What you really are is something that can't even be contained by the universe of time and space. Don't accept the ego's evaluation of you. It does not see truly.

GARY: Yes, I have to remember that what I really am has nothing to do with the lies I've been thinking for eons. People, even Course students, have had this guilt forever, and it's not representative of the truth. I need to remind myself of that, and remember to undo it.

ARTEN: Then remember these words, Gary, and don't be afraid to live as though you truly believe them, for the Holy Spirit *does* see truly:

You are altogether irreplaceable in the Mind of God. No one else can fill your part in it, and while you leave your part of it empty your eternal place merely waits for your return. God, through His Voice, reminds you of it, and God Himself keeps your extensions safe within it. Yet you do not know them until you return to them. You cannot replace the Kingdom, and you cannot replace yourself. God, Who knows your value, would not have it so, and so it is not so. Your value is in

God's Mind, and therefore not in yours alone. To accept yourself as God created you cannot be arrogance, because it is the denial of arrogance. To accept your littleness *is* arrogant, because it means that you believe your evaluation of yourself is truer than God's.

Yet if truth is indivisible, your evaluation of yourself must *be* God's. You did not establish your value and it needs no defense. Nothing can attack it nor prevail over it. It does not vary. It merely *is.* Ask the Holy Spirit what it is and He will tell you, but do not be afraid of His answer, because it comes from God. It is an exalted answer because of its Source, but the Source is true and so is Its answer.[5]

GARY: I love that. I really need the reminders to help me keep going. And I know you said this would be the last discussion in this series of visits. Do you think there'll be another series of visits?

ARTEN: Why don't you try to digest this series first? I think you know by now the reason we've kept appearing to you is that undoing the ego is a process, and as you go along you keep getting the Course on deeper and deeper levels. The realizations keep coming to you as the ego keeps going from you.

GARY: Cool. So I'll keep undoing the ego with my mind's power to choose. But you know, some Course students, or people who think they're Course students, are saying you've got to forget about the mind and think with your heart. They say you can have love only with your heart. You know, the "heart of Christ consciousness" and all that stuff.

PURSAH: I hate to disappoint them, but you can't think with your heart. Your heart is part of the body. It doesn't have a little brain in it. And the brain is just part of the body too. The mind is not in the brain. The brain is in the mind. Do you remember Phineas Quimby?

GARY: Sure. He healed Mary Baker Eddy, the founder of Christian Science.

PURSAH: He was the facilitator of the healing. Her mind was the healer. Eventually she had a relapse, but the seeds had been planted, and she went on to help many. And Quimby was a visionary, a true pioneer of the mind. He understood that all illness is of the mind, as is all healing. By the way, Mary wrote and said a lot of interesting things.

GARY: One of my favorites is, "Truth is immortal; error is mortal."

PURSAH: Yes, and by the way, we understand that people who emphasize the heart are talking about love, and there's nothing wrong with talking about it. But you won't find real, permanent love by talking about it, or by trying to be more loving, or even by trying to emulate J. You'll find it by undoing the barriers to it. You should keep looking to forgive anything you've placed in between yourself and your true nature. The ego is a formidable illusion. It's like a machine. It keeps persisting, which is why you've got to be vigilant. Always remember this vital quotation from the Course:

> Your task is not to seek for love, but merely to seek and find all of the barriers within yourself that you have built against it. It is not necessary to seek for what is true, but it *is* necessary to seek for what is false.[6]

GARY: So it'll always come back to the fact that salvation is undoing, and forgiveness is the way to undo the ego. Then love, which is what you are, will be there naturally. But you can't skip the undoing part, or your love will be temporary, mixed in with the ego, and your mind will be a mixed bag. Without the complete healing of the Holy Spirit you'll stay stuck on psycho planet forever.

ARTEN: Yes, or a reasonable facsimile thereof. Whether it's this planet or another, only the form changes. The content remains the same. You've spoken about the Course in what, 30 countries and 44 states? Despite the excitement of it, haven't you realized that people are basically the same everywhere?

GARY: Yeah, that's true. You go to China, and you get the same kinds of questions you do anyplace else. A guy raises his hand, and he wants to know how he can get along with his mother-in-law.

ARTEN: And you know the Course well enough to give him an answer.

GARY: The Holy Spirit knows the Course well enough to give him an answer. Speaking of the Holy Spirit, I remember the story of how Lieutenant Colonel Stanislav Petrov of the Soviet Union saved the world from nuclear annihilation back in '83, and I'm glad he's gotten some recognition for that, since you told me about him back in the '90s. But it makes me wonder: You said he listened to the Holy Spirit to make his decision not to launch the nuclear missiles. Does the Holy Spirit often intervene in world situations?

ARTEN: What the Holy Spirit does is speak to *everyone* through the right part of the mind. Of course the person has to be willing to listen. Adolf Hitler's mind was 99 percent influenced by the ego, and the Holy Spirit was not listened to by him. There was no willingness. Everybody has at least 1 percent Spirit, even Chairman Mao, who killed way more people than Hitler. That's because you can't destroy the truth, you can only cover it over. On the other hand, you have someone like Gandhi, whose mind was 99 percent influenced by Spirit, and he was more than willing to listen.

Because of duality, it stands to reason that a lot of people are in the 50-50 range. They have a chance, but they have to make the decision to listen. If they listen, they become more like Gandhi. That's just an example, of course. You don't have to influence world events the way Gandhi did. But if you feel guided to do so by Spirit, then go for it. The important thing is that the mind is moving in the right direction. It's becoming more peaceful, and peace is the condition of the Kingdom.

PURSAH: Over the eons, people have been fascinated with the struggle between good and evil, between what they've perceived as God and the devil. Well, this is one of the things the Course says about the devil:

> The mind can make the belief in separation very real and very fearful, and this belief *is* the devil. It is powerful, active, destructive, and clearly in opposition to God, because it literally denies His Fatherhood. Look at your life and see what the devil has made. But realize that this making will surely dissolve in the light of truth, because its foundation is a lie.[7]

So the devil is really separation and the mind's belief in it. After all, what is war but separation? What is projection, the blaming of people, inquisitions, torture, and punishment but separation? What is all violence and terrorism? How can you have judgment, and all its tragedy, without separation? The devil may be blamed, but the belief in the seeming separation from God and the endless symbols that go along with it will always be the cause.

All the sorrows of your life are caused by some form of judgment, which makes the belief in separation real, but you have it within yourself to end all suffering with forgiveness, and dissolve the ego thought system. The devil disappears along with it, for they are one and the same.

ARTEN: Everything changes with the Holy Spirit. If you give the endeavors of your life to the Holy Spirit, that's a spiritual gift. You mentioned the movie with Matt Damon. Even though he didn't say it verbally, it was clear that in the movie his psychic gift was eventually transformed into a tool that was used by the Holy Spirit for His purposes instead of for the ego's purpose of separation. That idea is in beautiful harmony with what the Course says about people who have such a gift:

> Any ability that anyone develops has the potentiality for good. To this there is no exception. And the more unusual and unexpected the power, the greater its potential usefulness. Salvation has need of all abilities, for what the world would destroy the Holy Spirit would restore. "Psychic" abilities have been used to call upon the devil, which merely means to strengthen the ego. Yet here is also a great channel of hope and healing in the Holy Spirit's service. Those who have developed "psychic" powers have simply let some of the limitations they laid upon their minds be lifted. It can be but further limitations they lay upon themselves if they utilize their increased freedom for greater imprisonment. The Holy Spirit needs these gifts, and those who offer them to Him alone go with Christ's gratitude upon their hearts, and His holy sight not far behind.[8]

PURSAH: Remember, the Holy Spirit knows your value was established by God, not the world. In this all are equal. The next time you're tempted to get down on yourself, feel unworthy, or get discouraged, remember us, remember J, remember the Holy Spirit, and remember God. Once you get up to the level of Spirit, we are all the

Holy Spirit, for we are the truth. You can't win with the lies of the ego, but you can't lose with the truth of the Holy Spirit.

ARTEN: When you work with us you're helping to uncover the love, which is Spirit that exists in everyone's mind. There's a corollary between love and the Kingdom of Heaven you should think about. Answer this question honestly: What is the most real thing you have in your life? What means the most to you?

GARY: Well, the most real thing I have in my life is my experience, and the most real experience I have is love.

ARTEN: Yes! And isn't it interesting that the most real thing you have in your life is something that's invisible, something you can't see? You can't see love. Yes, you can see love in action, but you can't see love.

Now, can you see the Kingdom of Heaven? No. It can't be seen with the body's eyes. Yes, you can see symbols of it briefly, but you can't see the Kingdom. Isn't it interesting that the most real thing you can have in your awareness is something you can't see?

Do the work to remove the blinders that prevent you from seeing that which cannot be seen. As you know, the Kingdom of Heaven *can* be experienced. And it's this experience that gives you a glimpse of the truth you can never forget, making it impossible for you to ever fully believe in the ego again.

PURSAH: When Helen Schucman met Ken Wapnick for the first time, she'd already been told by Bill Thetford that Ken was a very interesting man. She gave Ken two sections from the Text of the Course to read. After reading them, Ken knew the Course would be his life's work. He had intended to live in a monastery, but just reading two sections of the Course changed his life. The two sections were "For They Have Come," which contains a lot of lovely metaphor, and "Choose Once Again," which really brings the Text home, like the ending of a great symphony. I'm going to recite for you a part of "For They Have Come." Perhaps you'll understand why it meant so much to Ken, and why he went on to dedicate his life to the Course.

GARY: So this is from the very first part of the Course Ken ever read?

PURSAH: Yes. It's talking about those who have heard the Call to awaken, and are redeeming the world with their Holy Sight:

The blood of hatred fades to let the grass grow green again, and let the flowers be all white and sparkling in the summer sun. What was a place of death has now become a living temple in a world of light. Because of Them. It is Their Presence which has lifted holiness again to take its ancient place upon an ancient throne. Because of Them have miracles sprung up as grass and flowers on the barren ground that hate had scorched and rendered desolate. What hate has wrought have They undone. And now you stand on ground so holy Heaven leans to join with it, and make it like itself. The shadow of an ancient hate has gone, and all the blight and withering have passed forever from the land where They have come.

What is a hundred or a thousand years to Them, or tens of thousands? When They come, time's purpose is fulfilled. What never was passes to nothingness when They have come. What hatred claimed is given up to love, and freedom lights up every living thing and lifts it into Heaven, where the lights grow ever brighter as each one comes home. The incomplete is made complete again, and Heaven's joy has been increased because what is its own has been restored to it. The bloodied earth is cleansed, and the insane have shed their garments of insanity to join Them on the ground whereon you stand.

Heaven is grateful for this gift of what has been withheld so long. For They have come to gather in Their Own. What has been locked is opened; what was held apart from light is given up, that light may shine on it and leave no space nor distance lingering between the light of Heaven and the world.

The holiest of all the spots on earth is where an ancient hatred has become a present love. And They come quickly to the living temple, where a home for Them has been set up. There is no place in Heaven holier. And They have come to dwell within the temple offered Them, to be Their resting place as well as yours. What hatred has released to love becomes the brightest light in Heaven's radiance. And all the lights in Heaven brighter grow, in gratitude for what has been restored.[9]

GARY: Thanks, Pursah. That's really beautiful. I know there's a lot of metaphor in that, but it reminds me of how the world will end.

PURSAH: Yes, but don't forget the basics. The Course says:

The world will end when its thought system has been completely reversed. Until then, bits and pieces of its thinking will still seem sensible. The final lesson, which brings the ending of the world, cannot be grasped by those not yet prepared to leave the world and go beyond its tiny reach.[10]

GARY: I'm ready to go beyond its tiny reach.

PURSAH: You already have! You're a metaphysical wild man. It's fun to work with you, brother. You can grasp that the thought system of the world must be *completely* reversed. You can't give faith to one illusion. They're either all true or all false.

ARTEN: It's getting to be time to close our discussions for this series of visits. There's no hurry absorbing all that we've talked about. Read your notes again. You know the Course needs repeating to be understood, and that any new realizations must be applied a great deal in order for them to do their job in allowing the Holy Spirit to heal the unconscious.

We'll leave it up to you to call on us if you need us. We'd never leave you comfortless, any more than J would. If and when the time comes that another series of visits is called for, we'll be here for you. If not, we'll always be in your mind as the Holy Spirit. We love you, and we'll be together forever in God.

GARY: Thanks so much, Arten. You too, Pursah. I love you both. Words will never be able to tell you how grateful I am. But I guess you know. You know everything. And by the way, I forgive you for a decision you've stuck with ever since the beginning of our meetings. You said you weren't going to tell me much about my personal future, because you didn't want to deprive me of my forgiveness opportunities. I didn't like that at first, but I can see now it was for the best. My forgiveness lessons wouldn't have had the same impact if I knew what was going to happen. I guess the Holy Spirit really does know best. You've earned my trust.

ARTEN: The ladder to enlightenment will be steadily climbed by all who are willing to listen to the Holy Spirit. J promises that you will be successful:

High has the ladder risen. You have come almost to Heaven. There is little more to learn before the journey is complete. Now can you say to everyone who comes to join in prayer with you: *I cannot go without you, for you are a part of me.* And so he is in truth.[11]

PURSAH: As your journey comes to a close, you'll feel an all-encompassing gratitude to God, who you acknowledge as your creator and the only reality:

The ladder ends with this, for learning is no longer needed. Now you stand before the gate of Heaven, and your brother stands beside you there. The lawns are deep and still, for here the place appointed for the time when you should come has waited long for you. Here will time end forever. At this gate eternity itself will join with you.[12]

Gary, we ask you to join with us at the level of the mind and become One with us in God. Spirit knows no separation, and we shall be forever whole. Hear this prayer before there are no ears to hear it with, for all that is visible will soon be gone:

We are eternally grateful for the immortal, indestructible nature of our being. Fear cannot enter a mind that is only Spirit. All ancient thoughts slip away, for there is no world to remember, and nothing remaining to forgive. We soar beyond the limitations of finite thought. The joy is unimaginable. The love unspeakable. There has never been such fullness. Nothing is left out, for everyone and everything that appeared to travel the world of illusions has awakened.
Our home is perfect, for we have never left. Heaven's song has never stopped. The little gap that was never there has long been healed and has vanished. No opposites exist to hide the truth. We are forever taken care of here. Only abundance, beauty, and life abound. There is no guilt or forgiveness, for neither is needed by the innocent. We have made the decisions that set us in the right direction, where we could not fail to once again be where we belong. Our Father is pleased; He knows that His Own will always be within Him.

God, Christ, Spirit: these are words without meaning here. No distinction remains in perfection. The holiness of our love is all that there is. Time has vanished. We have returned to our rightful place. And so we disappear, into the Heart of God.

Appendix

Outline of the Lifetimes Examined in This Book

Chapter 2, Lifetime #1

Names	J: Saka (male), B: Hiroji (male)
Time Period	700 B.C.
Location	Japan
Religion	Shintoism
Relationship	Friendship

Chapter 2, Lifetime #2

Names	J: Shao Li (female), B: Wosan (male)
Time Period	600 B.C.
Location	China
Religion	Taoism
Relationship	Romantic

Chapter 3, Lifetime #3

Names	J: Harish (male), B: Padmaj (male)
Time Period	500 B.C.
Location	India
Religion	Hinduism
Relationship	Cousins

Chapter 4, Lifetime #4

Names	J: Takis (male), B: Ikaros (male)
Time Period	500–450 B.C.
Location	Greece
Religion	Plato's Academy
Relationship	Fellow students of Plato

Chapter 5, Lifetime #5

Names	J: Rahula (male), B: Siddhartha Buddha (male)
Time Period	450–380 B.C.
Location	India
Religion	Nondualism
Relationship	Child–Parent

Chapter 6, Lifetime #6

Names	J: Y'shua/Jesus (male), B: Nadav/Phillip (male)
Time Period	0–55 A.D.
Location	Jerusalem
Religion	Pure nondualism
Relationship	Ultimate Follower–J's equal

Index of References

*A*ll quotes used from *A Course in Miracles*© are from the Third Edition, published in 2007. They are used with permission from the copyright holder and publisher, the Foundation for Inner Peace, P.O. Box 598, Mill Valley, CA 94942-0598, www.acim.org and info@acim.org.

In the following Index, please follow the examples below to correlate the References to the numbering system used in *A Course in Miracles*.

T-26.IV.4:7. = Text, Chapter 26, Section IV, Paragraph 4, Sentence 7.

W-p1.169.5:2. = Workbook, Part 1, Lesson 169, Paragraph 5, Sentence 2.

M-13.3:2. = Manual, Question 13, Paragraph 3, Sentence 2.

C-6.4:6 = Clarification of Terms, Term 6, Paragraph 4, Sentence 6.

P-2.VI.5:1. = Psychotherapy, Chapter 2, Section 6, Paragraph 5, Sentence 1.

S-1.V.4:3. = Song of Prayer, Chapter 1, Section 5, Paragraph 4, Sentence 3.

A Note from the Author about *A Course in Miracles*:
What It Teaches, and Its Relevance to Jesus and Buddha.
1. T-1.VI.2:1. 2. Introduction. 3. Introduction. 4. M-21.1:9-10. 5. T-31.VI.2:1. 6. W-pl.201.h. 7. T-10.1.2:1. 8. W-pl.158.4:5. 9. T-18.II.5:12. 10. Introduction. 11. T-6.II.6:1. 12. W-pl.169.12:1. 13. M-28.2:2. 14. T-5.II.h 15. T-20.VIII.7:3-5. 16. C-1.1:1. 17. T-I.I.29:3.Principle 29. 18. T-22.II.10:1. 19. T-I.I.5:1. 20. T-2.II.I:11-12. 21. W-pl.132.6:2-3. 22. T-12.III.1:1-3. 23. W-pl.201.h. 24. T-8.III.4:2. 25. T-6.II.12:5. 26. T-31.VIII.6:5. 27. T-21.in.1:5 28. T-23.III.6:1. 29. T-1.II.3:10. 30. T-3.IV.7:12. 31. T-31.VIII.1:5. 32. T-31.VIII.9:1-3.

1: The Ladder to Enlightenment.
1. T -28.III.1:1-2. 2. T-6:V.C.2:8. 3. T-27.VIII.3:1. 4. T-31.VIII.3:1. 5. T-27.VIII.6:1-5.

2: From Shintoism to Lao-tzu: Early Peak Experiences.
1. T-31.VIII.9:2.

3: A Time as Hindus.
1. T-18.VII.5:7. 2. T-18.VII.5:7-7:3. 3. T-18.VII.7:7-8:3. 4. M-27.7:3.

4: Plato and Friends.
1. Plato, in *Timaeus*, 27d. 2. T-20.III.9:1-2.

5: Siddhartha and His Son.
1. M-4, 1.A.6:11.

6: The Final Times of J and Buddha.
1. T-6.V.C.2:8.

7: Gnosticism.
1. The Gospel of Truth, 1.22.12-21, in *The Nag Hammadi Library*, page 40, edited by James M. Robinson, published by Harper Collins. 2. Ibid., 28. 30-32. 3, page 43. Both used by Dr. Kenneth Wapnick in his book, *Love Does Not Condemn: The World, the Flesh, and the Devil According to Platonism, Christianity, Gnosticism, and* A Course in Miracles, pages 251-252. 3. C-1.1:1, in Manual for Teachers. 4. M-4.I.A.6.4-5.

8: J Channeled, 1965–1977: This Time the Truth Will Not Be Buried.
1. W-p1.200.5:1-2. 2. T-18.II.6:1. 3. T-13.VII.17:7. 4. T18.II.5:12-14. 5. T27.VII.8:1-3. 6. T-10.I.2:1. 7. M-12.6:6-9. 8. Introduction.6-7. 9. T-27.VII.13:1-5. 10. T27.VII.14:1-8. 11. T-28.II.7:1. 12. T-19.II.6:7-8. 13. W-p1.182.1:1-6. 14. T20.VIII.7:3-5. 15. T-27.VIII.10:1-6. 16. T-17.I.5:4-5. 17. T20.IV.1:1. 18. T.30.VI.1:1. 19. T-8.VI.9:8-11. 20. T-5.I.5:1-7. 21. T-9.III.I:1-8:11. 22. T-9.IV.4:1-6. 23. T-9.V.6:3. 24. T2.V.A.11:3. 25. T-1.III.7:1. 26. T-3.IV.7:12. 27. W-pII.361-365.h. 28. T-29.VII.1:1-3. 29. W-pII.I.4:4. 30. W.pII.I.I:1-4. 31. T-8.III.4:2. 32. T-8.III.4:5. 33. T-3.VI.5.5:7. 34. T-16.III.7:7-8. 35. T16.V.14:1-2. 36. W-pl.134.6:I-10:4.

9: The Importance of the Mind.
1. T-4.IV.8:3-4. 2. W-p1.155.1:1-5. 3. W-p1.132.6:2. 4. W-p1.186.14:2. 5. W-p1.188.1:5. 6. W-p1.189.1:1-2. 7. W-pII.3.1.4. 8. T-31.VIII.6:5. 9. M.26.2:7-9. 10. S-2.II.1:1. 11. M.i.2:1. 12. T-16.VII.3:2. 13. T-6.II.6:1. 14. W-p1.23.2:2. 15. T-31.VII.15:5-7. 16. S-3.II.3:1. 17. S-3.II.3:4. 18. T.26.VII.4:7. 19. T.26.VII.3:1-2. 20. Preface. xiii. 21. T.26.V.5:4. 22. M-5.III.2:11-3:9. 23. M-6.3:1-2. 24. T-18.IX.13:1-14:5.

10: The Ladder Disappears.
1. T.28.II.12:5-7. 2. T.15.IV.3:1. 3. T-12.VIII.3:1-8. 4. Suzanne Berry. 5. T-9.VIII.10:1-11:7. 6. T.16.IV.6:1-2. 7. T3.VII.5:1-4. 8. M-25.6:1-9. 9. T26.IX.3:1-6:6. 10. M-14.4:1-3. 11. S-1.V.3:5-10. 12. S-1.V.4:1-5.

About *A Course in Miracles*

The Combined Volume, Third Edition of *A Course in Miracles* is the *only* edition that contains in one place all the writing that Dr. Helen Schucman, its scribe, authorized to be printed. It is published solely by The Foundation for Inner Peace, the organization chosen by Dr. Schucman in 1975 for this purpose. This Combined Volume also includes the supplements to the Course: Psychotherapy: Purpose, Process and Practice and The Song of Prayer. These sections are extensions of the Course principles, which were dictated to Dr. Schucman shortly after she completed *A Course in Miracles*.

About the Author

*G*ary R. Renard underwent a powerful spiritual awakening in the early 1990s. As instructed by two ascended masters, Arten and Pursah, who appeared to him in the flesh, he wrote his first bestselling book, *The Disappearance of the Universe,* over a period of nine years. He was later guided to speak in public, and has been described as one of the most interesting and courageous spiritual speakers in the world. Gary's next two books, *Your Immortal Reality* and *Love Has Forgotten No One,* were also bestsellers.

Over the past 14 years, Gary has spoken in 44 states and 31 countries, and has been the keynote speaker at numerous *A Course in Miracles* conferences. He is also a recipient of the Infinity Foundation Spirit Award, which is given to those who have made a meaningful contribution to personal and spiritual growth. Past recipients include Dan Millman, Ram Dass, Gary Zukav, James Redfield, Byron Katie, and Neale Donald Walsch.

More recently Gary has been busy teaching (and sometimes introducing) *A Course in Miracles* with talks and workshops all over the world. He has done hundreds of radio and print interviews, appeared in nine documentary movies, recorded 60 podcasts with Gene Bogart, posted dozens of videos on YouTube, created three audio CDs for Sounds True (one of which has over seven hours of unedited material), made a music CD and a meditation CD with Cindy Lora-Renard, filmed several DVDs, and is developing a television series based on his books. He has also written the forewords for seven books, answered tens of thousands of e-mails, developed the largest *A Course in Miracles* study group in the world (the D.U. Discussion Group at Yahoo), and had his books published in 22 languages. For his growing body of steady readers, Gary is the "go-to" guy when it comes to cutting-edge spirituality. Website: www.GaryRenard.com.

Hay House Titles of Related Interest

YOU CAN HEAL YOUR LIFE, the movie, starring Louise Hay & Friends
(available as an online streaming video)
www.hayhouse.com/louise-movie

THE SHIFT, the movie,
starring Dr. Wayne W. Dyer
(available as an online streaming video)
www.hayhouse.com/the-shift-movie

REMEMBERING THE LIGHT WITHIN: A Course in Soul-Centered Living,
by Mary R. Hulnick, Ph.D., and H. Ronald Hulnick, Ph.D.

RESILIENCE FROM THE HEART: The Power to Thrive in Life's Extremes,
by Gregg Braden

*SOUL SHIFTS: Transformative Wisdom for Creating a Life of Authentic
Awakening, Emotional Freedom, and Practical Spirituality,*
by Barbara De Angelis

10 MESSAGES YOUR ANGELS WANT YOU TO KNOW, by Doreen Virtue

THE UNIVERSE HAS YOUR BACK: Transform Fear to Faith,
by Gabrielle Bernstein

All of the above are available at your local bookstore,
or may be ordered by contacting Hay House (see next page).

We hope you enjoyed this Hay House book. If you'd like to receive our online catalog featuring additional information on Hay House books and products, or if you'd like to find out more about the Hay Foundation, please contact:

Hay House, Inc., P.O. Box 5100, Carlsbad, CA 92018-5100
(760) 431-7695 or (800) 654-5126
(760) 431-6948 (fax) or (800) 650-5115 (fax)
www.hayhouse.com® • www.hayfoundation.org

———

Published in Australia by: Hay House Australia Pty. Ltd.,
18/36 Ralph St., Alexandria NSW 2015
Phone: 612-9669-4299 • *Fax:* 612-9669-4144
www.hayhouse.com.au

Published in the United Kingdom by: Hay House UK, Ltd.,
The Sixth Floor, Watson House, 54 Baker Street, London W1U 7BU
Phone: +44 (0)20 3927 7290 • *Fax:* +44 (0)20 3927 7291
www.hayhouse.co.uk

Published in India by: Hay House Publishers India,
Muskaan Complex, Plot No. 3, B-2, Vasant Kunj, New Delhi 110 070
Phone: 91-11-4176-1620 • *Fax:* 91-11-4176-1630
www.hayhouse.co.in

———

Access New Knowledge.
Anytime. Anywhere.

Learn and evolve at your own pace
with the world's leading experts.

www.hayhouseU.com

Printed in the United States
by Baker & Taylor Publisher Services